Roderick Cavaliero is a writer and historian, author of *Italia Romantica: English Romantics and Italian Freedom*, *Admiral Satan: The Life and Campaigns of the Bailli de Suffren*, *Independence of Brazil* and *Strangers in the Land: The Rise and Decline of the British Indian Empire* (all I.B.Tauris).

'Mr Cavaliero has a splendid tale to unfold and he tells it excellently. His colourful account of "a worthy machine running down" is an unusual and Sitwellian piece of historical evocation.'
Sunday Times

'Delightful . . . the author's modesty matches his erudition and wit. An absorbing and valuable book.'
The Tablet

'The hundred years' story of the decline [of the Knights of St John and Malta] is told in detail and with authority . . . *The Last of the Crusaders* brings this era poignantly and accurately to life.'
The Times

'With scholarship and wit Roderick Cavaliero describes the decline and fall of the Knights of Malta.'
Alfred Duggan, *Daily Telegraph*

'A splendid piece of history writing . . . a great tale to tell . . . told splendidly. *The Last of the Crusaders* will continue to hold a cherished place on many a bookshelf.'
Sunday Times (Malta)

Tauris Parke Paperbacks is an imprint of I.B.Tauris. It is dedicated to publishing books in accessible paperback editions for the serious general reader within a wide range of categories, including biography, history, travel and the ancient world. The list includes select, critically acclaimed works of top quality writing by distinguished authors that continue to challenge, to inform and to inspire. These are books that possess those subtle but intrinsic elements that mark them out as something exceptional.

The Colophon of Tauris Parke Paperbacks is a representation of the ancient Egyptian ibis, sacred to the god Thoth, who was himself often depicted in the form of this most elegant of birds. Thoth was credited in antiquity as the scribe of the ancient Egyptian gods and as the inventor of writing and was associated with many aspects of wisdom and learning.

THE LAST OF THE CRUSADERS

The Knights of St John and Malta in the Eighteenth Century

Roderick Cavaliero

TPP

TAURIS PARKE
PAPERBACKS

Published in 2009 by Tauris Parke Paperbacks
an imprint of I.B.Tauris & Co Ltd
6 Salem Road, London W2 4BU
175 Fifth Avenue, New York NY 10010
www.ibtauris.com

First published by Hollis & Carter in 1960
Copyright © 1960, 2009, Roderick Cavaliero

Cover image: 'View of the Bay of Malta', engraving by Barthault.

ISBN: 978 1 84511 729 0

A full CIP record for this book is available from the British Library
A full CIP record is available from the Library of Congress

Library of Congress Catalog Card Number: available

Printed and bound in India by Thomson Press India Ltd

CONTENTS

ILLUSTRATIONS

PREFACE

WHEN *The Last of the Crusaders* was written nearly fifty years ago, little study had been made of the Mediterranean City states, and of the conflicts of religion and commerce that both enriched and threatened them. Fernand Braudel, in 1949, established the inner sea as one of many voices, a sum of individuals but, despite the rich seam of sources present in the island, Malta found no place in the index, and in the magisterial three volume *Civilization and Capitalism from the 15th to the 18th Centuries*, Malta of the Knights receives only two mentions, the only substantial one of which is that the knights depended on Sicily for the wine that was a 'sovereign remedy to break their fevers'. Professor Lionel Butler and his *pépinière* of Crusader historians at St Andrew's University had begun to mine the archives, but the first, and, alas, the only volume of a *History of the Order of the Hospital of St John* reached 1310. Transference to London University as head of a constituent college, followed by his untimely death, prevented Professor Butler from taking the History as far as the Order's time in Rhodes. For a serious history of the Order, covering both the Maltese and modern periods, we have had to wait for H. J. A. Sire's *The Knights of Malta* and for Jonathan Riley-Smith's magisterial short history of the Order, *Hospitallers*.

When in 1970 the Council of Europe and government of Malta organized an exhibition of the work of Mattia Preti, the catalogue carried a bibliography of works on the Knights in all languages, showing a rich monograph literature but little sustained work on the impact of Malta of the Knights on the surrounding Mediterranean lands. Peter Earle's *Corsairs of Malta and Barbary* made a significant contribution to this, supplemented by Christopher Lloyd's *English Corsairs on the Barbary Coast*. Earle regretted that no latter-day Braudel had attempted a history of the Mediterranean in the seventeenth and eighteenth centuries. Professor John Bromley, in volume XI of the *New Cambridge Modern History 1688–1725*, included a chapter on the guerres de course (corso) at the turn of the two centuries, in which Malta received prominent treatment, appearing for the first time in the hundred year war between France and Britain, fought across the Atlantic, in the Bay of Bengal and latterly in the Mediterranean. Barbary, the principal object of the Christian corso, constitutes a prominent feature in the works of Professor Linda Colley, *Captives* and *The Ordeal of Elizabeth Marsh*. The economic and social implications of a large work-force of short-term and ransomable prison labour is only now becoming better known.

A spate of books in France, listed in my *Admiral Satan, The Life and Campaigns of the Bailiff de Suffren*, have rescued the French navy, whose objectives were different from those of its principal rival, from the reputation of always being on the losing side, and helped to establish how much was learned about the seamanship of its great captains in Malta under the Knights. Dr Sire refutes the prevailing belief, which I once held, that the Maltese navy throughout the eighteenth century was in terminal decline, pointing out its very considerable achievements in conducting the corso, and carrying out police actions which it was inconvenient for the major Mediterranean power, France, to undertake.

The principal quarrel I would have with my own work is that it is too deferential to the Knights, whose return after their expulsion by the French was opposed by the people whom they had ruled for over two hundred years, as is so conclusively proved by Desmond Gregory in *Malta, Britain and the European Powers, 1793–1815*. The Order was, in fact, an occupying power and the Maltese had neither fought for it nor risen in its favour. Secondly I would modify statements about the decadence of the Order during its last century in Malta. That the eighteenth century was merely waiting for Napoleon and Beethoven to blow in a new age was still prevalent in the 1950s, partly a hangover from the Second World War which seemed to have proved the greater resilience of democratic institutions over dictatorship. Today we are better aware that the Romantic wind which blew across Europe after 1789 had been largely blowing over the century as Europe was enriched by inventions, commerce and colonies, and administrative reform had been gearing up nations to modernity since the end of the wars of religion. Malta under the Knights in the eighteenth century, was a very successful society, by comparison with its close neighbours, and the Knights provided an efficient if not a popular environment in which the island prospered. When the revenues of the Order were cut off from France it became a successful joint stock company whose principal investor has withdrawn its capital, open to takeover. Nations that had shown little interest in Malta when ruled by its managing director, then became aware of her importance as the naval base she had been since 1565. Britain being in possession became the successor occupier mainly because Napoleon's expedition to Egypt, and the election of a Tsar of Russia as Grand Master, brought home to her the island's potential value to both France and Russia, rivals for empire in the gorgeous east.

I like to think that *The Last of the Crusaders* helped to transform the Knights of Malta from subjects of curiosity and romantic fiction to important players in the game of Mediterranean politics. The archives in Valletta are being mined for information about both the occupiers and the occupied, notably John Montalto's *The Nobles of Malta, 1500–1800*, and much work has and is being done on the last days of the Knights in Malta, the complex matter of the Russian–Polish priory, the election of the last Maltese Grand Master, and on the Maltese intelligentsia and its part in the French invasion. Finally, in an article in a Festschrift in honour of Dr Giovanni Bonello, (The Order of St John and Britain, 1792–5 in *Celebratio Amicitiae*, published last year in Malta by the Fondazzjoni Patrimonju Malti,) Roger Vella Bonavita has elucidated how Admiral Hood came to enrol Maltese sailors in the attack on Toulon in November 1793 (page 208), and what happened to them. The best tribute a man can give to his former pupil is that he wished he had written it.

Inevitably time and scholarship have revealed inaccuracies. The most egregious are on page 207 where the British consul in Malta, Angelo Rutter is said not to have known the name of the British Under-Secretary of State for Southern Affairs. He did. On page 152 it is stated the Grand Master, Emmanuel de Rohan served with the Bailiff de Suffren in his 1781–3 campaign in the Bay of Bengal. He did not, but he did serve his caravans along with Suffren between 1748 and 1752. On page 149 Cavalcabo presented the portrait of the empress Catherine II to Grand Master de Rohan, not to Pinto. Two misspellings: Villeneuve Bougement should read Bargemont (page 276) and Kutchuk Kainardje (page 158) is more accurately spelled Küchük Ki'narja (Kaynardzha). Finally I must acknowledge the generosity of the Fondazzjoni Patrimonju Malti (the Maltese Patrimonial Foundation) for allowing the illustrations which it used in its Malta edition of *The Last of the Crusaders* in 2001 to be used again in this.

Roderick Cavaliero

Grand Master Pinto de Fonçeca (1741-73)

Chapter I

MALTA AND THE HOSPITAL

IN 1798 Napoleon Bonaparte captured the island of Malta and in doing so virtually destroyed the last effective Crusading Order in Europe. The Knights Hospitaller of St John of Jerusalem survive to this day; their only rivals, the Order of Teutonic Knights, had succumbed to enforced inanition long before the Hospitallers ceased to be a force in European politics. It was partly chance, partly a robust constitution that kept the Knights of St John going for so long. They have existed for nearly nine hundred years.

The Hospitallers, as their name implies, had first maintained and protected in Jerusalem the pilgrims' hostel that had been founded by pious merchants from Amalfi. Their patronal saint was St John the Almoner, but at some period of their lively history confusion had arisen over the identity of this little-known St John and the Hospitallers adopted as their patron and protector the more powerful Baptist, whose feast-day became the most solemn festival in the calendar and whose arm was purchased from the Ottoman Emperor Bajazet to become their most treasured relic. In 1113 Pope Paschal II transformed the loose body of devoted Hospitallers into a religious Order following the rule of St Augustine. The first rector was a Provençal (some say Amalfitan) called Gerard who was traditionally endowed with the soubriquet Blessed. In 1119 the Hospitallers were confirmed by Calixtus II and in 1120 elected their first Grand Master, another Frenchman, Raymond de Puy. From that moment they grew in wealth and prestige and became an important, often violent force in the Crusading Kingdoms of Outremer. The monarchs of Europe endowed them with extensive lands, and the Popes granted them equally extensive spiritual privileges. The Hospital remained, throughout, their chief care, but the Hospitallers had, perforce, to become warriors. The younger ones accompanied caravans of pilgrims to Jerusalem and apprenticed themselves by fighting before they learned to nurse. In the uncertain and dangerous epoch in which they served the sick and the poor the Hospitallers were expected to be more adept with the sword than with the scalpel, and as military was more advanced than medical science, the Knights of St John became a closely knit élite corps whose cavalry was feared by Crusader and Saracen alike and whose power often held the balance between contesting princes. It was inevitable that the early statutes demanded exceptional qualities from their members. They were religious, obliged to take monastic vows; they were soldiers obliged to have both the physique and the means for their profession. In the service of God all men are equal, but in the service of the Hospitallers tradition, inheritance and skill with the sword and lance were pre-eminent qualities. The Order of St John was a democracy, but the membership of this democracy was open only to the well-born. The Knights were recruited exclusively from what was to become the aristocracy of Europe.

The years in Palestine saw their evolution into a Crusading Order with a rigid code of laws and a rigorous discipline. But in 1187 Jerusalem fell to Saladdin, and as he disliked the Knights Hospitaller perhaps more than any other of his foes, after the Battle of Hattin he had massacred them without pity, an unexpected act of ferocity on his part. For a time they held various forts—Krak des Chevaliers till 1271, Margat till 1285, and St Jean d'Acre, which fell six years later—and then they were expelled from Palestine. They went first to Cyprus and thence, in 1308, to Rhodes, which they conquered from the Byzantines. There they stayed for 214 years, a thorn in the Ottoman flank, building themselves a huge, gaunt, fortress-like city, and taking to sea in galleys to become pirates in Christ and a force of terror and destruction in the Levant. There, too, in the words of Gibbon, they "neglected to live, but they were prepared to die, in the service of Christ", until

2

the end of 1522, when Suleiman the Magnificent's encircling advances rendered the island impossible to retain. The Ottomans landed, besieged the city through the winter and forced the gallant old warrior Villiers de l'Isle Adam to capitulate. This time the Knights abandoned their Hospital with the honours of war. The oxen dragged the cartloads of archives, cartularies, deeds and benefactions to the waiting ships and the Grand Master stepped off Rhodes in full view of the respectful Turks in the middle of a snowstorm. The Levant had come at last under the Turkish peace.

The European monarchs had watched the last outpost of Christendon fall in the East with only parting regret and fatalistically accepted the position, His Most Christian Majesty actually coming to terms with the Sublime Porte. Alone, Charles V held that his personal duty to Europe lay in meeting the Ottoman menace and had launched a counter-offensive against the van of Islam. In 1510 the Spaniards captured Tripoli. On 23rd March 1530, unable to do better for them, the Emperor signed a Deed of Infeudation with de l'Isle Adam and made the Order of St John the perpetual and unfettered sovereigns of Malta and Tripoli. Malta was his own *feudum* as King of Sicily. He made two conditions: the anchorages of the island were to be closed to all ships of nations at war with the Kingdom of Sicily, and on the accession of every new sovereign the Order's ambassador was to swear homage and fealty to its feudal overlord and to present him each year with a falcon.

Malta was Charles V's last despairing offer, but, with Khair ud-Din Barbarossa raiding the Italian coast to find beauties for his master's harem, the presence of a vigilant, experienced naval force in the narrow waist of water between Sicily and North Africa might act as a deterrent. It probably did not enter his reckoning that the unfertile, unpromising island controlled the most vulnerable link in any trading communications in the Mediterranean. With the whole Levant in Turkish hands, he could not envisage the day when a trade route would stretch from the Echelles of Damietta, Sidon and Tripoli in Lebanon past Malta to Marseilles, Barcelona and the Atlantic.

The island lies sixty miles from Cape Passaro, two hundred and twenty from Tripoli and two hundred from Cape Bon. She forms the apex of an equilateral triangle controlling these two points. No ship sailing through the canal, as the waters were called between Sicily and Malta, could escape the galleys of St John. If Charles V did not see the importance of his move, Suleiman did. Between May and September 1565 he spent what has been computed at thirty thousand lives in an attempt on the island that failed. The siege was one of the most fearful in modern war, and the besiegers and besieged performed prodigies of valour. Then, after considerable and nearly fatal delay, the European monarchs staged the *Gran Soccorso*, but when the Christian ships sailed across from Sicily, Suleiman's forces had already been thwarted to the point of withdrawal. The most famous siege of the century, for the successful outcome of which Queen Elizabeth I of England ordered special prayers in the churches, constituted a defeat for Suleiman, and the hero of Europe, Jean de la Valette, the Grand Master whose indomitable courage had won through, had made the Knights of Rhodes into the Knights of Malta and established them once more as a potent force in the Mediterranean. The results of that siege were to last a further 135 years, and upon the glory of their victory the Knights were to live with decreasing vigour until 1798.

Tripoli had not lasted long. The battle with disease and heat was lost before the final Moorish attack and Malta became the bulwark of Christianity in 1551. It was a small island, ninety-five square miles in area, with fresh-water springs, a few stocky pines and carob trees, and a deep-water anchorage forming a perfect natural harbour. After the comparative size and fertility of Rhodes, the reports which the Knights received of Malta's uncongenial terrain jarred unpleasantly on the ear. Rhodes had been able to supply the Order, its garrison and the Rhodians with enough to eat. Malta could not. Rhodes was set deep in the flesh of the Ottoman world, and short, violent jabs could be made with comparative safety from its harbours. Malta was many miles from the Levant and the seas were fickle and more dangerous. Rhodes was far away from Europe, so that the difficulties and dangers of life there appealed to that quixotic strain in the European who will forsake his home and family to become a Conquistador. Malta was too close. Service would be more like a tour of duty in an uncomfortable frontier post, to be vacated at the first opportunity, and the decline and the fall of the Hospital can be dated from the end of the Great Siege. Many factors contributed. In 1571, at Lepanto, in which the galleys of St John participated, Ottoman naval power was checked, and the threat from the Turk declined. The Unholy Alliance of France and the Sublime Porte increasingly embarrassed the Order, a great number of whose members were French. Growing prosperity and decreasing danger worked their corrosive effect on the martial vigour of the Hospitallers. Finally disputes and dissensions in the Order itself, whose sense of unity declined as the temper of the perpetual war against Islam was tarnished, made its ultimate destruction inevitable. The process was slow, not immediate. The Maltese, who had until the advent of the Knights lived a life dominated by fear of Moorish slave raids, grew and multiplied under their benign administration and became the finest sailors in the Mediterranean. The chief engine of the Order, the galley, officered by the cream of Europe's second sons and cadet nobles and crewed by a motley association of Europeans, wreaked its havoc on Moslem shipping and kept open the waters of Southern Italy. The Maltese corsairs became the fear of the Eastern Mediterranean, and the profits to be made induced as many Knights to make their profession as had the spiritual gains of earlier centuries. To be a Knight of Malta was no empty distinction. The Hospitallers lived and fought hard; they were operating a navy second to none in the Mediterranean, of which no ship ever struck her colours and surrendered to the enemy; they were prosecuting a Crusade in which there were gains to be made both in this world and in the next. In 1655 and 1657 they took part in attempts to seize the Dardanelles and block them, in league with Genoa and Venice. In 1664 the Knights attacked Algiers and in 1707 they assisted the Spaniards to hold Oran. The galleys co-operated in endless cruises against Barbary shipping and the Order's troops were involved in the heroic defence of Candia which the Venetians sustained between 1667–9.

Whenever there was a Crusade to be mounted, whenever grosser causes led the flotillas of Venice, Rome, Spain or France against Islam, the Knights were invited to assist. The chronicles of Bosio, Dal Pozzo and Vertot are scored with accounts of such engagements and encounters, when the van of the war against Islam was occupied by the Knights Hospitaller. But the occasions for military glory grew increasingly infrequent as the Porte became a respectable power and as the commercial interests of France and Venice in the Levant restricted the field of Christian free-booting. Towards the end of the seventeenth century, the greater part of the Order's crusade was spent in cruises round the home waters of Sicily and Sardinia to the west, and of Crete and Morea to the east. As long as the unprincipled states of Barbary, who were uninfluenced by the policy of the Grand Signor, continued to menace Christian shipping, the galleys of St John maintained a regular *Corso*, thrice-yearly cruises in search of the squadrons and pirates of Algiers, Tunis and Tripoli: they seldom failed to make prizes. The record of the Order throughout the seventeenth century showed a vast credit list of captures, firings, sinkings and forcings aground. The number of Moslem slaves in Malta far outnumbered those in other hands. The profits of the *Corso* went to the embellishment of the huge cathedral-like churches that were built in every village, and the rumour of a Maltese vessel in Turkish waters was enough to send all shipping back to port.

But there was a term to this activity. The Holy War was a venture steadily losing its glamour and its utility as Turkey became an ally to be used against Christian powers and as the nature of Europe subtly changed after the relief of Vienna. Pope Innocent X had bravely tried to launch a Holy League against the Crescent, but save for those Mediterranean nations that feared the ever-present possibility of slavery in North

6

Africa and those lands that had once been overrun, the great European powers paid mere lip service to the war against Islam. When Narborough in 1675 freed all British slaves in Tripoli at the point of the gun, he liberated the Maltese too, because he had received provisions from the Grand Master. He did not liberate all the Christians there. Had at any time a concerted naval offensive been launched upon the Barbary Regencies, they would have been destroyed, all their slaves freed and the trade lanes secured. But no such campaign was ever mounted. Instead a *modus pugnandi* was evolved between the powers that disputed the seas, in which certain laws were kept and a licensed anarchy prevailed. Spain, Sicily and Tuscany did not make their peace with Turkey until well into the eighteenth century; Malta, by virtue of the Order's statutory and perpetual war against the enemies of the Cross, never did. Until events dictated a new rationalism in the Mediterranean, Malta, bulwark of Christianity, was a naval base directed against the Moslem. Her survival in that capacity had three causes. First, the Knights did a valuable job in keeping the waters clear. Secondly, the navy of the Order provided a first-rate training for a number of potential officers in the navies of Christian powers. Thirdly, and probably most important, Malta's strategic value in the centre of the Mediterranean meant that were she to be held by any other than a neutral, international Order, she would at once become disputed territory.

The Knights left Malta for good in 1798. Their history has been written in great detail by members of their own Order and by the Abbé Vertot, who published his immense work in 1726. The last years in Malta have never been chronicled. They reveal a gradual and steady decline, a story of spoiled hopes and blind fears, of bursts of vigour and long periods of listlessness and dispute. It is a sad story of a worthy machine running down. The fault did not lie entirely with the Knights, represented so often as leading lives of degenerate licence in their island fortress, debauching the local inhabitants, grinding down the Maltese over whom they exercised a lordly and indifferent sway. In the growing complexity of European politics, the existence of an international order of chivalry engaged on a crusade became an anomaly which was difficult to reconcile with a Europe of governments who had long since tacitly agreed on abandoning wars of religion. A small power only functions in a power vacuum or by kind permission of its protectors. The vacuum had ceased to exist by 1698, but the protectors, particularly France, did not choose to remove that permission until Napoleon Bonaparte landed his first troops at dawn on 10th June 1798.

Chapter II

EIGHTEENTH-CENTURY CRUSADERS

WHO were the Knights Hospitaller entitled to carry the eight-pointed cross emblazoned upon their person, the four arms signifying the Christian virtues of prudence, justice, fortitude and temperance, the eight points the beatitudes these virtues bestowed and its colour the incandescent whiteness of knightly purity? They were the younger brothers and second sons for, unless the Pope granted a dispensation, the wearer was a monk.

But he was a monk with a difference. He had not abandoned the world; he was not a priest but a lay brother. He wore no distinguishing costume but the cross. He was free to move about the world but at the same time he had taken a vow of poverty, chastity and obedience. It was a strange and difficult vocation.

In Rhodes the Knights had been obliged to live in convent, in a special *collachium* cut off from the rest of the island. In Malta, though Valetta was called the conventual city and younger Knights were encouraged to live in barrack-like hostelries known as Inns, this distinction was not kept. Older men and particular families were allowed to build their own houses and to live often outside the city walls, like gentlemen of leisure.

As the responsibilities of the Order grew, so did the pious bequests, and in order to assist in the collection of revenues and in the maintenance of its lands, the system was adopted of assigning those Knights who had done their apprenticeship or "caravan" a self-supporting estate known as a "commandery". For the upkeep of this he was responsible, as a steward, who should pass it on when he relinquished it in as

9

good, if not better, condition. Of the revenues, however, he was obliged to send a certain percentage to the Treasury of the Order, and this was known as his responsions. These commanderies were grouped into Priories—of which there were nineteen—and the Priories into Tongues. There were eight of these, of France, Auvergne, Provence, Castile, Aragon, Italy, Germany and England. In 1540 the Tongue of England disappeared in all but name before the rapacity of Henry VIII. It provided ten martyrs for the Order.

Many Knights Commander lived as country squires on their commanderies; some appointed bailiffs and lived at court; some occupied positions of trust in the convent. As a Knight was promoted, so he would enjoy *smutition* from a poorer to a richer commandery. In theory the richest went to those who had deserved them, but, with powerful friends at court, merit was not always the test. Others who were Ambassadors or Captains of galleys with considerable expenses to meet were allowed to hold as many as three commanderies. The advantage of the system was to give the Commander a close personal interest in the source of his income, guaranteeing the Treasury its regular tithe and acquitting it of the burden of maintenance. The danger was that it slackened the sense of belonging to a community and encouraged ambition after material rather than spiritual benefits.

Though a Knight might live most of his days as a country squire, he could not acquire heirs to his body or his fortune. In theory, too, he was the possessor of no goods; what he enjoyed, he enjoyed by permission, what he left was the spoil of the Order. Many possessed enormous private fortunes, and apart from one-fifth that could be willed away, they accrued to the Treasury on their demise. Some then lived to the hilt, liquidating capital; others, perhaps more, considered their personal incomes at the disposal of their Order, for which they would reap the credit while alive and the glory when dead. The treasures of Malta were their legacies.

Not all the Knights were rich; there were many poor men with ancient pedigrees and humble means for whom the commanderies were intended—but on the whole the Order was rich and composed of rich men. It did not escape the envy its enormous wealth attracted. Protestant monarchs had sequestered its lands; Catholic sovereigns cast greedy eyes on its untouchable riches. The Holy Father himself was not above laying a tribute on the Priory of Rome. Yet they were not sufficient. The colossal works of the Order were first conducted from the resources of the Treasury, but as the centuries passed, the value of money decreased as the revenues failed to rise. The upkeep of the navy, the Hospital, the fortifications and a diplomatic service proved an endless drain, and the Order in the eighteenth century found itself often in debt.

The Knights of Malta, then, were religious brothers, expected to keep their vows and to lead exemplary lives in the face of every temptation that the world had to offer. To enter the ranks of the Hospitallers, no religious vocation was needed, no aptitude for hospital work, for fighting, for administration, for holiness. The intrinsic nobility of the candidate, revealed by an unsullied pedigree, was, in the glorious legend of Europe's aristocracy, sufficient to ensure his capacity for all these things. The privileges of birth enjoined the duties of nobility: the Order, because it was a republic of aristocrats, was the last organization in which the nobility of Europe carried out the duties for which it had originally been created.

Over half the Knights of the Order were French, whose three Tongues disposed of 272 commanderies in all. Their paternal and maternal grandparents had to be *gentilshommes de nom et d'armes*; an aspirant had to prove eight quarters of nobility. The Italians demanded only four quarters but two hundred years of recognized nobility. Since the Italian nobility was rather patrician than royal, this proviso was to ensure that the candidate's family had respectable origins. Families that had made their name in banking and commercial industries and still maintained the business were not excluded. The Tongues of Aragon and Castile (which included Portugal) also required four quarters and their chief preoccupation was to ensure that there was no Moorish or Jewish blood in the family. The

Germans were most strict: sixteen quarters had to be shown and each family had to be received into the Assembly of the Circles of the Empire and have entrance into all noble Colleges. If any quarter failed, so did the candidate. No civil nobles, no premier magistrates qualified and royal bastards were denied admission, other Tongues admitting the legitimized issue of royal misdemeanours. The Tongue of Germany, too, refused to admit German-speaking candidates who lived outside the boundaries of the Holy Roman Empire, and resisted most bitterly any attempt to include outsiders. This exclusiveness explains why so few of the distinguished members of the Order were Germans: the field for recruitment was too narrow.

Each candidate's application was closely scrutinized. The local Priory set up a commission of four to examine the documents, it called witnesses and visited the candidate's family. The "proofs" were then sent to Malta, and re-examined by the Head of the Tongue, followed by a special council, and finally by the Venerable Council of the Order. If they were accepted, the Grand Master sent to Rome for a papal brief. The Pope alone could grant dispensations if any quarter were missing. The Priory of Portugal alone, where the genealogies of all noble families were lodged in the Royal Archives, did not conduct the preliminary investigations. Yet dilutions in the noble blood were accepted. Rome often upheld appeals for dispensation, and in Italy particularly the *haute bourgeoisie* found the doors eased open by Papal protection. Nobility, however, was not a quality you could acquire; it was born in you and like a good wine needed years of maturity to bring it to full flavour. There were bitter protests. In 1715 the French Knights wrote to the Regent Orleans protesting at the continuous stream of dispensations requested by the royal house: "Of all the privileges that men enjoy, the antiquity of nobility is the greatest. It is above all ranks or dignities, above the gift of Kings, who may only give it birth: it is the passage of time, the course of centuries that gives it honour and glory."

Dispensations never, however, dispensed with the necessity for aspirants to be noble born. It was possible to become something less than a Knight and still to wear the cross. A Servant-at-Arms was not a noble, but he enjoyed a vote in the Councils and was eligible for promotion. It was not impossible, though exceedingly unlikely, for one to become Grand Master. Conventual Chaplains—priests of the Order—were recruited from the lesser gentry and wore the cross. Neither Servant-at-Arms nor Chaplain could spring from stock engaged in any "vile or mechanic art", or sordid commerce. The senior Chaplain was the Grand Prior, the Order's own Bishop, for Knights were not subject to the ecclesiastical jurisdiction of the Ordinary. Lastly there were the Donats, without rights but with the privileges of knighthood, entitled to wear a half-cross, their reward for services rendered. They were permitted to marry. Professed Knights were known as Knights of Justice; there was a growing number—like the famous Metternich, who proudly wore the cross on every occasion—of Knights of Devotion, awarded the cross *honoris causa*. With these, who numbered latterly most of the great names of Europe, we are not concerned.

Two other classes must be mentioned: the Knight of Magistral Grace, created by the Grand Master without *proofs* for signal services to the Order, and Knights Commander in *ius patronatus*. In this case, important families may have endowed the Order with lands, reserving the right to nominate the Commander, who was subject in all things to the Statutes. Often the Pope allowed a "family" commander to marry and to retain the cross: there were many of these dispensations in the eighteenth century.

Promotion within the Order was by seniority. Because of this, a limited number, usually a hundred families, were allowed to enter children at birth. These enjoyed seniority as soon as they reached their sixteenth birthday. Every entrant paid his *passaggio*—a deposit originally paid by an aspirant Knight to the patron who conducted him to Jerusalem—computed in the sixteenth century at 260 golden crowns. It was like entry to an exclusive public school. At twelve, a future Knight might be sent to Malta as one of the twelve pages, where he waited upon the Grand Master, and received an education at his expense from senior Knights and special tutors. These pages were usually chosen from poorer families.

At fifteen, the page returned to his family for a year in which to digest his experiences. Regular profession could be made at sixteen, but only after a year's novitiate. Those who had not served as pages could therefore begin their novitiate at fifteen, but in later centuries it started later, profession following after the eighteenth birthday. A candidate could serve his novitiate only up to his twenty-fifth year; after that a special dispensation was needed.

The novitiate was spent in Malta in a communal house under the instruction of a Master of Novices, always a Knight Grand Cross, and two other senior Knights. It was passed, or should have been passed, in religious services and communal prayers, all novices taking Communion together on set days, and exercising three days a week at swordsmanship, sabring and musketry. But novices were only young and often high-spirited. Discipline became so lax on occasions that in 1770 the Grand Master was constrained to write to his Ambassador in Rome that, unless hooliganism were stopped, the noble houses of Europe would have second thoughts about sending their sons to Malta at all.

When the novitiate was over, the novice returned to his Priory for six months where he might take a commission in his monarch's service. If all reports were favourable, he would proceed to take his vows. This ancient ceremony was usually carried out in the church of the Priory. The candidate presented himself in secular habit, after being absolved of his sins, before a Knight deputed to receive him. He would carry a lighted candle to represent Charity; this he would hold throughout Mass, at which he would receive Communion. The Knight receiving him would warn him of the gravity of his vows, especially that of obedience. He would ask four questions: Was the aspirant already a member of any religious Order? Was he married? Did he owe money to the Treasury? Was he an unredeemed slave? The last question dated from Palestinian days, when Knights were received more readily, in camp or on the field of battle. The candidate then laid his hand on a missal and made the following promise: "I vow to God, to Saint Mary, ever a Virgin, Mother of God, to St John the Baptist, to render henceforth, and for ever, by the grace of God, a true obedience to the Superior which it pleases Him to give me and who will be the choice of our Religion, to live without property and to guard my chastity."

He thus became *un serviteur de messieurs les pauvres malades* and was consecrated to the defence of the Church.

The receiving Knight then pointed to the eight-pointed cross. "Do you believe that this is the Holy Cross upon which Jesus Christ was secured and died for the redemption of our sins? This is the sign of our Order, which we command you to wear always on your garments." The new Knight kissed the cross and the knightly mantle was placed across his shoulders, the cross covering the heart. He was then solemnly warned that "if ever in fighting for Jesus Christ against the enemies of the Faith, he should turn his back and abandon the standard of the cross to take flight in a war so just, he will be despoiled of the Holy Sign as a prevaricator and cut off from the Order like a rotten and gangrenous limb." The mantle was then secured by a cord round his neck. "Receive the yoke of the Lord, because it is sweet and light, under which you will find repose for your soul. We promise you only bread and water, and no delicacies, and a modest habit of no price."

The candidate had now left his fathers and become a Knight of St John; he had a paramount duty to his Order.

This dignified and simple ceremony was a final profession. It could only be dissolved by death, dispensation or disgrace. A ceremony existed for the spoliation of a Knight and his discharge from the Order. But so serious was dismissal that it was seldom invoked.

The newly-professed Knight was under no obligation to go to Malta until he was twenty. But before he could be promoted, he had to perform four caravans, unless exempted by special

Grace of the Grand Master. Each caravan was a cruise, lasting at least six months, in the galleys. As service in the sailing ships of the Order proved so attractive in the eighteenth century, the caravan period upon them was raised to one year to prevent the galleys from being denuded of *caravanisti*. The galleys were not at sea all that time but the *caravanista* was on active service for the whole period. The caravans ensured that nearly every Knight had some experience of practical naval matters. Their ignorance of more theoretical aspects of seamanship, however, grew so alarming in the days of more complicated sailing that the Grand Master in 1782 added a school of Mathematics and Nautical Sciences to the recently founded University and made it obligatory for all novices, *caravanisti* and Knights in the service of the Order, whether at sea or in the regiments, to attend. While not actually on board ship, and for some time after completion of his caravans, if a Knight did not at once go home he would lodge at the Inn (*Auberge*) of his Tongue. Here he slept communally, and ate communally—by fours off a single platter—under the presidency of the Pilier. The Pilier received an annual subvention of sixty scudi per year per Knight, but what with the elderly Knights who were to be maintained at his expense and the rising costs he was nearly always out of pocket. In 1678 a French writer was amazed at the cheer he found at one Inn, fruit and vegetables of wonderful freshness, excellent bread, meat and game of the greatest variety and no shortage of ice, brought by a special merchant from the summit of Mount Etna. In 1741 the Knights of Provence nightly raided the Pilier's table because their food was so bad. Oxford colleges have similar tales to tell. A Knight who was lucky might find himself commanded to the Grand Master's table—the fabulous Cotoners in the seventeenth century had as many as a hundred seconded to their company for entertainment. Sir William Young in 1772, used to the great houses of Europe, was struck by the fact that "the Grand Master is always served at table by the Knights in person, who, whatever their pretensions to rank or distinction on the continent or in their native country may be, never sit or are never covered in his presence ". Those Knights who set up house—many lived in palaces their families had built when Valetta was first constructed—saw to it that they lived well, and as frequent boats called at all the ports of the Mediterranean, cooks from Cataluña, Parma, Bresse or the Tyrol would send in their orders regularly.

Caravans completed, the Knight would return to his own land, there to enter the service of his monarch, or to live at his own or his family's expense until he qualified for a commandery. Those who stayed in the island joined the fleet as officers or became administrators. A good naval officer, however, stood the best chance of promotion and Grand Masters refused to accept powerful intercessions on behalf of second-rate candidates for the captaincy of a galley or a man-of-war. Later in the eighteenth century when the galleys became largely obsolete, the Grand Master gave way more often. It was not always possible to refuse requests for commanderies and offices of state, but on the matter of naval commands the Grand Masters were strict. The Captain of a galley had to be at least twenty-five, had to have completed his caravans, had to have been professed for ten years. The number of Knights commanding in the navies of France, Spain and the Italian states is testimony to the value European monarchs placed upon their training and experience in the fleets of Malta.

The caravans, however, were not wholly productive of good. Towards the end of the eighteenth century, as the ships went out on more and more fruitless cruises, they had the opposite of the desired effect. One distinguished knightly Polonius in a treatise for other members of his family who might become Knights considered that by 1764 they merely gave young Knights opportunities for duelling, gaming and scandal-mongering.

High spirits and horse-play were not confined to novices, and one of the major problems of life in Malta for a young Knight was finding something to do. With its restricted size and limited resources, the island was invaded for periods of the year by large numbers of hot-blooded, proud young men, who had not moderated undergraduate high spirits with the virtues of temperance. They were thrown together in precocious youth into communal life, many of them touchy on points of honour and resolved to cut a dash. High spirits often began a rag which degenerated into violence; often some real or pretended insult to their dignity would bring the young men into open revolt. Riots reminiscent of the town and gown conflicts of English university cities were rare, but unpleasant, and they did not go down well with the local population, who walked in dread of them.

For a Knight of Malta was a privileged being, subject to discipline according to the statutes of the Order, not the laws of the land, but while he was immune from the attentions of the local police, it did not mean he was free to do as he liked. If he broke the rules, he could be arrested, but only at the direct command of the *Maestro Scudiere* or the Pilier of his Tongue. He could be imprisoned only in the castles of St Angelo and St Elmo, and he stood trial before his equals. A conciliar committee tried his case, and his punishment was at the hands of the Grand Master. The supreme penalty was dismissal from the Order and consignment to the secular arm. This was rarely applied, the first being considered serious enough to meet most crimes but unrepentant heresy. Life imprisonment was more common. For light offences, the Knight might cool his heels for a period in St Elmo. Appeals were often made by his family to his monarch to intercede for him, but over and above the Grand Master there was only the Pope as supreme head of their religion. Such an appeal should only have been made after the judicial processes had been completed, but there was an irregular short cut. The offender might appeal to the Inquisitor, the Papal representative in the island, who might then send it direct to Rome. This was the cause of endless trouble, as Rome did not always care to send the appeal back to Malta, and the Grand Master, whose relations with the Holy See were always delicate, had to insist respectfully, and often unsuccessfully, that the appeal was irregular. Because Rome upheld so many appeals it became customary for a Knight who knew he was in trouble to appeal straightway before any judgment had been pronounced, and the ill-effects of this were most noticeable towards the end of the eighteenth century.

Discipline was always a major problem. The oath of obedience was a religious oath, taken by one member of a religious body to its head, and in Catholic countries the Order could call on the secular arm to arrest offenders against its statutes. Disobedience struck at the whole body of the Religion. But as the eighteenth century progressed, the acts of defiance became more frequent as the activities of the Order were circumscribed. Duties and obligations that survived from the more active centuries grew irksome and unpleasant, a series of gross breaches that went virtually unpunished set a bad example. As a Grand Master was not expected to live long, an action of defiance against the ruling head was often calculated to constitute an offence only so long as he was alive; his successor might be counted upon to pardon the offender. It was not uncommon to find Knights who were in serious trouble under one Grand Master enjoying positions of trust under another. Intercessions from monarchs, prelates and ministers of state were a powerful force militating against absolute severity in an Order whose members were related to the highly placed and where statutory penalties, drawn up when the Order was a militant, fighting force, were sometimes unnecessarily harsh.

The second oath of the triple vow was that of chastity. The cynics and wits of the eighteenth century were quick to relish the inconsistency of an Order whose members were vowed to poverty and chastity but who kept enormous establishments in which they installed their women. Patrick Brydone, a stout Protestant of the Establishment, who visited Malta in 1770 described the departure of the galleys for a cruise off Tripoli: "There were about thirty Knights in each galley, making signals all the way to their mistresses who were weeping for their departure upon the bastions; for these gentlemen pay almost as little regard to their vows of chastity as the priests and confessors do."

A similar observation was made by Sir William Young: "Their vows are chastity and charity and obedience to the canons of the Order: these they trangress every day: with respect to the first, almost every Knight has his mistress publicly, who is called his *Commare* or Gossip."

This harsh judgment is partially corroborated by the old Polonius mentioned already, a worthy Knight called Camillo Spreti. The ladies of Malta he had found very pressing, inquisitive and flattering, and because the island lay very close to the torrid zone, the women were hot and wanton by nature. "Guard yourself at night time," he advises his nephews, "against the evil women, who, completely enveloped in their mantles and filling all the streets, pursue their abominable trade of allurement, importuning the passers-by while seeking to cloak their sin under pretext of begging alms."

It would be too much to expect five hundred Sir Galahads to survive the temptations of a free-and-easy world. But this very delight in the inconsistency evinced by eighteenth-century writers must put us on our guard. The Knight of Malta provided a ready-made type for the sentimental novels of the day, and in many French *romans* of the eighteenth century we find a prominent part played by a Knight of Malta—always young and handsome, always professed against his will, usually enamoured of some gentle lady who perforce became his mistress. The exemplar of a sensitive, melancholy, refined lover, with noble background and an impediment to marriage, was immortalized in the Chevalier des Grieux.

Sometimes the hero of these romances is a Don Juan, a perfect bad character who ought to be good, a sometimes heartless, more often sentimental, seducer of noble beauty. The plots, however, are set outside Malta. When in *Les Liaisons Dangereuses* the Chevalier d'Anceney had killed Valmont in a duel, he remembered his neglected duties. "I shall go to Malta," he wrote, "and finish with my life of pleasure, and there I shall religiously keep these vows that will separate me from a world, of which, young as I am, I have had so much to complain."

Conditions in Malta were severer and life at no time was a riot of degenerate pleasure. There were scallywags, it is true, but when Coleridge, who was for six months secretary to the first British Governor of Malta, averred that every Knight attached himself to some family as their patron and friend to whom the honour of a sister or a daughter was sacrificed as a matter of course, then he must be disbelieved. The slander that some two hundred and fifty families of the island were willing to allow the debauchery of their women for the dubious value of a Knight's protection is wholly inconsistent with the severe and intense private morality which has always been a characteristic of the Maltese. That there was a small circle in which a Knight might find the pleasures of both table and bed is true, but the universal depravity of morals, so indignantly claimed by the British who took over in 1801 and categorically affirmed by the very Treasurer of the Order who played Quisling to Bonaparte's invasion of 1798, was part of a propaganda campaign to justify the transfer of power that occurred at that time.

The obligations of celibacy were often irksome to men who considered their vows the tiresome accompaniments to a life they had not chosen themselves. Towards the end of the eighteenth century little attempt was made to disturb what was discreetly hidden. Yet, if the regulations were blatantly defied, retribution was harsh—imprisonment for the Knight, exile for his paramour. The tone, however, was low enough for the rigorists, and the same Treasurer, Bosredon de Ransijat, in his *apologia pro rebellione sua*, stated that troublesome husbands had actually been "removed" with official approval. Yet the Grand Master he castigated by name struck with the greatest severity at offenders.

The Maltese, in general, did not mix with the Knights; their wives were forbidden to hold or attend receptions, while their husbands kept the doors firmly closed to all comers like

Dr Bartolo. They were allowed to attend Mass, but only wearing a thick black veil which covered their faces in such a way that only their eyes—*qui sont les plus beaux du monde*—were visible. A writer in 1678 believed that a young Knight would find life intolerable without the diversions of feminine company, and said that they were not hard to find. But it was always risky. A jealous husband or common informer was only needed to inform the *Maestro Scudiere* for the machinery of law to strike and the cells of St Elmo to be opened. They were frequently occupied.

Camillo Spreti warned his nephews against coffee-houses where the idle "mis-spend their time, speaking ill of others, impugning both reputation and honour". He was afraid they would be involved in a duel. Duelling was most strictly forbidden as it was both "a sin to draw on a brother and a crime of *lèse-majesté*", punished by long stretches of imprisonment. Duels there were: outside the strict air of the convent they were sometimes fatal, but throughout the eighteenth century there is no record of a fatal encounter in Malta. The bloodletting of an earlier age gave way to the pinpricks that satisfied honour.

Spreti wanted his nephews to map out their day with intellectual and athletic exercises, such as the study of music or navigation. This was not, however, easy. The *caravanisti* were often men of rudimentary education, loath to apply themselves to study. Intellectual pursuits were limited, and as the intelligentsia of the island were almost wholly the local clergy—not necessarily the Conventual Chaplains, only six of whom were Maltese—with whom relations were often strained, little incentive was provided until the palmy days of piracy declined and the prospect of long periods of enforced idleness became a grave social problem. A press was established in Malta only in 1747, a hundred years after the initial proposal had foundered in a long quarrel with the Inquisitor. In 1763 the Bailiff de Tencin bequeathed as part of his spoils an entire library of twenty thousand volumes, later installed in a handsome neoclassical building erected at the expense of the Spanish Bailiff

Perez de Sarrio in 1776. "I have deplored all my life", de Tencin wrote in his will, "the ignorance that reigns in the Orders of Religion." By 1798 the collection had swelled to fifty thousand volumes: it contained all the classics of European literature, though nothing by Tencin's dangerous contemporaries, Voltaire, Rousseau or the Encyclopaedists. An attempt was made to leaven the collection with some mathematical, medical and scientific treatises, but perversely it contained nothing on seamanship. In addition to the library the eighteenth-century Grand Masters and Bailiffs held *conversazioni*, but these were often the occasions of scandal and intrigue.

Relations with the local Maltese nobility and *bourgeoisie* were not close. Spreti, with all his good sense, wrote contemptuously of their intelligence and of their provincial manners. As a result, he believed, "of the wrongs and discourteous treatment they had suffered from a few extravagant fellows among the Knights", they kept very much to themselves, for, on arrival, so the story goes, the Hospitallers had proved a little too gallant with the ladies. Whatever the reason, the aristocracy lived in the ancient city with their "limited education, their spirit spiced with prejudice, their air of savagery, their welcome cold and their conduct dissimulating". In reality they had little reason to fraternize with the Knights, who might always snub them. In every office of the island but that of Bishop and Grand Prior, who were sometimes Maltese, the lowliest Knight was a more important person than the highest Maltese. There were otherwise only six Maltese members of the Order—all of them Conventual Chaplains. The aristocracy was not eligible for membership, and families like the Siculo-Maltese Parisios got their sons in because they were born in Sicily and their proofs were accepted by the Priory of Messina as Sicilians. It was not until 1756 that a Maltese, the French consul Abela, was given a Cross of Devotion and in the eighteenth century a number became Donats. But the Maltese on the whole preserved towards their overlords the same detachment that the Venetians showed their Austrian rulers in the nineteenth century. There was little love, though often genuine and deserved mutual respect, and much disdain and obsequiousness between them. Towards the end of the eighteenth century there were occasional outbursts of hostility.

In 1769 a university was founded on the spoils of the dispossessed Jesuits with degrees recognized by Rome, and the Grand Masters saw a chance to mend the rift by bringing novices and scions of the local aristocracy together in a common education. Towards the end of the century, there were signs of a precocious activity. The press produced a number of medical tracts. The local *literati* tried their hand at odes and masques to commemorate the endless junketings of an international Order, though to our modern ear we must admit that they merit praise only for the delicacy in which the sycophancy was couched. The *salon* in the absence of any fashionable and cultivated lady was impossible in Malta, but Maltese scholars were making their names abroad, becoming members of French and Italian academies. Numerous contacts with the world of letters, arts and commerce acted as a leaven in a population wrapped too long in "African isolation". Arabic studies were made the concern of a university chair and enquiries initiated into the supposed Punic origin of the Maltese tongue. In 1782 the Parisian Academy of Inscriptions was able to reconstruct some of the missing letters of the Phoenician alphabet from two *cippi* discovered in Malta with inscriptions in Punic and Greek. No less a man than the Captain-General of the Galleys, the Bailiff de Freslon, who became Librarian, and the Knight Louis de Boisgelin took a lively interest in the astonishing Neolithic temples that were being properly excavated for the first time. Local antiquarians, the Donat Count Ciantar and the Conventual Chaplain de Soldanis, helped to foster an intellectual coterie that studied the history, archaeology and language of Malta. Ciantar became a member of the Paris Academy of Inscriptions; Antonio Vassalli, Professor of Arabic, wrote the first scientific grammar and dictionary of the Maltese language.

In the realm of experimental science too a new interest was being shown. Grand Master Pinto set up a laboratory, in which Cagliostro claimed to have worked, and the celebrated geologist Déodat de Dolomieu, a Knight of the Order, conducted many of his most important surveys while in Malta. He accompanied the Bailiff Camille de Rohan on an embassy to Portugal in 1778 and studied the volcanic formation of that country. He then proceeded to examine the volcanoes of Sicily and Naples as well as the climatic and geological features of Malta. He persuaded the Grand Master to set up an observatory in the suburb of Floriana, which flourished from 1782 to 1789, when it was destroyed by lightning. His collection of natural objects and specimens of stone became one of the most extensive in Europe and was lodged in his house at Valetta. With the Grand Master de Rohan, an enthusiastic amateur, and one or two other Knights who play a dubious role in our story, he numbered Sir William Hamilton as a fellow researcher. Dolomieu's fame was to be perpetuated in the discovery and classification of that magnesian limestone which is today called dolomite. In the late 'eighties his relations with the Grand Master cooled, and in 1790 he bequeathed his unique collection to the U.S.A. on condition that a similar collection of geology and fauna of the New World should in a hundred years be made to France. He was enrolled by Bonaparte as one of the savants to accompany him on his Egyptian expedition and was accordingly present at the fall of Malta. Dolomieu was one of the most distinguished Hospitallers. His intellectual curiosity and avidity for work were untypical of his fellows, few of whom he liked, but he had his following and amateur science was an interest of some of the older members of the Order who returned to Malta to enjoy the climate and the fruits of their seniority.

But these intellectual opportunities did not attract more than a small number. Even the enthusiastic sailors had to be entertained while on shore, and towards the end of the century Grand Master de Rohan tried to break down the mutual exclusiveness of the Maltese and the Order by holding soirées to which women were invited and patronizing the theatre of which he was an enthusiast. He even created new titles and held all-night balls, an event unheard of in earlier days. Despite the relaxation and the veneer of cosmopolitan civilization, the mixture of garrison town, hospital, naval dockyard and monastery was not one in which the gentle arts flourished. The alternative attraction of gambling was stronger. Though card games for profit were strictly forbidden, and despite periodic attempts to enforce the regulations, the vice persisted, and was patronized even by the Bailiffs.

The objection to gambling was that it helped to dissipate money which by the Knight's vow of poverty should have belonged in one way or another to the Order. Though Knights could do what they liked with their own, it was better they should spend their money on building or good works. They should not spend it on expensive clothes. Sumptuary laws promulgated in 1697 and 1741 put an embargo on clothes made from brocade or cloth of gold or silver, on all lace fringes and trimmings, on gold or silver buttons and knots or bows of gold or silver thread. The penalties were confiscation of the offending garment, which would become the informer's, and three years in St Elmo. The decree was so effective that Knights of different nations did not attempt to compete in styles of dress. Brydone in 1769 found all the "Knights and commanders have much the appearance of gentlemen and men of the world. We met with no character in the extreme. . . . The French skip, the Germans strut, the Spanish stalk are all mingled together in such small proportions that none of them is striking."

On ceremonial occasions the Knights appeared in full dress —the captains of the galleys in red surcoats and gold braid, the officers with tricornes and white stockings, all with the red silk soubrevest blazoned with the white cross of St John. In convent, they were expected to wear the habit—a black cloak with the white cross embroidered over the left shoulder, black vest, breeches and hose. They could carry a sword, through the handle of which they would loop the clumsy stole that hung from the neck down the left side and was embroidered with the symbols of the Passion. This costume was worn on formal rather than ceremonial occasions and always by the Piliers in their Inns. The walking-out costume would be cut, modestly, in the fashion of the day.

The French formed the majority in the Order, with their three Tongues. The Germans, because they were allowed to complete their caravans by service on the Turkish frontier, were the least numerous. At times there were Poles, Magyars, Englishmen, Peruvians, Swedes and Russians aboard the galleys—some as *caravanisti*, some as cadets under training. Navarrois were part of the Aragonese Tongue; Portuguese, with their Grand Priory of Crato, of the Castilian, along with South Americans. Savoyards and Jacobite English were usually Knights of Italy; the Swiss had commanderies in the German and Italian Tongues. Poles belonged until 1776 to the Bohemian Priory of the Tongue of Germany with Silesians and Magyars. Belgians, Alsatians and Lorrainers were Knights of Germany. The divisions followed a linguistic pattern long out of date. In 1776 the King of Sardinia wished to reserve the commanderies in his kingdom for his subjects only, and after an arduous and expensive diplomatic shuffle the various states of Italy followed suit. The English Tongue in 1783 was revived to incorporate the Bavarians and Poles, both of whom had set up new Priories, and Frederick the Great after the conquest of Silesia refused to let Imperial subjects hold the commanderies there. The international flavour of the Hospitallers wilted under the nationalism of the monarchs of Europe: only in Malta were national differences ignored, for there the Knights were Hospitallers first and foremost in an island where all Christian monarchs were equally honoured. The internationalism of the Knights was another anachronism of the century, and the Order's virtual extinction after 1798 coincided with the holocaust of principalities and powers that had defied the new rationalization of Europe.

In that new rationalization many Knights felt uncomfortably aware that the times were running against the Order. In the palmy days of the Holy War there had been plenty to do of one sort or another, but as the Turks became the allies of Christian powers and as the war against Barbary was progressively whittled down, so the Knights became the victims of the ambience they had created for themselves. Many hoped for a placid life on their commanderies, studiously ignoring the summons that came periodically from Malta when the island was believed to be in danger. France would not allow Malta to fall to the Turks, so why should they uproot themselves to make the long and tedious journey? "That which mortifies me above all," wrote the indignant Ambassador in Paris to the Grand Master in November 1722, "is the lack of courage shown by our French Knights. I am ashamed to belong to the same nation as they. . . . They say that alarm is taken too easily in Malta, and at the wrong times, that the voyage will ruin them, that they will leave the Order. Others aver that these alarums will put off many families from having their children received as Knights of Malta." His worst fears, however, were not realized, as the lists of professions right up to the end of the century show.

This attitude was a sad degeneration from earlier days, but there were still enough good men in the Order to keep it useful and effective. By the second half of the eighteenth century, however, the number was running short. The really good men, like the Bailiff de Suffren, made careers for themselves in the service of their own monarchs. The mediocre stood out for their rights and lived correct, dutiful but unrewarding lives. The lazy ones, the greedy ones, the rebellious ones quarrelled among themselves and, with little else to do, tore the fabric, thread by thread, to tatters.

Such, then, were the Knights, a mixed company of expert sailors, good administrators, philanderers and loafers. Many were bored, most were rich, on the whole they were brave. In earlier days they had shown a quixotic valour that was deeply tinged with buccaneering: the savage mien of soldiers fighting in a war in which quarter was neither expected nor asked for was softened by their duties in the Hospital, where the proudest and bravest were required to wait upon the sick, however dirty or humble. They were in Malta to promote and assist the legend of Europe's aristocracy, and they carried on into the late modern age the principles for which Europe's aristocracy had been created. They were men of the sword whose job was fighting, protecting and serving. In the duties of a Knight Hospitaller, the term *Noblesse oblige* found positive meaning—they were defenders of the faithful, the weak, the pious, the humble, the good, servants of the sick, the maimed and the diseased. The greatest legend of Christendom, enshrined in the gestes of chivalry, found active expression in an Order at once monastic and chivalrous. A Knight Hospitaller was a walking model for the virtues of a Lancelot and a Roland.

By the eighteenth century something of this picture had been modified. The Order had become more like a school for cadet nobility, the most compact and useful international body in a Europe of growing nations, and it provided a reflection and reminder of Europe's past and of the potentialities of her future. But though the Catholicism of the Order was strictly maintained, a large number of its Knights did not escape the moral indifferentism of the century. They continued to give the Order *bon ton* but seldom devoted religious service. A high level of good behaviour and a business-like devotion to duty was, in most cases, the best that could be expected. A society managed entirely by elderly staff officers—which is an adequate description of eighteenth-century Malta—undoubtedly lacked a certain elasticity and suffered from defects of imagination. Dullness was the keynote of life in the island. The tone set at the top was of mild urbanity with a meticulous and fussy insistence on discipline and precedence. High spirits, explosions of violence, crime and criminality there were, but, despite the incredulity of contemporary witnesses and the malice of those who did not believe in monastic pretensions, immorality and flagrant breaches of discipline were not the rule. The atmosphere of Malta was like that of St Cyr, and, as a forcing house for officers of the marine and for useful soldiers, as good a military academy as existed anywhere at the time. However much Gibbon taunted and polite society coughed behind its hand, the spirit of the Order was not hypocritical; even the most advanced of its enlightened members would not have held that the sum of its virtues was less than that of its vices. The aristocrats of Europe, when they were allowed to find a job worthy of their rank, were usually men who believed in what they were doing.

Chapter III

THE LAW AND THE ORDER

THE Abbé Vertot in his massive work on the Order of St
John compared its constitution to that of Venice and in
doing so proved unwittingly that the first city states of
medieval Europe modelled themselves upon the monastic
Orders. The Knights Hospitaller were the bridge between the
religious City of God and the secular City of Man. It was a
Republic of Aristocrats.

The constitution vested the supreme legislative authority in
the Chapter General, a council of all Knights and Servants-at-
Arms of whatever degree in whom was reposed the sole power
to amend the statutes that were binding on them all. Originally
the Chapters General were to meet every five years; this was
soon lengthened to ten, and by the fifteenth century the loose,
inchoate and often anarchic Chapters General met with
increasing infrequency. After 1631, another was not to meet
until 1776. As a complementary process the power of the
Grand Master and his council of dignitaries increased. The
Order in fact was administered by councils. The Chapter
General itself used to resign all effective power to a committee
of Sixteen, one Bailiff and one Knight from each Tongue, and
this had the effective legislative power—subject always to the
approval of the Pope.

The day-to-day administration was carried on by the
Venerable Council composed of a corpus of dignitaries. For
judicial purposes this was swelled by the addition of two
representatives from every Tongue and of every Grand Cross
to become the *Complete Council*. This was the highest criminal
court in the Order before which all offenders were tried. It
could also be called upon to ratify the decisions of the last and

most important council—the *Sacred Council*. This was responsible for policy decisions on questions of statecraft. To it every Grand Cross had the right to belong, though not everyone cared to attend its meetings. It had no collective or individual responsibility and legally no member could be excluded. It had therefore the features neither of a cabinet nor of a cabal. As the eighteenth century wore on, the Grand Masters, in common with the absolutist princes of their day, began to work with what was called a *Congregation of State*—a small cabal attended only by their nominees. It became an executive body responsible for decisions that did not affect the constitution of the Order and that concerned rather Malta as a state than the Order as a religious body. Its duties or indeed its constitution were never closely defined and it was an irregular combination that grew up from motives of expediency without reference to the statutes. In all councils over which the Grand Master presided he had two votes and jealously reserved the right to propose the agenda. Towards the end of the eighteenth century a conservative, constitutional party made its complaints felt that the real power of the Grand Master was so great that the ancient democracy of the Order was in danger.

The Grand Master enjoyed power in two capacities: as head of a religious order and as prince of Malta. As the second he was an absolute prince, owing nominal feudal vassalage to the King of Sicily. His nearest parallels were the Electoral Prince Bishops of Germany. As the first he was a constitutional monarch, subject to the statutes, to the decisions of the Councils whom he could not defy, and to the Pope. The Pope enjoyed absolute spiritual dominion over the Order and had to approve of every decision that affected it. The Order liked to believe that even his power was limited by the statutes, and as late as 1953 it was arguing that as it was a sovereign body the Pope had no power over its constitution except to withhold his consent to any change it might decree. Throughout the Order's existence in Malta the Pope effectively held the balance between constitutional anarchy and Grand Magisterial despotism. On the whole the Popes behaved scrupulously in observing the statutes, but they were often inclined to interfere where they had the power, especially in granting gratuitous dispensations to individual Knights from compliance with the more rigorous rules of the Order.

The Grand Masters held office for life, and when one died, a new one had to be elected within three days. "The intrigues are ceaseless in this place," wrote a French visitor in 1678, "as in all countries with an elective head, where very often particular interests put men on the throne who would never have aspired to it had they not been pushed forward by those who hoped to make their fortunes out of them." "During these three days [before an election] there is scarce a soul that sleeps in Malta", wrote Brydone. "All is cabal and intrigue and most of the Knights are masked to prevent their particular attachments from being known."

Every attempt was made to render the inevitable intrigue nugatory, but as the three-day limit restricted the selection to those Knights already in the island, canvassing and caballing could have successful results; a Bailiff likely to be *magistrabile* was not above discreetly playing himself in with likely supporters. But the system was not an easy one to break. Every voter—who had to have at least three caravans done and to be eighteen years old—met in the chapel of his Tongue in the conventual church, except those of the Lieutenant's Tongue who met in the nave. The Lieutenant, often the favourite, was not allowed to vote. He was the officer elected when the Grand Master was moribund and was in charge of the Order in the interim period. Each Tongue then elected three Grand Crosses by ballot. The twenty-four then proceeded to elect a President of the Election who was now out of the running and the Lieutenant stood down. They then chose a triumvirate of one Knight, one Chaplain and one Servant-at-Arms. The twenty-four now dispersed and the triumvirate chose a fourth and the quadrumvirate a fifth and so on until there was an octumvirate of one from each Tongue. A further eight were then chosen, one again from each Tongue, but in all sixteen there was not one Grand Cross. The sixteen, composed of eleven Knights,

two Chaplains and three Servants-at-Arms, elected the Grand
Master, the President of the Election having the casting vote.

Bribery was impossible, though accusations were often made
that the Grand Masters had committed simony in promising
rewards to potential voters. But most Knights who were
magistrabile were content to spend money lavishly before the
election to give the impression that they would be as generous
in power as out of it. In effect the Grand Masters were those
whom the Knights had generally agreed to elect, or com-
promises between various factions. As the number of Knights
resident in Malta in the eighteenth century decreased, so the
canvassing became more intensive.

The Grand Master was always a man of some experience in
the Order and nearly always selected from the Bailiffs. These
were the highest dignitaries of the Order. Their title had
originated in the Holy Land where they were the heads of
priories in Jerusalem, but it had been extended to anyone
dignified by the award of a Grand Cross. Some of the Bailiffs
held titular bailiwicks of venerable origin, the Morea, Negroponte, Acre, the Holy Sepulchre; there were twenty-two in all;
twenty-two more were Grand Priors. In France, Spain and
Portugal these were the direct nominees of the Crown, princes
of the royal blood and infantes. All these and any others had a
right to a seat in the Sacred Council. Bailiffs *d'honneur* were the
creation of the Grand Master and often of the Pope. The
eighteenth-century Popes created so many that the title grew
cheap.

The most important Bailiffs, however, were the heads or
Piliers of the eight Tongues. They were always rich men—
for it was an expensive business being Pilier—usually old men,
and always holders of a particular office, though the effective
work was often done by a younger Lieutenant. The Pilier of
Italy was the Grand Admiral—a desk-side job like that of the
First Sea Lord. The Pilier of France was the Grand Hospitaller,
that of Provence the Grand Commander (*Gran Commendatore*),
the President of the Treasury. The Pilier of Auvergne was
the Grand Marshal, the senior military commander; the Pilier

of Castile the Grand Chancellor, who sealed the bulls; the Pilier of Aragon the Grand Conservator, responsible for the upkeep of the charitable foundations and bequests made by past members of the Order and for paying out the subsistence rates to the Knights on caravan or living in the Inns. The Pilier of Germany was Grand Bailiff, in charge of the fortresses and look-out posts, while the Pilier of England had once been in charge of lightly armed Palestinian mercenaries called the Turcopoles, used for fighting off raids. In Malta, the office, held by a Grand Master's nominee as the Tongue of England was no more, administered the watches and sentries posted throughout the islands.

This departmentalism was never wholly successful. It was designed to give everybody an office to aspire to and to prevent any one Tongue from dominating the offices of state. In fact it led too often to violent squabbles over pretended infringements on one Tongue's province by another, to long series of second-rate men achieving position by sheer seniority. But that seniority did ensure experience. Like the Papacy and the Italian Republics, the Order was governed by old men. That was, as well as being a weakness, also a strength, for despite its exclusive caste there were men of devotion and capacity who graduated to positions of trust through service at war and ten years' statutory residence in Malta. One could not be a Pilier without experience of both. But it also meant that young men were continually kept in subordinate capacities, and this in the long run was demoralizing. The younger men were often the Lieutenants and had, in the Pilier's absence, seats on the Council, but they had a long time to wait for their reward. As war and disease killed off fewer as the centuries wore on, the competition became that much greater. By 1776, de la Platière could write: "The fortress maintains as many applicants, hangers-on, common jobbers and women as the Papacy at Rome. There are the same intrigues, the same solicitations, the same planning for future contingencies, the same money paid out, and perhaps more fermentation. One hears nothing but 'How old is he?' 'How is he?' 'When will

35

he die?' Their health is only of interest because it may give out at any time and make way for somebody else."

Much of this jobbery and speculation came from the power of the Grand Master to give away once every five years a commandery in each Priory, whose responsions he would enjoy himself. The gift was in his own hands, though limited for political reasons to nationals of that Priory, and as there were nineteen Priories (the Priories of St John of London and of Ireland were defunct) a Grand Master reigning ten years might dispose of twenty-eight. Pinto in his long reign of forty years gave away upwards of a hundred and twenty, some of them worth two thousand pounds a year. "There is more to gain from paying court to the Grand Master", wrote the anonymous French visitor of 1678, "than to many other more powerful princes." All visitors spoke with wonder of the perfect outward respect accorded to the ruler.

The Grand Master expected this from the oath of obedience. He controlled every movement of his Knights in convent; they had to seek his permission to leave the island, to spend the night out of Valetta, to set up house. His orders were final unless, in the case of a dispute between him and one of his subordinates, the case was referred to the *Sguardio*, a session of the eight Piliers, presided over by the Grand Marshal, which decided where the rights lay. The Grand Master could only reverse the decision of the *Sguardio* by an appeal to a Chapter General or to the Pope. In the eighteenth century the *Sguardio* was seldom invoked as recalcitrant Knights found it easier and more opportune to appeal through the Inquisitor to the Pope straightway.

The Grand Master's titles were Serene Highness and Eminence, as he enjoyed a rank equivalent to a cardinal deacon. The King of France addressed him as "Mon Cousin" and like other monarchs he received embassies covered. In 1607 the Emperor accorded the Grand Masters the title of Princes of the Empire, and at the courts of Versailles, Rome, Madrid and Vienna the envoy of the Order enjoyed the rank and honours of an ambassador. The Captain-General was entitled to a return salute, gun for gun, from the fleets of Catholic powers.

Though towards the end of the eighteenth century these were largely empty honours, they were not considered so in Malta, for the Order depended upon the goodwill of all European powers. The nations with Tongues or Priories were represented in Malta by a Knight Grand Cross appointed by the Grand Master and he enjoyed the protection of his sovereign. Non-Catholic powers were allowed a consul, also appointed by the Grand Master and always a Roman Catholic subject, but he was allowed neither a patent nor a salary; when there were disputes with those powers with whom there was no accredited envoy of the Order, the ambassadors of the Protecting Powers (France, Spain, Austria, Portugal and Naples) would take up the matter at issue in the capital concerned.

Financially the office of Grand Master was not a lucrative one, but most of them were rich. As befitted their power and prestige, they maintained a complete court in their gaunt palace in Valetta. It was modest in size and, unlike most European courts, even the Papal court, it was entirely devoid of the influence of women, for the female relatives of the Knights seldom came to live in Malta. The activities of the Grand Master's court were ceremonial and utilitarian and rather dull! The senior courtier was the Seneschal, and always a Grand Cross. Under him were the Master Squire (*Maestro Scudiere*) and *Maître d'Hotel*. The administration of the Palace was in the hands of a Procurator of the Treasury, a Receiver of His Eminence's revenues, a *Chambrier-Majeur* and a *Sous-Maître d'Hotel*. A *Premier Ecuyer* supervised the stables and equipage, a Falconer the hunting. The two palaces outside Valetta were each under a *Sous-Maître d'Hotel*. Three officers of the Grand Master's corps of guards—a body, set up in 1701, of 100, later raised to 150 picked men—four secretaries for his Latin, Italian, French and Spanish correspondence, a governor for the pages, an almoner in charge of his charities and alms-giving, four chaplains, and a *credancier* for his commissariat completed the court and were all Knights or Servants-at-Arms. His *Intendant des Affaires* was a Maltese and looked after the farms on his estate. This little court was amplified by ostentatious Grand Masters with Knights seconded to their service to keep them amused at their expense and was served by a host of unpaid male servants—valets, cooks, dishwashers, servers, ostlers, janitors, *fenestrarii*, cess-boys enlisted from the Moorish prisoners of war in the Great Bagno—a considerable economy, for the money to run this establishment was not unlimited.

Beside the court there had grown up a considerable bureaucracy, in which occasionally a Maltese held a position of trust—for example, the Grand Viscount (*Gran Visconte*), the senior police official responsible for the good behaviour of everyone except the Knights, who were the responsibility of the Master Squire. But out of 261 officials in 1742 in the service of the Hospitallers, 45 were Grand Crosses, 173 Knights, 17 Conventual Chaplains, 13 Servants-at-Arms and 13 Maltese. The last were usually the judges in the various tribunals. The busiest departments were the Congregation of War (4 Grand Crosses), of the Galleys (4 Knights), of the Ships of the Line (1 Grand Cross and 3 Knights), of Armaments (4 Knights) and the Commissioners for Caravans (2 Grand Crosses). Other concerns of the Government: the upkeep of the fortifications, of the buildings of the Order, of the public works, of the Mint, of the powder factory, of the magazines, of the Bagno, the enrolment of soldiers, the granting of flags of convenience, the administration of spoils, the committee of nobility, the Public Health Office (known as the Quarantine with its excellent lazaretto), the supervision of novices, the redemption of slaves, the government pawnshop, all were the concern of small committees usually composed of a Grand Cross and one or two Knights each. There were two commissioners each for alms, for beggars, for sick women; two proctors for widows and fatherless daughters; two *Prud'hommes* for the conventual church; a Bailiff Protector of the Ursuline nuns; two proctors for catechumens—usually slaves or Protestant sailors under instruction in the Catholic faith. Most important of all was the staff of the Sacred Infirmary, about which more will be said.

A Bailiff Grand Castellan was in charge of the law courts, the High Court of Justice being known as the *Castellanìa*. Its judges were Maltese but the Fiscal or Chief Prosecutor was a Servant-at-Arms. All cases save those concerning Knights among themselves were heard here, and the first appeal could be made to the Grand Master's Court of Audience (*L'Audienza*) composed of Grand Crosses. The final appeal was to the Grand Master himself. Maritime litigation, of which there was plenty in an island that lived largely off the profits of privateering, was heard in one of two tribunals: the *Magistrato degli Armamenti* and the *Consolato del Mare*. The second was created in 1697 and modelled on the Consulate of the Sea at Barcelona and designed to expedite justice. It was a prize-court in which four merchants (later six) sat as consuls to deal with all claims and counter-claims, as well as to arbitrate in cargo disputes, wage claims, recovery of debts and alleged ill-treatment of mariners. Prior to 1697 all such disputes had been heard in the *Magistrato*, but this tribunal was not a secular one but a tribunal of the Order and, as such, subject to the final jurisdiction of Rome. As the disappointed parties began inevitably to appeal against all judgments to Rome, thus embarking on a tedious and complicated litigation that could prolong the case indefinitely, the Grand Master set up the *Consolato* as a prize-court in his capacity as sovereign prince of Malta and so subject to no higher authority than his. The Inquisitor, Papal representative in the island, refused to accept his competence to do so and the eighteenth century witnessed a long juridical battle between Rome and Valetta as to whether the Grand Master had a dual and separate role as secular prince and ecclesiastical superior.

Malta under the Hospitallers had evolved into a city state of some complexity. The Maltese never doubted that it was a despotism, though a benevolent one. They felt increasingly as the centuries wore on that they were denied the position in their own society that they had enjoyed under previous sovereigns. This feeling was largely illusory, but the prosperity of Malta under the Knights created a mercantile class that was irked by the status of second-class citizens. In the days of the Aragonese kings a small feudal aristocracy had, it is true, enjoyed a measure of autonomy in the Popular Council, though whether this was legislative, or merely consultative, nominated or elected, has never been decided. Under the Knights they were not consulted. The Popular Council was invoked by name when the burgesses and nobles of the Five Cities of Notabile, Cospicua, Vittoriosa, Senglea and Valetta elected their Jurats. To these elected officials due honour but not power was given. The Jurats—a title of venerable antiquity —had once been deputed by the Aragonese Viceroys to appoint the judges in the civil courts, to sit as appeal judges and to exercise criminal jurisdiction. Under the Hospitallers the Jurats of Notabile retained this privilege, while those of Valetta, which was a post-Aragonese creation, were the judges in the *Castellania*. The title was also given to the chief merchants of the island appointed by the Grand Master to control the buying and selling of corn and the administration of the public bank known as the *Università*. The senior Jurat of Notabile, the Captain of the Rod, was a Maltese noble who had the right of the Grand Master's audience at any hour to lay the grievances of his nation before him. His rod of office could be carried before him by a page, a privilege shared with the Piliers alone, the Grand Castellan and the Fiscal. The Jurats of the Three Cities (Senglea, Vittoriosa and Cospicua) carried the Grand Master's baldachin in ceremonial processions and occupied seats of green silk in the collegiate churches in which at their entry the congregation stood.

In the finicky and costly ceremonies in which the Order engaged, the Maltese played a passive part, though at the ceremonial induction of a new Grand Master into the ancient capital of the island lip-service was paid to the traditions and civic pride of a long-memoried people. At the entrance to the city the Grand Master imitated a practice of the Aragonese viceroys before him when he received from the Jurats the keys to the gates, in return for which he swore to uphold the liberties and franchises of the Maltese people. The procession from Valetta was in full state—the Grand Master's gilded coach drawn by six Arab steeds, a present from the Bey of Tripoli, with its Moorish postilions in the Grand Master's own livery, jogged through streets dressed with flags and banners, past fountains running wine, to the music of kettledrums and trumpets. The cortège of a hundred coaches was met by the Captain of the Rod and the cavalry of the island, who escorted it to the suburbs of Notabile. There, after Mass in the Augustinian church, the Grand Master was robed in the long black mantle of his office, full like a cardinal's, with an ermine-lined soutane of black silk emblazoned with the eight-pointed cross. He was girt with a silk cord and small scrip that denoted him the Father of the Poor, and on his head was placed the fluted, flat-topped biretta that was his distinctive headgear. He then walked to the gates of the city where he met the Bishop and received the keys from the Jurats, who swore homage on bended knee. His entry was made to the fanfaronade of cannon on the bastions. Latin speeches, eulogies, Mass, *Te Deums*, gifts and audiences crowded the morning, to be followed by a twenty-one course dinner to the strain of a string orchestra at which the Knights and nobles sat down to relays of food while the Grand Master played a hand of cards with the Captain-General.

In the afternoon the Spanish and Portuguese Knights performed a carousel in the yellow waistcoats and turquoise vests of a brigade of dragoons, executing a complicated manœuvre on horseback to the admiration of the plebs, while a carnival coach representing the Order's triumph over Barbary passed the loggia of the Jurats' palace from which the new Grand Master flung down largesse into the frenzied crowd. Less extensive, but no less flamboyant ceremonies followed at a later date when the Grand Master rowed across Grand Harbour in his gilded barge to receive the keys of Vittoriosa, while the Jurats carried his baldachin into the church of St

Lawrence where the cardinal's hat offered to La Valette was on display.

The Grand Masters had no coronation. They were just shown to the people. Indeed there was no crown, but only the biretta. He wore a cardinal's ring and carried an admiral's baton, the symbols of his spiritual and temporal authority. But the later Grand Masters hankered after something more. Verdale at the end of the sixteenth century had set a ducal coronet above his arms, and Vilhena in the 1730's displayed this coronet encircling the biretta in his portraits. Pinto converted the coronet into a crown. It is displayed upon the table in all portraits thereafter, a symbol of their aspirations to royal estate.

A Grand Master's death was equally solemn. His body was exposed in the Council Hall of the Palace, robed in the magistral habit, guarded by relays of four pages dressed in hooded garments of black, one of them keeping off the flies with a fan. Four knights garbed as heralds held the banners of His Eminence and of the Order at the four corners. To his right were lain the armour of La Valette, tutelary genius of the Order, and the sovereign's baton. This was broken ceremonially in the conventual church by his seneschal and thrown upon the catafalque after the solemn intonation of the Office of the Dead. His Master Squire added two golden spurs and the Treasurer of the Order his purse. These relics of his sovereignty were interred with him in the sumptuous mausoleum he had prepared for himself in the chapel of his Tongue.

The Grand Masters lived and died as great princes, and they presided over an Order that was believed to be immensely rich. But as the eighteenth century progressed, this wealth, though considerable, was increasingly more apparent than real. The revenues of the Order came from responsions, an annual ten per cent, sometimes five per cent, rarely thirty per cent of the annual revenue of each commandery. Another source of income was from Mortuary and Vacancy payments, first raised in 1631 to build a novitiate and seminary and retained as a permanent tax. *Mortorio* consisted of the entire revenues of the commandery from the death of the Commander to the

1st May following; *Vacante* took up the entire revenues of the commandery for a year after that. It was possible for a new Commander not to draw any revenue from a commandery for eighteen or more months. Then there were Spoils, four-fifths of a dead Knight's assets, the proceeds of timber sold from the woods of the Priories, occasional emergency taxes levied on commanderies to provide special pensions or meet special needs—all these and the responsions were collected by an official in each Priory known as the Receiver and shipped aboard the galleys to the Treasury in Malta. This was a bureau of seven Knights responsible under the Pilier of Provence for the administration of finance. The estates of the Hospitallers, too, were free of the normal taxes of the country in which they lay, but Catholic sovereigns latterly cast greedy eyes on the untouchable wealth their ancestors had alienated for ever. In 1608, after a long argument as to whether the Hospitallers were bound like other religious orders to pay the *quinzièmes* and *vingtièmes* laid on the clergy by the Kings of France, or whether they formed a sovereign order immune from them, the Grand Master accepted a compromise in the *Composition des Rhodiens* whereby the Order accepted a quittance from the capitation tax and *vingtième* at a far lower rate than it would have paid had it been listed as a religious body. Other nations, except Spain, followed the French example, and the Pope was not above laying occasional impositions on the Priory of Rome. But these burdens were passed on to the Commanders themselves, who had to pay their share in addition to responsions.

The responsions, however, were fixed by statute in 1631 and were not raised until the Chapter General of 1776. The commanderies were largely agricultural or forested land and the revenues did not rise proportionately to the fall in the value of money. Nor did they keep level with the expenses of the Treasury: ceaseless building, bigger and better walls, constant refurbishing of weapons, extensive replacements of galleys and in 1701 the creation of a squadron of men-of-war, a foolish competitive struggle with richer sovereigns to maintain embassies and Grand Priories in sumptuous state, all contemporaneous with the falling off of revenues from privateering, costly outlays on men and munitions from abroad at times of threatened invasion, soon caused the expenses to exceed the revenues and drove the Order to repeated loans, either raised in Genoa or from the local Maltese in the *Università*. The Order's credit was good, but the interest merely increased the deficit. Then in 1776 the Order, while its accounts were dangerously unbalanced, took on the commanderies of the centuries-old Order of St Anthony, founded in the Crusading era as a minor Hospitaller society to care for those afflicted with the malignant fever known as St Anthony's fire. Prestige drove the Order to outbid the Comte de Provence and his Order of St Lazarus and, in the illusory hope that by 1879 the Antonine revenues would show, by compound interest, a steady annual profit, it accepted a crushing annual burden of 62,000 livres as pensions to the ex-Antonines and a cash payment —raised in Genoa at three per cent—of one million livres as indemnity to the Lazarites. The union cost the Order 300,000 livres a year before the National Assembly confiscated the French commanderies in 1792. Folly such as this was the penalty of an ambition that the revenues could not sustain. The Embassies, too, cost a pretty sum, and did not reap commensurate results. Rich rather than experienced Knights were often given them because they were prepared to meet the expenses from their own pockets, but professional diplomacy, of vital importance to an Order whose importance was declining, was not a career that appealed to more than one or two of the Knights, who were, like Sagramoso, conspicuously successful at it. Sailors make good diplomats sometimes—like the celebrated de Suffren in Paris—but not on all occasions. And the Knights of St John were sailors first and foremost.

The greatest expense of the Treasury was towards the upkeep and manning of a navy far larger than the size of Malta seemed to admit. Up till 1700 the navy consisted of a squadron of seven galleys; after that date a squadron of line ships was inaugurated to allow more effective pursuit of the swifter sailing ships of Barbary. The galleys were rowed by a crew of prisoners of war, Moor and Turk, and Christian as well if taken voluntarily serving aboard infidel men-of-war. To these were added criminals, usurious Jews, and the most miserable of all, the *buonavoglie*, who signed on for a lump sum to spend sometimes the rest of their lives chained to an oar, little better and often more hopeless than a Moslem slave. In addition to the regular vessels of the fleet the Order had one or two tartans, 22-gun light raiders, numerous galliots and many lightly-armed coastal craft on the constant alert for enemy shipping in the vicinity of Malta. The galleys never went entirely out of service, but with the more effective use of sail they were less often used for raiding in the eighteenth century than for ceremonial escort duties to foreign princes and dignitaries, and for fetching the Order's responsions from the *caisses* at Barcelona, Marseilles, Venice and Genoa. The active crew of these ships were Maltese, among the finest sailors of the Mediterranean, tireless, ingenious and brave. "The Maltese cannoneers", wrote Houel in 1787, "are the best in the world; it is partly to their skill that the vessels of the Order owe their success in combat. It is rarely that, on the second run in, the masts of the enemy are not brought down and she does not lose her head for fear of being taken a prize." The galleys each carried a troop of soldiers, a mixed gang made up of many different nationalities, who boarded the enemy; these were officered by the Knights and *caravanisti* who went to sea, ten to a dozen on each galley. The efficacy of the naval training on board both the galleys and the men-of-war was acknowledged even in the days of decline. At different times, Swedes, Danes and Russians saw service before the mast under the flag of St John, and when Catherine the Great wanted to organize a galley fleet on the Baltic she asked for a Knight of Malta to assist her. French sailor Knights included the Chevaliers Tourville, d'Hocquincourt and the Marquis de Valbette in the seventeenth, and the great Bailiff de Suffren de St Tropez in the eighteenth century.

During the palmy days of the sixteenth and seventeenth centuries there was constant work for the galleys and for the big armament of privateers sailing under the Grand Master's flag. But, as we shall see, their success was too thorough. Barbary corsairs did not cease to be a menace until they were eliminated by the French occupation of Algiers in 1830, but their threat was localized by the constant and unstinting watchfulness of the Order. Its range of activities was, however, restricted by various pacts which first the French, then the Italian maritime Republics made with the Porte and with the Regencies. Predatory activity had entirely ceased in the Levant and Adriatic by the second half of the eighteenth century, and as the financial difficulties increased, fewer ships were able to put to sea. But they swept the waters of Italy and kept the sea between Cape Bon and Cape Passaro clear for shipping of all powers, and when other sovereigns cooled, the King of Sardinia remained a steadfast supporter because the Order kept the island free of pirates by maintaining a perpetual cruise in her waters.

Malta's independence depended upon the multiplicity of services she could render to as many powers as possible. These included Protestant powers as well as Catholic ones, and not only those with interests in the Mediterranean. In 1739 the Order lent a number of skilled mariners to assist an imperial push down the Danube against the Turks. Spain in particular it assisted by cruising the ships and galleys off the coasts of Malaga when she was at war with Britain and her own ships could not safely go to sea. France and the maritime states of Italy, and to a lesser extent Great Britain, used the services of Malta most.

In all disputes between Christian powers the Order was obliged to observe the strictest neutrality. Within Maltese waters ships were free from privateers and asylum was accorded to the vessels of any nation not at war with the King of Sicily. But by the Donation of Charles V these were excluded from Maltese harbours. In 1689 the storm-shattered fleet of the Duc de Guise was denied admittance to Grand Harbour for this reason and Louis XIV could only reproach his ancestors for not foreseeing such a contingency when the Donation was witnessed, at the special request of the Grand Master, by all the monarchs with Knights in the Order. To soften the embarrassment of a complete closure, it was the practice thereafter to admit French—and British—ships to St Paul's Bay and Marsa Scirocco and the French used this concession in 1727 and 1733 when they were at war with the Empire. It was justified by the legal quibble that the Donation only referred to fortified anchorages. It would have been tactless to offend the Order's chief protector.

France's connections with Malta were particularly close and the services the Order could render all nations were of particular value to her. As a safe asylum for privateers, merchantmen and men-of-war Malta was most useful. As a recruiting ground for sailors in peacetime she was also valuable, though in time of war belligerents were expressly refused permission to take on men or arms, unless they were at war with the Moslem. They could take on at all times fresh supplies and water. This rule was only relaxed once, for Admiral Hood in 1794, but the times were then peculiar. The sailors that could be recruited were not, however, Maltese. These were too good as sailors and too valuable for the fleet of the Order and for the many privateers to be spared for foreign service. But there were always many sailors of different nationalities from all over the Mediterranean at a loose end in Malta, and the Order was glad to get rid of them as they were often the cause of trouble. The English had a habit of encouraging galley slaves and *buonavoglie* to desert to their ships, refusing to hand them over as the French and Spanish did, with the proud excuse that the British flag flew only over free men.

The Hospital's services were provided free to the sailors of all nations—though after three days non-Catholic seamen were obliged to accept the visits, but not necessarily the arguments, of a Catholic divine. The French *chargé d'affaires* was peculiarly well placed to hear of piratical activity in the Levant and to pass on to Marseilles the latest news of depredations and warnings of dangerous areas. But most important of all, Malta became an excellent convenient half-way house for the Levantine trade, and merchants increasingly used the facilities of the island for doing quarantine, which was less arduous than it was in Marseilles and more efficient. Many of them bonded their goods in Maltese warehouses to save the costs of re-transport from Marseilles to the Italian and Adriatic ports. The British had their consul, whom they shared with the Dutch, and many British ships had occasion to be thankful for the neutrality of Malta as they were hotly pursued by French warships. But for every British ship that used the island, there would be ten, or even fifteen, Frenchmen.

Short of Malta's becoming a French island she could do little more for France. As a neutral island she was an inviolable haven for French privateers and merchantmen in time of war, and it was commonly held in England that Malta was a French naval base and that the Order's neutrality was diplomatic humbug. There was some justice for this view, though the same facilities were scrupulously accorded to all powers, even France's Protestant enemies. The Order also assisted France in her occasional forays against the Regencies. When France was at war with Tripoli in 1728 the galleys cruised off Algiers and Tunis to deter them from sending assistance though they were not at war with France, and the line ships kept watch off the Morea for Turkish battleships which the French could not attack. In the Tunisian war of 1741, France used Malta unashamedly as an advance base and the galleys blockaded Tunis to prevent the beleaguered shipping sailing out with Algerian or Tripolitanian flags. The combined fleets of France and Malta swept the Mediterranean Sea clear of Barbary raiders and could have destroyed piracy for ever. But France wanted North African trade without colonization, and Malta wanted booty. So valuable had Malta's services been during this war that the Court of Versailles made a great exception to its golden rule and permitted the ships of the Religion to hoist the French flag in the Levant if they met *soltanas* of the Turkish fleet while looking for Barbary raiders. The ambassador in

Paris too was accorded the honours of the Louvre, the right to drive a coach into the courtyard of the royal palace—a distinction reserved for princes of the royal blood and the ambassadors of major powers.

It was in France's interest to keep Malta dependent but also strong enough to look after herself. The purchase of weapons and munitions of war was never denied, even though at a time when France was herself at war. While not assisting from her own budget, she was exercised about the financial solvency of the Order and prepared to help her out of embarrassing situations like the loss of huge sums in the chaos following the collapse of John Law's grandiose schemes.

If the French felt that they could call automatically upon the assistance of Malta as a satellite, the kingdom of Naples and Sicily argued closer claims of feudal sovereignty. With the umbrella of four more powerful states these would have been easy to shrug off had not Malta been dependent upon Sicily for foodstuffs. By an ancient privilege the Knights were entitled to extract from the island supplies of corn, biscuit meal (they had a ship-biscuit factory at Augusta) and meat, without paying any royal duties. The amount had been fixed before the island's population began to grow rapidly, so that the duty-free supplies were soon inadequate. The Maltese, accustomed to cheap bread, did not fancy paying a higher price, and cheap bread was one of the basic principles of domestic policy in the island; in consequence representations were often made to have the allowance, known as the *tratte*, raised. The King of Sicily, whether he were Austrian, Spanish or Bourbon, knew that Malta was virtually dependent upon his allowing these supplies to be shipped to the island. Knowing too that the Order disliked subsidizing corn prices even when it could afford to, he was able to use them as a bargaining counter with the rulers of Malta, whom he regarded as feudal vassals. Corn diplomacy meant that the Order had to be circumspect: alternative sources of supply were tried, corn from the Levant, beef from Tunis, and on one occasion the King of Sardinia offered to provide what Sicily had provided on the same terms, but expense and uncertainties of various kinds made them unattractive.

The reign of the Bourbon Charles VII was the most uncomfortable for Malta. Charles saw the Order as an anachronism whose services to his kingdom, which were purely protective, could be rendered unnecessary with the creation of a Neapolitan navy and a truce with the Porte. He achieved both, and when in 1741 he forced the Pope to accept the revolutionary Concordat, he saw an opportunity to stop the extensive drain of money that left the kingdom for Malta every year. He decided to bring the prioral and other churches of the Order under the terms of the concordat and to submit them to the levy of a tenth of their revenues from the Bishop and further impositions from the crown. The Regno of Sicily then proceeded to offer the King a donation of 300,000 scudi and included the Order's commanderies in the levy. This touched the Grand Master on the raw, and it was only the growing pressure of first the Pope and then France that persuaded Charles the time was not yet ripe for squeezing the Order.

The Grand Masters feared most that the monarchs of Europe would sooner or later begin to step up the comparatively modest demands they had made on the Order in the time of the *Composition des Rhodiens*. The distinction drawn between the Hospitallers and other religious bodies may seem academic, but it was vital. The economy was dependent on revenues from abroad and every argument and every stratagem had to be used to see that these were not reduced more than could be helped. If the Neapolitans had got away with this, who knew what might follow? The Knights were not clergy who lived off their estates offering only spiritual services in return; they maintained a hospital and a fleet in the service of Christ that were expensive to run. They fully earned their privileges and exemptions. And they were able to retain them as long as their protectors, especially France, were prepared to support them diplomatically.

The Order of St John called itself sovereign, though the title was only added by Czar Paul I, and even today it constitutes an international body, capable of rights and duties under international law, like the United Nations. This sovereign identity has no regard to the possession of land; in the eighteenth century Malta was its title deed and property. It was vital for the Order to assert its independence and to operate independently of any foreign power as far as possible. This was not easy to do, and the Grand Masters were forced to accept increasing dependence on their neighbours. But they kept up a noble show of independence in their fortress isle, which it is now time to describe.

Chapter IV

BUILT BY GENTLEMEN FOR GENTLEMEN

MALTA, the largest island of the archipelago, was usually visited from Syracuse, and the *speronaro*, a light bark with a pointed prow and propelled by sail and oar, could accomplish the journey within a day. The visitor would first sight Gozo, the traditional home of the nymph Calypso, the more fertile but less heavily populated of the two larger islands. Then Malta would loom up with its ancient fortress of Notabile perched on a ridge of rock spanning the island and the massive walls of Valetta jutting into the sea along the beak of land on which the city was built.

This was the most famous fortress in Europe. The combined skill of such military engineers as Laparelli, engineer of Grand Duke Cosimo dei Medici, Floriani, designer of the walls of Rome for Pope Urban VIII, Maurizio Valperga, lent at special request by Victor Amadeus of Savoy, had contrived to erect a network of walls that would have presented to any besieging army insuperable problems of attack—if ever they could have been adequately defended. Louis XIV, on being shown the plans of the last line of fortifications to be built, the Cotoner Lines, remarked: "*C'est un très bel ouvrage, mais pour être utile il faudrait qu'il fût ici.*" By the opening of the eighteenth century the lines were completed—though work on the fortifications was constant, since an army of slaves was required to keep them in good condition. They had, over a century and a half, grown widely from the makeshift walls and ditches which the Knights had had to throw up against the Turks on their first arrival. Not only was Valetta itself impregnable, but it was protected by a double series of bastions beyond its suburb,

Floriana; the entrances to the harbours were protected by forts, and on the far side of Grand Harbour a further double line of walls forming a semicircle was aimed to prevent the enemy from establishing a base there.

Valetta was perched on a peninsular of rock, defended at the tip by a star-shaped fortress called after St Elmo, who was formerly widely venerated as the Patron of sailors. Between St Elmo and the city itself was a ditch from which the walls rose sheer. On the harbour sides, straight from the water's edge, the naked rock had been reinforced by blocks of hard sandstone to form steep, canting ramparts thirty yards high. At the neck of the peninsular, enormous, diamond-shaped bulwarks jutted into the rock cut away to form a steep, dry ditch, so that bastion and natural stone fitted like the jagged edge of a jigsaw puzzle. There were only two gates out of the city, one by the harbour side called the Marine Gate and the other at the neck called St George's Gate. Both were approached over a drawbridge. Within this box-like enclosure Valetta rose in a cluster of flat-roofed, pumpkin-coloured houses, floating like some enormous stone galleon without masts.

To right and left of Valetta were harbours, the famous Grand Harbour to the east, with its three coves lying over against the city and a deep prong of water receding half a mile inland; on the west was Marsamuscetto, a wider bay shaped like a dented kidney. Both were nipped at their mouths by narrow promontories of land, so that Valetta stood on a tongue barely touched by two mandibles of rock. That on the eastern side of Grand Harbour was a natural bastion, a cliff face rising straight where in the seventeenth century a Florentine Knight, the Chevalier Ricasoli, had constructed a fortress at his own expense. To force the island's defences by sea, while not impossible (it was threatened by Captain Augustus Hervey, third Earl of Bristol, in 1758), would achieve little, for once inside Grand Harbour the ships were at the mercy of guns from two forts, Sant' Angelo and St Michael, themselves on two smaller tongues of land that jutted out from the opposite shore at right angles to Valetta. Away from these two tongues, like Valetta themselves cut off from the mainland by severe entrenchments and bastions, a double line of walls and ditches, completed in 1686, cut off both the approaches to the deepest creek in the harbour, where the galleys moored, and the peninsular cities that flanked it.

The island of Malta, shaped not unlike a scarab, is deeply indented on the Sicilian side with coves that afford deep anchorage to the largest ships of today. Towards Africa, the coastline is sheer, deep and impenetrable. From time immemorial the inhabitants of Malta have been obsessed by the idea of a fortress, and the pattern for their immense lines of defence can be found in the line of their south-western coast. By their peculiar vulnerability the Maltese had been compelled to think in terms of security: under the Knights this was carried to extravagant lengths. The extraordinary inlet that forms Grand Harbour, radiating into creeks and branches like a hydra, is deep water throughout. The surface is seldom rough, however hard the storms rage, and the ground rises steeply on all sides but the farthest. Round this, the intricate defence works had been built: the Arabs had thrown up a small fortress on the promontory later reconstructed as Sant' Angelo, and the Normans had built a square fortress at the tip of Mount Sceberras, the site of Valetta, later remodelled as St Elmo. The Knights were to modify and complete these pivotal points of defence, and to construct an entirely new city besides. All round the entering ships, bleak walls rose and the clustered houses looked down on to all parts of the deck. Beyond the walls, the architecture of the island followed a similar pattern. The Reverend Henry Teonge, Vicar of Spernall in Warwickshire and chaplain of HMS *Assistance*, visited Malta on his way to Tripoli in 1675. "Here needs no sentry," he wrote in his diary, "for there is no getting over the outer-most wall if lease were given . . . and were an army of men in the midst of the cytty, yet their works were but in the beginning, for each house is a castle."

Valetta, the nerve-centre of the island, was the centre of life.

Originally the creation of Grand Master Jean Parisot de la Valette, she was the conventual city, and the centre and capital of this tiny principality. The walled *collachium* of Rhodes had become the walled city of Valetta; the walls were the limits of the convent. Within them the Grand Master was in absolute control; whom he would he admitted, whom he would he excluded. The Bishop, though allowed a palace, had no jurisdiction there; the Inquisitor had no specific right to enter. The Grand Master was father superior, sovereign and mayor all in one. No other city was ever built for an aristocracy solely, to be a fortress, a convent, a pleasure centre, a thriving mart and a seat of government all at once. Fortunately for Valetta, the encircling bastions prevented this confectioner's creation from degenerating into a muddle of conceit and flourish. Though housing the proudest and bluest blood in Europe, the appearance of Valetta is remarkably bald and un-assuming; its splendour is restrained. In the early days of the Order the monastic rigours of convent life, remembered by the older members who came from Rhodes, were to be reproduced in a city that was primarily a fortress. The Knights had en-dured the Great Siege in the jumbled medieval cities of Borgo and L'Isla—the first renamed Vittoriosa, the second rebuilt and rechristened Senglea after Claude de la Sengle. Mount Sceberras, never built on because it lacked water, was the only spot on which a new city could be built without having to indulge in wholesale demolition. La Valette was unwilling to endure another siege in the vulnerable and awkward peninsu-lars across the water: adopting a simple grid design that took no account of the rise and fall of the surface of the rock, sometimes very steep, he hoped at first to be able to level the whole summit of the hill and to create a table on which to lay out his city, a beautiful wax model of which he had sent to Philip II of Spain. This stupendous task was never completed: in fact the construction of the city, always against time for it was never known when Suleiman might launch another attack, was almost too great a work for the impressed workers—as many as eight thousand of whom were estimated as labouring daily. Yet in five years two miles of outer defences had been completed, and in spite of the reluctance of the Knights, who were comfortable enough where they were, the convent was duly translated with great pomp from Vittoriosa on 18th March 1571. The building then proceeded fast.

The Roman grid design had the virtue of simplicity. It did, however, leave little room for architectural distinction, and as the regulations laid down the size, style and pattern of building, the result was a series of bleak monastic-like blocks upon which the architects were unable to lavish any exuberance. With the exception of a few private houses that with the abandonment of strict conventual life families were encouraged to build on vacant lots inside and outside the walls, the buildings of Valetta matched with a bleak severity of design, the severity of her streets, of monastic rule and of military discipline. The most prominent architect, a Maltese, Gerolamo Cassar, designed most of the Inns with simple lines. They rose rapidly in the locally quarried stone that was so white at first that it was believed to be a cause of trachoma, without elaboration, complete units in themselves, with their own bakeries, slaughter-houses, storerooms, detention cells and *bagni*. Though intended to be Inns, they succumbed to the dominant motif of Maltese building and became fortresses.

In the eighteenth century, a hundred years of security tempted a freer approach to building. Grand Master Perellos erected a magnificent gate to the suburb of Floriana with false pillars of stone carved in the shape of cannons, the *Porte des Bombes*; Grand Master Zondadari placed the *Consolato del Mare*, or prize-court, in a sumptuous palace emblazoned with his own arms; Manoel de Vilhena embellished Notabile with a new gateway and Magistral Palace in a tasteful and elegant baroque, sacrificing solidity for grace and line; Pinto constructed a long line of opulently decorated warehouses for the merchants who were increasingly using Malta as an entrepôt for their goods, and erected a customs house which attempted, if it did not quite succeed, to capture the lyrical beauty of Venetian civic buildings. He also refaced his Inn of Castile in elaborate plateresque. Decoration was no longer confined to the churches: the Grand Court of the Castellania was given a new doorway with the figure of Justice, a demure angel worthy of the art of Serpotta, and attendant cherubs in stucco. De Rohan's reign saw the completion of a library in a happy marriage between the late baroque and neo-classical styles. Civic building began to match religious until the dead hand of British Indo-Colonial architecture was laid on the island and the nineteenth century became an age of effortful mediocrity.

Once inside the Inns, the embellishments of a century and a half's uninterrupted peace could be seen at once. The comforts of palaces in the north were not properly reproduced in the heat of the 36th parallel: stone walls, barrel-vaulted ceilings and tiled floors gave the same half-oriental flavour that we have come to associate with Crusader architecture, though shortage of water made it impossible to use fountains lavishly. The inner cortile of the Magistral Palace was a shaded grove, containing plantains and arbutus, an arborial grotto to which was removed after the Knights had gone a bronze statue of the Order's profane tutelary genius Neptune, attributed to Gianbologna. The walls of the council-chamber were lined with magenta and canary brocades; the other Inns had huge blank walls which it was necessary to fill. The taste for rugs and arrases—Malta is a notoriously draughty place—could be freely indulged, while the walls and ceiling of the Inn of Provence were panelled and painted with arabesques and flowers, green, crimson, beige and blue, like a massive brocade. The innumerable gifts from various sovereigns in the shape of massive portraits of themselves had to be hung somewhere; paintings by Matia Preti, Spagnoleto and Spada stood side by side with portraits of Piliers and Captains-General and Admirals. Cut-glass chandeliers from Murano, arrases from Gobelins, rugs from Damascus and Sidon, panelled oak from Sicily, carved sideboards from Amsterdam, closets from Lisbon, armoires from Nurnberg, china from Dresden and Capodimonte, side chairs from Hamburg—the European-wide connections of the Knights could be perceived in every room.

The undisciplined, unprincipled days following their departure saw it all disappear somehow, unrecognizable and irreclaimable, mostly aboard the French vessels that capitulated to the English in 1800 and were allowed to take it away.

But the real glory of Valetta—and its greatest monument today—was the conventual church of St John. Dedicated to the Baptist, a portion of whose arm it retained along with an imposing list of relics, arms, knuckles, phalanges and pelvic splinters from some of the Apostles, the early Palestinian fathers and the desert eremites, which had been transported from the Holy Land, the church was built between 1573 and 1577 from designs by Gerolamo Cassar. As originally built, it was a plain edifice with derivations from the Gesù in Rome; as befitted a military order, their church is shaped like a nissen hut, a long semi-cylindrical tunnel, the faintly arched vaults of which are supported on enormous stone piers. The bays of this massive arcade lead into tiny chapels, lit from drum windows above the shallow oriental domes that cap them, each one dedicated to a different Tongue and its patron saint. The façade was as plain as any building in Valetta; two bell-towers flanked the central door, above which a balcony hung from which the new Grand Master was shown to his people on election. There was nothing more; but as the centuries passed, so this severe and monastic church was transformed into a mausoleum for the finest and best of European chivalry. The chapels were bedizened with costly marbles and the swords and helmets of ancient warriors who had bequeathed them to the church. In the Chapel of Our Lady of Philermos hung an ikon of a dusky Madonna attributed to St Luke, the most precious salvage, along with the Baptist's arm, from Rhodes. In the Chapel of France lay the jewel-bedecked sword of La Valette, looted by Napoleon and now in the Louvre, and his ceremonial Grand Cross that once hung from the neck of a Russian Czar, the most treasured relics of the Order's glorious arrival. Throughout the seventeenth and eighteenth centuries the church was enriched by successive Grand Masters who were expected to give some costly bequest to the furniture. The decorations had a predominantly martial quality, and in the reigns of the two brothers Cotoner the final splendours were given to the church in the columns of *verde antico* marble, which spring to the vaults in a polished milky green, bearing the ubiquitous cotton flower of the Cotoners above the twelve consecrating crosses. By the end of the seventeenth century not an inch of space was bare: from roof to pavement there was a pattern and mosaic of red, gold and brown; the gilded barrel vaults springing from these great shafts of olive green swung across a ceiling of midnight blue where the genius of Matia Preti had painted the life of St John the Baptist. On either side of these shining girders of stone, the arches of the aisle rose from great square blocks, carved intricately all over their toffee-like sandstone with flowering, ceaseless folds of heraldic leaf and acanthus. The eye can pick out *putti* in flight, like tiny Jacks in a sandstone beanstalk; it can discern bannerets and grotesques, trumpeting angels and heraldic arms, everywhere the eight-tongued cross of the Hospitallers: breastplates, helmets, double-headed eagles, the bowed heads of Turkish slaves, shaved, with their carrot-tops of hair and with drooping moustaches, all merging like sea animals among a waving, gently sinuous submarine weed, which folds about and conceals them. Everywhere the sensation of gilt cloys with the unnatural sweetness of a wedding-cake.

But the floor and the ceiling are the peculiar glories of St John's, and together make it a building unique in Europe. On the first, heraldry has run mad. Each Knight who died in convent was laid to rest in his conventual church, and above his bones, at great expense, was placed a slab built of inlaid stones, until every square inch was paved in an avenue like the Almanac de Gotha in mosaic. Every ingenuity was spent to fabricate variations on an original theme: the family arms, and laudatory epitaphs, are surrounded by designs of every kind. Arms and armour dominate: shields of onyx, cuirasses of jasper, helmets of lapis, drums coloured primrose and quivers shaded peach. Time's skeleton grins, Death blows his trumpet; weeping children shed transparent tears or hold tapers astraddle magenta sea-horses. Each multicoloured design is set against a ground of black, but the stone is lilac, saffron, rust and cherry —with gilt and gold throughout, like the gaily decked hearses that still bear the dead to their graves in the far south. In the floor of St John's, apart from the weapons associated with dealing death, is Death himself; crowned with laurel, an energetic skeleton snapping an hour-glass, or a grotesque dancer reaching from behind a curtain to snatch off a Pilier's hat.

Spanning this dance and epistle of death, between hoops of blazing gold, is the masterpiece of Matia Preti, *il Calabrese*. In fact the entire interior decoration of the church is his work, for, without changing its structure, he transformed it from a bleak tunnel to this extravagant display of international pride. He designed the carving on the walls, he envisaged the tesselated pavement, he ordered the gilding of the furnishings: between 1661 and 1665 he had covered the whole ceiling and the tympanum of the west wall with paint. In the vault of blue, the crowded tableaux unfold the history of St John and along the architrave of the aisle the sanctified members of the Order sit in respectful contemplation. Preti was a painter in the tradition of Reni, Cortona and Luca Giordano, and at the age of twenty-one he had come under the influence of Rubens, whom he knew personally. His painting has the master's simplicity and fluidity of line without his subtlety of tone and invention; he painted up to the age of eighty-six with deceptive facility. Of noble parentage, he was born at Taverna in Calabria on 24th February 1613; he was received as a Knight of Grace in 1642, though the Papal confirmation was nineteen years in coming. As a Knight he made it his duty to serve the Religion as their artist until his death, and St John's was to be his undisputed canvas. Scarcely a house in Valetta was without its Preti, and spells in Rome and Naples never affected his boundless fecundity.

But there was one greater than Preti. In the Chapel of St John Beheaded, on the south side, a long rectangular oratory with false windows and gilt wooden ceiling with canvases by

Preti, the stormy petrel of the seventeenth century has left his mark. Michelangelo Merigi da Caravaggio was for four and a half months a Knight of Grace too—from 14th July to 1st December 1608. He was to leave two paintings in Malta—a huge canvas painted for the decollation of St John the Baptist, in his fluent neo-realistic style, capturing in the strong but easy postures of his figures something of the familiarity with execution and violent death that marked his century. Then in the Chapel of the Tongue of Italy he painted a St Jerome, a half-nude portrait of a wiry and vigorous old man, an experiment in light and flesh tints, a study of energetic repose. It is believed that he painted a Magdalen for the same church, but it has vanished if he ever did; the portrait of that bluff old warrior Alof de Wignacourt, standing like a sportsman in his ceremonial uniform with his pages holding his helmet while he waits for the hounds of war to slip their leash, hangs in the Louvre. His stay in Malta, just short of two years, was too short for more paintings from a fastidious brush like his: his pupil and friend Lionello Spada stayed on and the Caravaggesque influence is noticeable in local paintings of the period. Caravaggio was expelled *in absentia* from the Order on 1st December 1608, in the very oratory in which his masterpiece hung. The charge of criminality was never specified, but it was rumoured that he had fought a duel. Over what drink or catamite will never be known: with Caravaggio, "when his cock is up then flashing fire will follow". At the culmination, perhaps, of a series of gross breaches of knightly conduct, his paintings completed, the Grand Viscount ordered his arrest. He escaped from Sant' Angelo and disappeared. In the next years he worked in Palermo and Syracuse, and the Knights had nothing more to do with him.

That no one should forget that the conventual church was a mausoleum for warriors, the Grand Masters ordered before their deaths magnificent tomb-pieces which they erected in the chapel of their Tongue and which, they imagined, reflected their personality and achievement. From their position of prominence, the proud, bewigged busts gaze steadfastly down upon the trophies of war. The tomb of Ramon Perellos is an inventory of the machinery of destruction. As the Order felt the anomaly of its existence in an increasingly secular world, its heads placed greater emphasis on splendour to satisfy both the martial basis of its constitution and the pride of its members.

Thackeray, travelling as Mr Titmarsh from Cornhill to Grand Cairo in 1842, found St John's "magnificent within, with a rich embroidery of gilded carving. A fitting place for this wealthy body of aristocratic soldiers who made their devotions as if on their knees and though on their knees never forgot their epaulettes nor their quarters of nobility." The floor too "is paved over with sprawling heraldic devices of the dead gentlemen of the dead Order; as if in the next world they expected to take rank in conformity with their pedigrees and would be marshalled into heaven according to their orders of precedence!"

The most important building after the conventual church was the Sacred Infirmary, the *raison d'être* of the Order. It was situated where Valetta begins to lower itself into the water and faced south-west, a bad orientation as it was protected from the bracing winds from the north by the city behind it and received the sirocco full face. It was a building of impressive length, the great ward measured 185 feet, but of little architectural distinction, though it had the only pitched roof in Malta.

The Hospitaller was the French Pilier, but the administration was carried out by the Commander of the Hospital with two *prud'hommes*, both Knights, as treasurer and commissary. The regulations of the Hospital were detailed and minute but whether they were carried out depended on the temper of the men in charge. Fear of sickness, the fatigues of the job made it hard to find a good Commander and service in the Hospital was looked upon as the most unpleasant duty attendant upon residence in Malta. In the early days it was expected that the Knights and novices would help in the Hospital as nurses, and each Tongue had its day on duty. The Grand Master himself would don the humble costume of a Hospitaller and wait upon the poorest sick in person. But by the end of the seventeenth century this admirable custom was in abeyance and in 1678 it was only the novices whom the French traveller noticed tending the sick with *une charité inconcevable*.

The Hospital was obliged to provide for the sick and wounded of all races, creeds and colours free of charge. No sick man was to be denied treatment, though, if he were a Protestant, a Greek schismatic or a Moslem he was to be confined to a separate ward. Slaves too were admitted. Knights and religious were not officially to be segregated from the common herd, but by the seventeenth century the members of the Order were occupying private rooms. The only mark of distinction officially allowed a Knight was to have two sheets instead of one. In the times of penury after 1793, all separate wards were suppressed.

Early visitors to the Hospital remarked with wonder that every patient, noble and commoner, rich and poor, slave and free, was served off silver plate, to increase, in the words of the regulations, "the decorum of the Hospital and the cleanliness of the sick". Chaplain Teonge in 1675 was impressed at the width of the ward (thirty-four feet): "'tis so broade that twelve men may with ease walke abrest up the midst of it; and the bedds are on each syd, standing on four yron pillars, with white curtens and vallands and covering, extremely neate, and kept cleane and sweete." He found two hundred beds in this ward, and numberless others in the various private rooms for the Knights.

But between 1675 and Teonge's eulogies and 1789 when the Hospital was next visited by an Englishman, the rot seems to have set in. John Howard, the celebrated prison reformer and pioneer of better hospitals, arrived in that year with letters from Sir William Hamilton in Naples, to add the Sacred Infirmary to his report on the principal lazarettos of Europe. The Grand Master gave him complete liberty to see for himself. The report is a dismal one. Gone was the silver plate, save for affluent patients, substituted by pewter, and this was dirty. The great ward, which everyone else admired, he found gloomy, its ceiling blackened with soot from the braziers. The beds were so filthy that the physician had to do his rounds with a handkerchief to his nose, and the closets, with which each bed was properly provided, were unemptied. He was appalled. A visit now and then from the Grand Master might achieve something, but the Commander was a raw young man; no one else would take on the job, and he had no authority. But the Grand Masters were no longer in the habit of paying regular visits and Cardinal Verdale had been the last to tend the sick with his own hands. There is only one record of a sudden visit, and that was from Ximenes in 1773, who found the wards undusted and the sheets unchanged and threatened the servants with the galleys. He did not repeat the visit.

Despite its imperfections, the Hospital took in large numbers. Teonge's 200 beds were in fact 370 with valances and 365 without, for fever patients. The average number of sick and wounded at any one time was between 350 and 400; in 1780, according to the Book of the Councils of State for April 1781, 153,333 sick, more than the entire population of the island, had received treatment at the cost of about tenpence a head (5 tari and 7 grani). The total cost was between 60,000 and 70,000 scudi a year. This figure included not only medical treatment but hospitality to pilgrims on their way to the Holy Land, who were lodged in the Hospital and provided with food and drink for the journey.

In 1678 the French visitor was so impressed by the diet served to the sick that "an invalid of the greatest wealth could not ask for any more from this regimen". Two hundred chickens were slaughtered daily to provide the broth. Howard made no comments on the food. The medical treatment was provided by six doctors, three senior and three junior, who worked in shifts, two on for two months at a stretch night and day. There were also six chirurgeons, or surgeons, who worked on a similar rota. The senior doctors and chirurgeons received 350 scudi (about £35) a year, the junior 200. In addition there were six *barberotti*, last-year medical students, paid some 60–120 scudi per annum, who administered the medicines and

64

did simple treatment. The Master of the Physic ran the pharmacy attached to the Hospital.

The regulations called for thirty-eight nurses in the Hospital, some of whom, however, did menial jobs. Howard found them "the most dirty, ragged, unfeeling and inhuman persons I ever saw". He saw, in fact, only twenty-two, and among them debtors and criminals, since the Hospital enjoyed the privilege of sanctuary. He could not resist the remark that de Rohan employed forty servants to look after his fifty-two horses and the magistral stables were far cleaner than the Hospital. There were forty-four slaves, all Christians, also employed in cleaning and each ward had its guardian (nine in all) who patrolled by night and saw that the regulations were kept. Howard was not impressed by them.

With all Howard's reservations, the Hospital did deserve something of its high reputation, and within the strictly limited medical theories of the day, its treatment seems to have been good, and patients came from overseas for operations for stone and cataract. In 1676 the Grand Master had founded a Chair of Anatomy and Chirurgy in the Hospital itself and the doctors, surgeons and barbers had to attend its lectures. A senior in the Hospital had to complete a course at the University and do two years' practical in the wards. An oral and practical examination was then conducted by the *proto-medico*, sometimes by the Hospitaller himself, with the other doctors. It is impossible to know but easy to suspect that this examination had a touch of the Irish about it, and that medical degrees were obtainable by giving correct answers to stock questions.

There was a large out-patients department, specially for syphilitics undergoing mercury treatment—applied daily by slaves or *forzati* for a farthing a day, three rolls of *white* bread, and a *quartuccio* of wine. Husbands and wives had to receive parallel treatment at the Infirmary and the Women's Hospital and to produce a certificate from the Bishop's court that they were not cohabiting! The Hospital took in foundlings and bastards, who would be deposited in a wooden cradle at the door, which spun on an axis and rang a bell. These were boarded out with foster-mothers at the expense of the Order with a daily allowance of fresh milk (Howard particularly noted the health of the foundlings), and at seven the girls were portioned out to various institutions and the boys were put under instruction with the chaplain of the Hospital. If they were strong they were destined for service with the army or navy; the girls who could find husbands could expect a dowry of 50 scudi from the Order. It was a bleak prospect, but Mediterranean people are not unkind to children and they were not abandoned to the gutters and the stews.

The ancillary services of the Hospital were extensive too. The kitchens provided food for the sick religious in the convents as well as for beggars at the door. Disused clothing, sheets and blankets were given to the poor women and old crutches and splints to lame beggars. One hundred scudi a month were distributed among the blind, scrofular and lepers. There was a hospital for women in Valetta, where Howard found 230 patients *in their own beds*, a condition he noted particularly, but he found it the most offensive-smelling hospital he had ever visited. At the foundling hospital he found the children clean, but pale from lack of exercise, and at the two houses for the aged poor in Floriana he found contented old men with their own small gardens, and the Governors paying a kindly attention to them.

A further extension of the services of the Hospital created a rudimentary welfare state: free prescriptions were provided to the slaves, the poor and religious houses, as well as to the Pages and students at the Hospital. Two Knights, as Commissioners for the Poor, drew up a weekly list of known sick who needed attention and these were visited daily by the doctors and some-times by the Commissioners, receiving a ration of white bread and a few tari. Their cases did not admit of their being taken to the Hospital but they were unable to fend for themselves. The essential humanity of this was that the sick were tended in their own homes, and no one need fear dying alone in the middle of a callous and negligent world. Extensive though these services were, they often existed only on paper. Howard had worse things to say about hospitals as celebrated, but his story is an indictment of the Order really far more damning than any other. The Knights existed as Hospitallers, but by the end of the eighteenth century they had ceased to take this profession as seriously as they should have.

The Grand Master had three residences and was lodged, according to Brydone, "more comfortably and commodiously than any Prince in Europe, the King of Sardinia, perhaps, only excepted". His Valetta palace had been built by Cassar after 1572 and in design was of little distinction, being a squat, ugly building over three hundred feet long. In this monastic palace the succeeding Grand Masters did their best to brighten up the scene. In 1705 Perellos bought for the council-chamber a magnificent set of Gobelin tapestries, a baroque zoological fantasy of the animals of the world. They cost him 18,000 livres, cheap at the price as the weavers, who had been unemployed during the war, knocked twenty-five per cent off the price. The throne room used on ceremonial occasions was lined with red damask and hung with gilt and ormolu mirrors, with a frieze of topographical frescoes illustrating the Great Siege of 1565. The upper rooms were approached by a pair of circular stairways with shallow steps to enable the Grand Master's sedan chair to be carried up. The size of the building denied the occupants splendid halls and stairways, but on a miniature scale the palace was impressive enough.

Some miles outside Valetta the palace of Sant' Antonio, a country house in the Spanish style, was set in the middle of a botanical paradise, with extensive stables and the famous orange gardens from which annual consignments of the Maltese orange and cases of bottled orange water were sent out to the first ladies of Europe. A third palace existed for his *villegiatura*, the castle of Verdala, called after its builder, Cardinal Verdale (1582–95). This was a square, squat turret, also designed by Cassar, on one of the higher eminences of the island, consisting of two vast, vaulted salons to catch the breezes of summer. Around it lay the *boschetto*, a thickly wooded area of pines, olives, myrtles and carobs, a game preserve and zoo, where the Grand Master could take the air unperceived, shoot, fly his falcons and admire his Corsican stags and Iceland deer, which the King of Denmark sent him, and the North African gazelles that arrived regularly as goodwill offerings from his perpetual enemies across the water, the Beys of Tunis and of Tripoli.

In 1732 Grand Master Vilhena, a great builder and benefactor, was present at the opening night of a theatre built at his expense in Valetta. It was a little jewel, with miraculous acoustics, able to seat five hundred in special boxes panelled with sylvan scenes, the stage and galleries a confection of gilt and gold. The opening play was Maffei's *La Merope*, and the women's parts were taken by the novices from Italy. The local Maltese were encouraged to come and the ladies of the aristocracy occupied the best boxes by right on first-nights. Originally the plays were mounted by the various Tongues in competition, but Grand Master Pinto introduced a professional company after, it was said, repeated protests from the Inquisitor over pages and novices taking the soprano roles. The theatre became a centre of social life in de Rohan's time, who while a Bailiff was a great patron. The Master of the King's Chapel at Naples dedicated a number of musical dramas to the Grand Masters which were mounted at his command, and in the course of the eighteenth century operas by Galuppi, Paisiello, Cimarosa and Pergolesi were presented. In 1796 a Maltese, Niccolo Isouard, became musical director and presented six of his own compositions, one of which was called *The Barber of Seville*. Isouard had completed his training in Paris and lived there throughout the Terror; in 1798 he returned to Paris after the capture of Malta to make a considerable reputation as a composer of operas much admired by Rossini.

Entertainments for the Knights became increasingly lavish in the eighteenth century as the Order, in common with the rest of Europe's aristocracy, cultivated the art of presenting itself for the amusement and edification of the people. In Malta where the Maltese were so often snubbed, where there were frequent shortages of bread and water, where there were few large personal incomes, occasions for bread and circuses were readily seized. The birth of a dauphin or infante, a royal wedding, were all celebrated with pomp. In 1729, to mark the birth of the Dauphin, a mock battle was staged in Grand Harbour between ten caiques from the galleys and a galliot manned by real Moors, accompanied by the racket of blank grenades and a torrent of fireworks to represent the firing of the Infidel ship. For three days carnival reigned, the galleys were illuminated and fountains ran wine. Louis XVI's marriage to Marie Antoinette was marked by a solemn ball in the Palace to which the ladies were invited and which continued until five o'clock in the morning.

While presenting a munificent front to its own Maltese, the Order also attempted to compete with other sovereigns in the matter of entertainment. Its sovereign identity needed public advertisement; though costly equipages and magnificent receptions became less and less possible as the financial condition of the Treasury worsened, outside the conduct of Grand Master's court itself there was not much pruning on ostentation. In 1728 the Bailiff de Chambrai accompanied an embassy to Lisbon when he was just a captain and was drawn into the whirl of banquets, balls, concerts and *soupers intimes*. In 1755 the line ship *San Giovanni* visited Baia, and the Lieutenant-General invited the Duchess di Castropignano to do the honours of his ship at a ball on board at which the French Ambassador led off with the Duchess's daughter and the guests feasted and danced until six o'clock in the morning. Four years earlier, the line ships visiting Lisbon again had become the centre of fifteen days' junketing; in 1787, the galleys *San Luigi* and *Vittoria* visiting Palermo, the Viceroy invited the officers to a ball in their honour in his palace. The reports all speak enthusiastically of the company, the ladies, the meats and the glitter; all of it in honour of the Knights Hospitaller, the Servants of the Poor.

But in 1783 the Servants of the Poor lived up to their reputation when a sudden and cataclysmic earthquake destroyed Messina and Reggio in Calabria. The Grand Master at once ordered the galleys to sea with the doctors from the Hospital, twenty chests of medicines and two hundred beds and tents. The Knights navigated the still-turbulent waters to land in shattered Reggio, but the Bishop, who had heard that the disaster was worse across the water, sent them to Messina. There the hillsides were covered with frightened and homeless people, but on informing the Neapolitan commander that the Knights had come to set up a field hospital, the Captain-General, the Bailiff de Freslon, was astonished to have the offer curtly refused on the ground that the King of Naples had amply provided for the sufferers. On going ashore to pay their respects to the commander a deputation was received in a barn and entertained to a sumptuous meal on furniture salvaged from the wreckage while the famished and half-naked Sicilians crowded round the door begging for food. De Freslon was a bluff Frenchman and he bullied out of the commander permission to land his surgeons and set up a food kitchen on the mole, where the Knights had to drive off the frenzied crowd with the flats of their swords in case the whole apparatus was thrown into the sea. When their supplies and themselves were exhausted, de Freslon returned to Malta but persuaded de Rohan to send a ship loaded with grain from the granaries and several shipments of biscuit. Even the King of Naples, none too favourably disposed towards the Order at that time, was nudged into reluctant gratitude.

Expeditions such as these were rare. And rarer too were those engagements with Infidel vessels that had once been the daily lot of the galleys. Turkish waters were put out of bounds by France and Venice, Barbary ships became more subdued and elusive; there was little excitement left for the young Knights in Malta. But though indifferentism and casualness grew as the eighteenth century passed, most of the senior Knights and Grand Masters believed that the Order had many useful years before it and that its services to Europe, though increasingly difficult to render, were no less important. As a school of life for the cadets of the greater houses of Europe the convent city state of Malta had much to offer. Accordingly the eighteenth century witnessed the creation of an efficient little state with a tolerably contented, prosperous people and a growing trade. The process of modernizing the various institutions did, as we shall see in later chapters, meet with resistance, and the ancient Catholic traditions of Malta and of the Order threw into relief the paradox of a modern, autocratically ruled state governed by a democratically ruled religious order. But the Catholicity of the Order was never in doubt, and Pinto, perhaps the deepest tinged by the scientific rationalism of his day, was a martinet for religious decorum.

The character of the Knights was bound to change. An increasing number were being admitted from birth with a view to securing a fat commandery or an agreeable sinecure early on in life; the deterioration in the finances forced the Order to accept dispensations to ensure the immediate payment of much-needed passage money or responsions. Grand Masters found it more difficult to resist the Pope and other monarchs who recommended their protégés to posts and commanderies. The admirable system of earlier days had run to nepotism, ambition and perversion at the end. This was a development of historical pressures. Throughout the centuries during which the Knights were at Malta there was a perceptible change in their attitude towards the world, the flesh and the devil. Despite restrictions, they managed to create for themselves an ambience in which they were not too uncomfortable: all-night balls, to which women were invited, theatrical performances, banquets and games were frequently arranged.

One of the remarkable things about Hospitallers is the absence of personal documents, from which one can trace the intellectual and moral progress of individual Knights. The two notable exceptions are the Bailiff and Lieutenant-General Chambrai, whose papers are a catalogue of his triumphs, and the Commander Dolomieu, whose letters reveal the whole of his splenetic and disappointed temper, and his passing disgust with the Order. Between the fictional hedonism of des Grieux and the real rationalism of Dolomieu came the many dutiful men, exposed from early adolescence but unsuited by temperament to the call of dedicated religious. They were too much exposed to the world, too little encouraged to resist it. A careerist might make a very good job of life in Malta, but the majority had to find a *via media* between the austerities of a perfect observation of their vows and the licence of as perfect an abandonment of them. In many cases the young Knights were without much incentive to do anything, neither their religious nor their military duties, and in most cases they could obtain dispensations from Rome to let them off the more fatiguing duties.

It is not surprising that many, anxious to discover some practical application of their portentous vows, thought they found it in freemasonry. Freemasonry itself owes much to the Crusading Orders, and the medieval mystique of the Hospitallers and Templars, their hierarchy, their appeal to the noblest instincts of man, their perfect obedience, their secrecy, seemed an obvious model for those who professed the regeneration of mankind as their object. A Lodge existed in Malta, presided over in the 1780's by a Bohemian Knight, Kollowrat, who enjoyed the protection of Joseph II who had refused to promulgate in his dominions the bull of Clement XII condemning masonry. Grand Master Pinto had during his reign banished six Knights for assisting at masonic meetings, but de Rohan, who had himself been initiated while in Parma as squire to the infante Duke, did not actively prosecute the ban, though he declined to lend his patronage. In 1785 there were, according to Doublet, de Rohan's French secretary, forty adepts, all Knights except himself and an anonymous Maltese, and Kollowrat asked the Duke of Cumberland, Grand Master of the London Lodge, for a constitution. He responded in 1789 by the creation of the St John's Lodge of Secrecy and Harmony, which numbered, so Doublet says, over four hundred Knights by 1792 and which observed the French ritual. The Lodge *incognito* dowered every year upon the feast of St John a young bride in every Valetta parish. In the end, news of its existence reached Rome, and the Inquisitor, Mgr Scotti, was instructed to order its dissolution. Scotti may have been a mason himself, but he could not ignore orders from Rome, and the Lodge was quietly dissolved soon after the officers of the visiting Venetian fleet had been enrolled in 1792. Its effects were sold to reimburse the treasurer for his expenses in obtaining a patent from London.

Freemasonry was one inconsistency practised by the Hospitallers: there were many others. The moral sinews had rotted with disuse and the Order had sunk into a torpor of military complacency. For over a hundred years there had been repeated scares but no attack, and as the enemy repeatedly failed to launch an expedition against the islands, so the military machine rusted. The Knights were primarily fighters and there was not enough fighting to do. The most celebrated sailor in the Order, the Bailiff de Suffren, earned his reputation in the French navy. The majority of the Knights hoped for a life of comfortable neglect, and to many, vowed from earliest infancy to a life of frustration, the threatened dissolution of their society in the 1790's was anticipated with little regret. This feeling was not universal: when Napoleon arrived in June 1798 he came to drive out an Order that had come near to making of Malta one of the more enlightened, more efficient and yet more Catholic states of Europe. That was the tragedy of its destruction.

Chapter V

MALTA GEROSOLOMITANA

In the city state of Malta lived a population variously estimated as from seventy to one hundred thousand souls. The travellers who came to Malta had a markedly favourable impression of the Maltese. The exigencies of living on a small island the cultivation of which entailed much hard and thankless work had bred habits of sobriety and thrift that are no weaker today than when Spreti wrote in 1763: "The country folk, accommodating themselves to the barrenness of the island, live moderately and parsimoniously, wherefore with good air they are usually long-lived, there being a great number of rubicund, vigorous and robust old men who are well over eighty and sometimes ninety years of age." Denon, Gentleman in Ordinary to the King of France, Member of the Royal Academy of Painting and Sculpture and later to be Bonaparte's artistic adviser in the looting of Italian collections, visited Malta in the late 'eighties and found "poverty so active, so industrious and so neat that it has the air only of abstinence".

To the travellers of the eighteenth century, covering Europe for the first time as tourists, Malta was a curiosity. The Maltese lived in the outposts of Europe; there was a lure of romance about them, but they were in themselves a dour and unromantic people. The Knights, habits of superiority being too deeply ingrained, had little to say about them. Spreti was harsh: "The Maltese men are of an ugly complexion, being almost all dark and of a Sicilian cast of countenance, but otherwise valiant in arms, as indeed they have shown. They are rude and barbarous in their ways, and their language makes them seem more rough than they really are, it being much akin to Turkish, since the Turk and Maltese can understand one another. [By Turk Spreti meant, of course, Moor.] They speak but do not write it, using for their script a corrupt Italian or Arabic. They are very fond of money and most industrious in the making of it."

First visitors were impressed by the difference between the Maltese and the Sicilians, the natives of that brigand-ridden isle giving a poor account of themselves. "Never have I encountered more propriety," wrote de la Platière, "more honesty, an air more impressive, more officious and yet more disinterested. The peasants have in all a physiognomy that is both lively and spiritual, and they are robust. Add to this the fact that in the commerce of life they are both faithful and sure. What a contrast to the Sicilians!" "On getting ashore," wrote Brydone, "we found ourselves in a new world. The streets were crowded with well-dressed people, whereas at Syracuse there was scarce a creature to be seen and even those few had the appearance of disease and wretchedness." Louis de Boisgelin, author of a *fin-de-dix-huitième-siècle* account of Malta, ancient and modern, recognized both the virtues and the vices of the people he learned to respect. "It is, perhaps, as much owing to the situation of Malta as to the different strangers who have visited and conquered the island that the Maltese have become very industrious, active, faithful, economical, courageous, and the best sailors in the Mediterranean. But notwithstanding these good qualities they still retain some of the defects generally attributed to the Africans, and are mercenary, passionate, jealous, vindictive and addicted to thieving." Denon found the "traders interested and artful in all their bargains, but they are scrupulously faithful in fulfilling every contract, which renders all commercial intercourse with them safe and easy".

The beauty of the Maltese women was the source of constant, often lengthy, comment. The Polish Comte de Borch was lyrical: "The fair sex is very fair in Malta, their principal attractions being a waist extremely svelte, a leg beautifully formed, an instep finely arched, a skin of dazzling whiteness, a bust of splendid proportions, hair as black as ebony and an extreme vivacity in their discourse and in their every action. This last quality persists even in women of advanced age and seems to give an elasticity to their enfeebled strength. So many attractions can only appear of an inestimable value to the Maltese men, and such is their jealousy that more than once tragic consequences have attended those imprudent florists who neglected the flowers in their own gardens to cultivate those in another's." De Boisgelin described the Maltese women as "little, with beautiful hands and feet. They have fine black eyes, though they sometimes appear to squint owing to their always looking out of one eye, half the face being covered with a sort of veil made of black silk, called a *faldetta*, which they twist about very gracefully and arrange with much elegance. . . . They are extremely fond of gold and silver ornaments and the peasants are often loaded with trinkets of these metals. Their dress consists of a short shift, a linen or cotton under-petticoat, a coloured upper one, generally blue and open on one side, and a corsage with sleeves. The back part of their neckerchief is fastened up to the head, and their hair which is smooth, well-powdered and pomatumed is dressed in front in the form of a sugar-loaf, much in the style of the *toupées à la grecque*, so long worn by the men. They ornament their necks with gold and silver chains; sometimes indeed with necklaces of precious stones. Their arms are loaded with bracelets, and their ear-rings are in general more expensive than elegant. The shoe buckles are extremely large and always either of gold or of silver."

A high standard of living accounted for this; during the carnival of 1765, the wives of the merchants in the Three Cities with business interests in Spain and Portugal sported richer and more sumptuous costumes than the ladies of rank. The men dressed with less style. The richer affected the French style, the more usual costume being, according to de Boisgelin, "a large cotton shirt and a waistcoat as large, with silver and sometimes gold buttons. To these are added a *caban* or hooded cloak reaching below the small of the back, and a very long girdle twisted several times round the waist in which they constantly carry a knife in a sheath. They also wear long and full trousers and have both legs bare. They never wear hats, but blue, red, white and striped stocking caps. People of better fortune usually carry fans in their hands, and wear blue or green spectacles."

The Maltese women suffered from near purdah. The Maltese wife was seldom seen out, except in church or at festas; she tended to keep to her home and family and each house was provided with a wooden balcony, closed in with glass like a birdcage, from which she could watch the world pass by without being seen. A country phrase held that "women should appear but twice in public—the day they are married and the day they are buried". But by the eighteenth century this was a dead letter and the more sophisticated families were beginning to mix quite freely with society.

Malta's proximity to the Arab world endowed it with a romance that was only heightened by the celibate Order that ruled there and the large Moslem population. Honorato Bres, a Servant-at-Arms and Librarian of the Order, noticed that the women had "in their physiognomy and gestures something of the passionate expression of the Orientals, but mixed with so much reserve that one would mistake it for modesty". Denon thought he detected the atmosphere of the seraglio. "In imitation of the Levantine and Eastern customs, it seems as if they limit the usefulness of the fair sex to the sole department of pleasure. Though living under a burning sky they possess the fair skin of the inhabitants of the north, with the impassioned expression of the Orientals; their beauty is neither Grecian nor majestic, but it is not on that account less seductive. With fine complexions, which they carefully preserve, they have almost all of them large eyes, in which love lies in ambush beneath their long eyelashes, which give them a pleasing air of languor not a little resembling modesty. Those of the country are said to be faithful to their husbands but the women of the city know no more how to resist the gold of the Bailiffs than the amorous sighs of the young Knights, and we accordingly find at Malta the utmost licentiousness of celibacy!

77

Their dresses display more of coquetry than magnificence. Elegance and neatness constitute their luxury. They have the custom of shaving themselves like men; but then it is with so much art that you must come very close to discover the voluptuous effect of this practice. The operation they perform very dexterously with broken glass."

Malta, too, had its own large Moslem population whose customs gave the island its more distinctive Oriental flavour which attracted the painter Favray to make his profession as a Servant-at-Arms and to concoct his Moorish paintings from life and from stories that returning merchants told of the Echelles. This Moslem population was made up largely, but not entirely, from the slaves, prisoners of war taken on board Moslem shipping. The galleys were rowed, the fortifications were built and maintained, the Grand Master's court was served by an army of Turks, Algerians, Tunisians and Tripolitanians and Egyptians. Those that had been taken on board ships captured by the fleets of the Order were the property of the Order. Those taken by privateers, after one-tenth had been offered to the Order, were sold by public auction. There were few households without their Moorish slaves. The surplus, if any, was sold or presented to foreign monarchs; the old and infirm were periodically exchanged for Christians in Barbary. The slaves were not ill-treated, though they could hardly be called comfortable. As Malta was one of the biggest slave-holders in the Mediterranean, she was able to enforce a sort of unofficial Geneva convention; if information reached Valetta that Christian slaves were being ill-treated in the Regencies, similar treatment was meted out to the Moslems in Malta. If a slave was wantonly executed in Constantinople, a slave would be executed in Valetta; if Christians in Algiers were denied the ministrations of their priests, the Turkish *cadis* would be imprisoned and held incommunicado; if a Bey increased the weight of the chains (eleven ounces for a Moslem in Malta, six for a Christian), the weight was increased likewise. The Moslems enjoyed complete religious liberty; they had their Mosque and cemetery, they kept their feasts and their fasts. They were not encouraged to turn Christian, as Moslem rulers were inclined to read compulsion in what was always voluntary, and the Grand Masters were often compelled to curb the zeal of the local clergy, led by the Inquisitor. Conversion, however, did not lead to liberty; a slave was a chattel of economic value. It led to lighter chains, slightly better living conditions and more congenial work. Renegy was not easy; conversion had to be genuine.

Because of the comparative difficulty of escape the slaves were allowed considerable freedom of movement. They were allowed to set up booths if they had the capital, which could be sent from home, and to sell wine and other goods which would help towards their ransoms. They could also sell part of their ration of three loaves of black bread a day at a regulation pittance. Their hard-earned savings could be confiscated for a misdemeanour and they themselves bastinadoed (regulation limit: one hundred strokes). On the whole the slaves were an industrious and peaceful section of the community. Desperate characters there were who were guilty of crimes of sex and violence, but no more numerous proportionately than the local inhabitants. Those in private employ were sometimes very well off. For striking the slave of the Bailiff of Negroponte, a Maltese was ceremonially drubbed under the eye of the Bailiff by his other slaves.

Slaves of the Order had to lodge at night in the Bagnos of the Four Cities, huge cavern-like prisons where they were at the mercy of the caprices of the *agozzini* or warders, who often tyrannized over them, threatening them with punishment for breach of the regulations and often depleting their savings by accepting bribes against punishment. They went to work chained in pairs, and their heads were shaved clean except for a carrot-top of hair that was allowed to grow like a pigtail; the iron ring had to be exposed on their ankle to show that they were slaves.

Ransoms were calculated on the slave's utility, and 1,000 scudi was considered a fair price for a man in the prime of life. The scales were rigorously kept to encourage reciprocity from

Barbary. Ransoms were paid through the heads of Christian missions in the Regencies and through the French *chargé d'affaires* in Malta. Malta's proximity to North Africa, and the constant trade being carried on between them under neutral flags, meant that contact was more easily maintained with a slave's family. In 1714 the crew of a Turkish vessel depredated by a Spanish corsair successfully begged permission to be enslaved in Malta. The French consuls in Malta occupied most of their time in negotiating ransoms. When Bonaparte released all the slaves held in Malta, there were 2,000—some fiftieth of the total population in the island. With four galleys in commission, needing about 300 rowers each, a permanent labour force of 1,200 was necessary, not to mention the slaves in the arsenal, the public works, the bandage factory, the bakery and the palace. The number of Moslems was always amplified by the addition of Christian slaves, that is, any Christian taken while voluntarily serving on board a Moslem warship, usurious Jews and *buonavoglie*, often more wretched than the slaves. In moments of emergency the Bagno was opened to Greek Christians, Jews and private slaves, all of whom might be a potential fifth column.

The Grand Master appointed a Maltese priest to act as consul for the slaves and he was often used as an intermediary to recover debts from the slave's home-town and even to run his business there. As this would enable him to pay his ransom sooner, it was in the interests of the Order to allow the consul full freedom of action. Moslems visiting Malta on the business of ransom enjoyed perfect immunity; emissaries of the Beys were received by the Grand Master and Bailiffs and invited to dinners and concerts. Despite the peculiar war that existed, large numbers of Moors roamed freely through the streets of Valetta protected by French passes, while ambassadors from the Regencies stopping off on their way to European courts were received with royal honours, lent the Grand Master's coach and lodged in one of his palaces. When Tiepolo was commanded by the citizens of Udine to paint a picture celebrating the admission of their nobles to the ranks of the

Knights of Justice, he filled the foreground of the Council Hall, where Pinto sat in state surrounded by his Bailiffs, with turbaned figures in every extravagance of Turkish dress. In the middle of the hot war, the Bey of Tripoli would send gazelles and Arab horses to his enemy across the water, and the Grand Master would return orange water and liqueurs. He even sent his doctor to cure a friendly Bey of Benghazi and in 1726 informed another friendly Bey of Tripoli that he would accept the good faith of a Tripoli merchant engaged on trade without a pass. In the 'eighties, Tripolitanians sailed in with passes granted in Valetta and in 1792 the emissary of the Emperor of Morocco arrived to ransom all his subjects and stayed as a personal guest of the Grand Master.

The emphasis on trade communications reveals that in the eighteenth century a change came over the traditional industry of the Maltese, which had been, since the Knights arrived in Malta, a large-scale privateering activity known as the *corso*. In this, roughly half the able-bodied male population had been employed in various capacities. Some of the privateers were local Maltese, some of them were foreigners; the crews were largely Maltese, though often foreign *armateurs* took the flag of Malta for their own ends. There were two such flags—the flag of the Order and that of the Grand Master. Furnished with either of these a corsair could sail against the Moslem, but he had the most solemn orders not to molest Christian shipping. It was this very prohibition that represented the weakness of their predatory power and the Turks cottoned on to it in the early years of the eighteenth century as their protective naval power declined. They would purchase French passports from the consuls in the Levant and sail under those. They would put cargoes and crews under Greek Orthodox captains and sail as Christian ships. They would acquire a pass from the Guardian of Jerusalem, usually a Franciscan responsible for the pilgrims to the Holy Land, who was empowered to grant pontifical passes. There was even a black market in Jerusalem patents in Malta where interested merchants would fill in blank ones for Turkish traders. With these passes the Turks were legally immune from depredation; very often they were only produced after a boarding had been made and a great deal of damage done, and then there would be claims in the prize-courts in the island and fat damages to pay. In fact it became increasingly hazardous to attack Moslem ships at all, since so many of them had passes, and though every ship was obliged to submit itself to the *visità* whereby the privateer captain could demand to see the ship's papers, fears of decoys, traps and ambushes made this seem almost as hazardous as a straight attack.

Malta's position as a privateering state with international obligations—which did not inhibit the Regencies—became by the end of the century almost impossible. In 1647, in response to representations from the Procurator of the Holy Land, the Palestinian coast was put out of bounds to all Maltese shipping. In 1697 the ten-mile limit of fifty years earlier was raised to fifty. In 1714 the Venetians closed the Adriatic to Maltese privateers on the grounds that they were imperilling the delicate relations between the Republic and the Porte. The Turks had discovered that the French were very sensitive about their trading posts in the Levant, and by threatening to sequestrate the goods in the French factories if Maltese privateering did not cease, they managed to persuade the French court to see that Maltese corsairs were kept out of the Levant. The Maltese were often innocent, as there were Sicilian and Monagasque corsairs quite as intrepid and violent; often too the Maltese flag was guilty of raids in forbidden waters, but the captain and crew were French, who, in the words of the French Minister of State, Pontchartrain, were "good-for-nothings, who on the pretext of making war on the enemies of religion only dream of pillaging, thieving and enriching themselves by any means to hand, however shabby". Threatened in 1714 and 1719, after repeated raids within the fifty-mile limit and after an Italian *armateur* had been cruising in the Levant with both the Maltese and Spanish flag, depredating equally Turkish and French shipping, the Grand Master had to withdraw every Maltese corsair from the eastern Mediterranean. It was useless for him to complain, as Zondadari did in 1720, that "if the

Maltese *corso* cease in the Levant, then the French flag will not be as respected as it is, and Greeks will take up the commerce of these waters and wrest it from the French".

The Greeks themselves played their part in bringing the dreaded Maltese corsair to heel. Greek schismatics as Christians had been immune from depredation and the Aegean had been largely closed to Maltese pirates on this count. But in 1702 the Inquisitor decided to set himself up as the champion of Greeks who had, he believed, been unjustly depredated. He objected to the new practice of hearing Greek complaints in the *Consolato del Mare*, whose constitutional existence he ignored, as the Grand Master refused to accept the higher authority of the courts of Rome. He began, therefore, to accept Greek plaints himself and to appeal from any adverse decision in the *Consolato* direct to Rome, where, the Grand Master ruefully admitted, "in all disputable cases we always come off worse, and in cases where there can be no dispute we never see the end".

Appeals to Rome became legion and the Grand Master could not do more than object. At first he tried to persuade the *Rota* to accept the justice of depredating Greeks engaged on provisioning the Turkish fleet. When this failed he sought to make a distinction between his flag and that of the Order. The Order's was granted in the name of religion, and any offences committed under it could in the last resort be tried in Rome. His own flag he granted as a sovereign prince, and as a sovereign prince he was the last authority in litigation concerning prizes made under it. Rome would not accept the distinction, and the Grand Master, hoping to make his point, ceased to give his own flag knowing that the *armateurs* preferred it, and warned the Secretary of State that they would buy the Venetian. This was a forlorn threat, since he had already had a brush with France over Maltese-based corsairs flying the Tuscan flag who had attacked Turkish shipping in the Levant and whom the Grand Master accordingly could not punish. The French Minister of State, Maurepas, refused to consider them immune from the Grand Master's jurisdiction since the captains and crew were Maltese. In the end he had to promise the French that he would allow no Maltese to fly any other flag but one of the two he could obtain in Malta.

Rome was not then likely to be deterred by this threat, and the Turks, noticing the success that the Greek appeals were having, began to put their cargoes under Greek captains. Grand Master Zondadari tried to impress Pope Clement XI, known to be not indifferent to the decline of Crusading zeal, with the fear that a decline in the Maltese *corso* would merely mean that the Turks would acquire those marine skills of which the Christians were still the master and so control the inner seas. The Greeks were not to be trusted. They claimed goods that were not theirs and came to Malta to spy out the land, finding out what prize cargoes were being brought in and sending information to their confederates who then proceeded to claim them. The Tuscans refused to recognize the immunity of a Christian vessel whose captain and half of whose crew were not Roman Catholics. Why should not Malta do the same? Rome refused and Vilhena wrote bitterly in 1722: "Not being able to support the many families reduced to the most deplorable poverty by this far too indulgent favour being shown to the Greeks in Rome, we shall be forced to introduce open commerce with the common enemy and so break the strictest rule of our Order." It was still largely bluff, since Maltese were already trading in a small way with Tunis, but by 1724 there were over one hundred unsolved cases before the *Segnatura* in Rome, most of them brought by Greeks, and only eight corsairs at sea, a sad decline from the twenty to thirty of happier times. One Greek from Patmos claimed that he had made a hundred per cent profit on claims settled in Rome against Maltese. By 1728 the entire *Corso* had been suspended in the eastern Mediterranean, and only four corsairs were operating from Malta, each flying the Tuscan flag. Further pressure from Rome brought the Grand Master to heel in 1733. Every corsair had to fly the flag of the Religion and be subject to the tribunal, the *Magistrato degli Armamenti*, and to appeals to Rome. "The Turks", wrote Pinto in 1765, "are now trading under any flag but their own and our *Corso* is reduced to attacks on Barbary pirates, whose ships are of no value. Such little profit is made from them that it is insufficient to keep those sailors that are wounded, to pay pensions to the widows, to give bonuses to captains and to meet those expenses that will prove necessary if my subjects, who are better sailors than those of other nations, are going to stay in the service of the Religion."

The *Corso* did not die. There was an average of four or five corsairs at sea every year but they could not sail east of Crete, and in 1781 the Grand Master, after fifty years' quiescence, began to issue his own flag again. But though the decline of the *Corso* meant financial loss in Malta, it cannot really be regretted. It was, at best, a negative blessing and it is arguable that much of the penury and backwardness of those Moslem nations that fronted the Mediterranean Sea in the seventeenth and eighteenth centuries may be attributed to the prolonged war of attrition that formed the staple activity of the maritime nations. Anyhow, with its decline something else had to be provided before the Maltese relapsed into the poverty from which the *Corso* had rescued them at the coming of the Knights. From 1740 onwards, the Maltese that had once sailed out to raid, began to sail out to trade. It was a change for the better.

The principal industry to benefit was the growing, spinning and export of cotton. Maltese cotton enjoyed a high reputation for durability and the plant grew so well, and so profitably, that by the end of the eighteenth century most of the available land in Malta and Gozo had been given over to it. Agriculture was a hard and precarious living: foodstuffs were easier to buy from Sicily than to grow at home and the population had not outrun the water supply. Cotton began to be cultivated at the expense of corn, barley and beans, as well as the hitherto extensively produced cummin for which the market was declining. From the scanty surviving records of the Douane, it is possible to trace a steadily ascending curve. In 1776 the cotton thread shipped from Malta weighed roughly 466 tons; by 1779 it was 825 tons; in the first six months of 1792 it was

684 tons and in the last eight months before the arrival of Bonaparte the total tonnage was 658, and that when the French market had ceased.

Cotton thread alone was exported. As spinning helped to maintain a high level of employment, the export of raw cotton was forbidden; the industry was run on family lines, the farmers that grew it often being the spinners and shippers as well. The quality of the thread was not high, that of the raw cotton being better, but home weaving was confined to stocking, coverlets and blankets. The value of the exports is hard to assess. De Boisgelin avers that between 1788–9 they were worth 2,750,000 livres—and that the gross product of Malta was valued at three million. De la Platière quotes an annual customs revenue of between 150,000 and 200,000 livres, the export duty being $3\frac{1}{2}$ per cent—though, if de Boisgelin's estimate is correct, this sum should be nearer 96,000. The biggest market was Barcelona, closely followed by Marseilles. After the outbreak of the French Revolution Spain absorbed the whole supply save for a small proportion that went to Italy, and it was shipped on vessels flying the Ragusan flag. When the British occupied the island in 1801 they permitted the Maltese to continue their trade with Spain, even though she was an enemy power. But as soon as the French market withered, and the cotton of Egypt and America poured into Europe via England, the Maltese cotton industry languished and died. It was rigidly protected while it lasted and was able to capitalize the most-favoured-nation terms offered to Malta by the Chamber of Commerce at Marseilles.

One of the reasons for Marseilles's benevolent attitude to Malta was the greater interest Marsilian merchants were showing in the island. In 1733 Grand Master Vilhena reduced the tax on a cargo transferred from one ship to another from $6\frac{1}{3}$ per cent of its value to 1 per cent. Thus merchants were encouraged to bond cargoes in Malta to await the best price in Italy or France. A nominal anchorage due was charged on ships that disembarked nothing, and ships and cargoes doing quarantine got very favourable terms; goods in bond were charged 1 per cent per annum—lower than in Marseilles itself. All this had the desired result. Malta became a transit port, and Marsilian merchants bonded their goods there when prices in Marseilles were fluctuating. Grand Master Pinto tried the experiment of declaring Malta a free port for certain periods of the year (though this concession only once covered the buying and selling of corn). He also built sumptuous warehouses to lease to merchants who wished to store the increasing volume of goods coming into the island.

Much of the merchant shipping was Maltese, used for the carrying trade. Some of these flew the French flag and so were able to trade with the Levant, Morea and Barbary. One of the most profitable activities was the exchange of money and goods, a commerce in which the Maltese showed great skill. The usual practice, according to Honorato Bres, was to sail from Malta with specie which was exchanged at a very favourable rate in Genoa; buying goods in Italy, mostly silks, the merchant then sailed to the Spanish mediterranean ports where silks were exchanged very profitably for other goods which were then transported to the Canaries, Cuba, sometimes even to Mexico and Peru. Some Maltese merchants were said to have had their factors in Philadelphia, U.S.A. They then returned with American goods, which they sold at a fine profit. This patient series of exchanges, showing a small profit each time, was typical of a frugal, hard-headed people who had wrung a living for centuries from a hostile soil. In 1751 the Marsilian merchants were complaining of the amount of French specie going to Malta, where it was accepted in exchange for foreign currencies, particularly the Spanish piastre, at better rates than in Marseilles. The piastre exchanged favourably against the Maltese scudo, and the louis-d'or better against the piastre. The Grand Master grew perturbed, as did the Chamber of Commerce in Marseilles, at the number of louis-d'ors in the island, where they were accepted as legal tender more readily than the local currency. In 1777 the commonest silver currency in the island was the ubiquitous Maria Theresa dollar. The Grand Master's own currency was the scudo, a silver coin bearing his image and arms, exchanging always at a higher rate in Malta than elsewhere as the Grand Masters pegged its exchange rate higher than it was worth. This was never exaggerated, as every now and then he had to try and raise a loan on the value of the scudo in Genoa. To add to this confusion, a great deal of foreign specie came into the island by way of responsions, and was used freely to oil the wheels of commerce.

In Marseilles the traders sometimes regretted the privileges they had been persuaded to grant the Maltese. They were not charged any dues on their cargoes—a privilege not enjoyed by French traders from the Levant. In 1753 the Director of Farms wished to prevent the Maltese traders from transferring their goods from one ship to another in Marseilles harbour as they heard of price fluctuations in the various ports of destination. Pinto warned him that if this practice were forbidden his subjects, they would move their business to Leghorn, Genoa and Messina and pursue their trade under English flags. The Marseillais would then lose the cargoes as well as the merchants, who were good customers, as nearly every Maltese company had at least a fifth of its funds in Marseilles.

The little island grew in wealth from its merchants as well as from its merchandise. In 1777 the French Comptroller-General Turgot wrote to de Rohan on the creation of Malta as an entirely free port. "Malta, if her port were free, would become of necessity and independently of any political measures the entrepôt of all merchandise from east and west. The money, which the traders from all the ports of Europe would lay out, would enrich the Maltese, and the increase of comfort be all the surer since, having no outlay to make, they could only gain." Such a design, he went on, would also render food shortages less likely, since there would always be supplies in the warehouses. Malta was better placed than Leghorn; Holland had just made Cape Town a completely free port. The increasing volume of goods passing through the island would amply compensate the Grand Master for waiving his $6\frac{1}{2}$ per cent tariff.

As the Maltese were not directly taxed, this tariff formed the greater part of the government's income from harbour dues. It was levied on leather from the Levant, Smyrna, Leghorn, Marseilles and Tripoli, on playing cards and writing paper from Venice and Marseilles, on tobacco from Lisbon and Brazil, on coffee from Leghorn and Susa, if it was brought in on a foreign ship. On cargoes aboard Maltese ships the due was 3 per cent of the value, but, according to de la Platière, foreign merchants avoided the higher rates. The greater part of the shipping that used the island was French; in the 1770's, 60 per cent of the ships doing quarantine in Malta were French. In 1780, of 207 ships doing quarantine, 132 were French, 17 Ragusan, 18 Venetian and 12 Maltese. There were no British.

The profits of the Corso had gone to the enrichment of the immense churches, of cathedral size, that sprang up in the seventeenth and eighteenth centuries to dominate the sprawling and pullulating *casales* that dotted the island. A generation of Maltese architects had followed Cassar to build and embellish with decorations of great wealth the fanes of the people. The profits of trade could be seen in the dress of the merchants' wives who had the latest French fashions sent from France, and in the solid, affluent building of town and country houses. The splendour and prosperity of Malta stamped the people with a fierce national pride and a spirit of independence vastly in contrast to that of their neighbours on all points of the compass.

Even the poor had something of this dignity; though they lived near subsistence level, they were not squalid. The farmers lived in their *casales* and trudged out to work on the fields. They lived frugally on "bread, peppers, onions and anchovies", the traditional manner of eating it being to scoop a hollow in a loaf of bread and filling it with a mixture of all these ingredients. "Give him an Arabesque beauty for his bed," wrote the Baron Riedesel in 1773, "and a mess of oil and onions for his board, and your Maltese will consider himself the happiest of mortals." On high days and holidays he might eat pork, but only then.

There were many holidays; in fact there were so many that in 1749 the Grand Master prevailed on the Pope to strike fifteen out of the calendar as the poor were suffering from enforced idleness. They were accompanied by jollifications in which the Knights and nobility played the feudal host. Each *casale* celebrated the feast of its titular saint, and the Feast of St Peter and St Paul was celebrated by the whole population, who gathered, if they could, at the Boschetto and ate fried rabbit, danced and drank in the orange gardens and under the pine trees by the light of Chinese lanterns. *La Luminaria*, or *Mnarija* as it was called locally, was so important an occasion that brides would have it written into their wedding contracts that their husbands should take them to the Boschetto every year, where they would sport their wedding dress. Weddings were arranged by the parents, and the sight of a potted geranium on the outer wall of a house was said to signify the presence of a marriageable daughter inside.

For the three days before Ash Wednesday the country people would flock into Valetta for Carnival. This was not as sophisticated as the Venetian, but a lot of money would be spent on finery and the Knights would descend into the frollicking and half-crazed crowd to throw off, like them, the inhibitions of a lifetime in three days of licence. The masked crowds played peekum and catch-as-catch-can, lord was servant, servant lord. Even so, the *sbirri* were on the lookout for lethal weapons—which had to be laid aside—and for women masked as men, men as women, and slaves masked at all. When in 1775 the Pope died and the Bishop requested the Grand Master to cancel the Carnival, he declined. Said the then Bailiff de Rohan: "One should not deprive the public of this fleeting recreation to which it looks forward so jealously and so avidly." The climax of Carnival, as indeed of many celebrations, was the *coccagna*. For this, cross-beams were set up against the guard-house of the Palace square to which were tied live poultry, pigs, kids, hares and partridges, baskets of fruit and eggs, sides of ham, strings of sausages, wreaths of oranges and other provisions, the whole structure being surmounted by a figure of Fame holding the Grand Master's flag, and approached by rope ladders. The assembled crowd, at a signal from the Grand Master, rushed for the ladders, and anyone who managed to bear out any trophy intact could keep it. He who reached the figure of Fame first received a special largesse from His Eminence. The noise must have been indescribable, the shrieks of the dismembered animals being drowned in the general din. "The people are particularly delighted with this entertainment," wrote de Boisgelin, "and do not suffer foreigners or soldiers to share in the profits of the festival."

The townspeople were, while being respectably dressed and shod, by no means over-sophisticated, and two of the best descriptions have been left by Englishmen who were in the island shortly after the Knights left. The characteristics of a people do not change quickly. Here is Coleridge on noise: "I have heard screams of the most frightful kind, as of children run over by a cart, and running to the window I have seen two children in a parlour opposite to me . . . screaming in their horrid fiendishness—for fun! But it goes through everything, their street cries, their priests, their advocates, their very pigs yell rather than squeak, or both together, rather as they were the true descendants of some half dozen of the swine into which the devils went recovered by the Royal Humane Society."

Pigs were allowed to roam the streets quite freely in the poorer parts of the town, acting as a dustbin service. They were locked in the houses at night, and surprisingly never stolen. Goats were milked on the doorstep. The dung of all these and other beasts of burden was dried on the rooftops both in the towns and *casales* and used for fuel. Coleridge does not mention the chickens kept in cages on balconies and roofs, crowing through the night and slaughtered daily.

The second description is from Thackeray's *From Cornhill to Grand Cairo*, written in 1844. "The streets are thronged with a lively, comfortable-looking population; the poor seem to inhabit handsome stone palaces, with balconies and pro-jecting windows of heavy carved stone. The lights and shadows, the cries and stenches, the fruitshops and fish-stalls, the dresses and chatter of all nations, the soldiers in scarlet and the women in black mantillas, the beggars, boatmen, barrels of pickled herring and macaroni, the shovel-hatted priests and bearded Capuchins, the tobacco, grapes, onions and sunshine, the signboards, bottle porter stores, the statues of saints and little chapels which jostle the stranger's eyes as he goes up the famous stairs from the watergate, make a scene of such pleasant confusion and liveliness as I have never witnessed before."

The Maltese were fiercely religious, and there was an air of almost Jansenist austerity about the moral climate of Maltese religion. They claimed to have been evangelized by St Paul and kept a portion of his arm in the Collegiate Church of St Paul. Though Biblical evidence was obviously in their favour, it was not until the reign of Benedict XIV that the Pope arbitrated in favour of Malta over its rival, the Adriatic island of Meloda.

Malta was the seat of a bishop, whose nomination lay with the King of Sicily by a procedure known as the *Terne*. The King was presented with a list containing three names: one of them had to be a subject of the King of Sicily, the other two could be Maltese or any other nationality. The Grand Master, who drew the list up, often included the name of the Grand Prior, who was on occasions both Maltese and the King's choice. It was not until 1889 that the British special mission to Rome insisted that the Bishop of Malta should be a Maltese.

The Bishop had his palace in Notabile and another in Valetta. He was permitted to grant patents to his curial clergy and *familiari*, and all tonsured clergy were immune from the legal processes of the land and liable only to judgment in the Bishop's court. It was a cause of constant friction between himself and the Grand Master. The position was complicated by the presence in the island, too, of an Inquisitor, who was effectively the Papal Nuncio and the one foreign *chargé d'affaires* who was not nominated by the Grand Master or subject to him in any way. The first Inquisitor had arrived during the reign of La Cassière in the sixteenth century to watch over the orthodoxy of the Knights. They were usually prelates marked out for promotion, twenty-five of the Maltese Inquisitors subsequently becoming Cardinals, and two became Popes Alexander VII and Innocent XII. The orthodoxy, or un-orthodoxy, of the Knights did not exercise them much and they spent their energy in being watchdogs of the Church. Their court and palace were in Vittoriosa—the Grand Masters refused them residence in Valetta—and they had a summer palace in the country, as elegant and charming as the Vittoriosa palace was gaunt and forbidding. The Inquisitor enjoyed, like the Bishop, his own jurisdiction over his patentees and *familiari*, and any disputes between one of these and a layman had to be decided in his court. No heresy need be involved. The paten-tees, always laymen, and *familiari*, usually laymen, enjoyed clerical immunity, and the Inquisitor had a habit of building up the number of these by splitting up his estates and letting them out to men as leaseholders; as such they qualified for patents and were prepared to pay for the privilege. They could not be arrested by the *sbirri*, they need not turn out when the Grand Master called up the militia, they could dishonour their debts and obligations with comparative impunity and they could evade the laws of the land. It was invidiously true that sentences in the Bishop's or Inquisitor's courts were mild. Patentees who undertook to insure ships and cargoes before the *Consolato del Mare* (which the Inquisitor refused to recognize) could refuse to pay when a judgment was given against them. Any *sbirro* who arrested a patentee, and it was impossible to recognize one as they all ignored the regulations to wear a tonsure and to dress as a cleric, might find himself arrested in turn by the Inquisitor's or Bishop's *sbirri*, and excommunicated until he made abject apology. In 1706 the Grand Master had obtained an order from Rome that merchants and slaves were not to be given patents, and in 1750 it was extended to cover shopkeepers, goldsmiths, drapers, victuallers and pharmacists who had been short-weighting and short-cutting, protected from the legal penalties by their patents.

Relations between the Grand Master and the two prelates

were nearly always bad, fomented by irritating clashes over their respective jurisdictions. The Grand Master was anxious to minimize the authority of the prelates; the Inquisitor, jealous of his position, was often prepared to challenge an injustice or to defend a principle on grounds of personal animosity; the Bishop, presiding over the largest educated body of the Maltese, championed the cause of clerical independence at the expense of good government. To our modern ear, dual jurisdiction, clerical immunities and rights of sanctuary sound fearfully cumbrous and unfair, but, though the administrative system in the island was improving, the judicial system was neither foolproof nor wholly just. Miscarriages of justice were not uncommon and the Church's patronage of fugitives often prevented them. Similarly it often obstructed justice. In 1777 the Grand Master was able to limit sanctuary to minor breaches of the law, committed through neglect or poverty, whose perpetrators might reasonably fear that the penalties at law, in an age that knew no remand system, would ruin them and their families. The opposition of the Church, in a land where there was no free speech as we know it, no independent press, though irksome and gratuitous and detrimental to efficiency, was alone what prevented the Grand Masters from setting up little divine-right states that were the curse of contemporary Germany.

Any animosity that may have existed between Church and State did not spread to the spheres of doctrine or morals, and, throughout the Order's history, the Church's divine authority was never challenged. There was a remarkable unanimity among the people as regards their faith, and this was not due entirely to the classic explanation of ignorance and poverty. Traditional religion had a great part to play in producing it, but also an advanced spirit of social responsibility among the clerics. The extraordinary rising of the priests in 1776 was largely inspired by a close sympathy with the sufferings of the common people, together with some hazy appeal to national identity, which the priests as educated Maltese and the spokesmen of their parishioners were the first to feel. When the

Maltese rose against the French in 1798 they were to be led by a priest, and the cause of the Maltese first found natural expression after the spoliation of their churches by Napoleon's commissars. The Maltese did not notice a disparity in wealth between their clergy and themselves. The churches, then as now, were lavishly and expensively decorated and furnished, but by infinitesimal contributions from the poor. A great deal of money was spent on festas, and the French thought in terms of millions of scudi when they saw the silver in the churches. But large religious foundations with corrupt manners and an impoverished lower clergy were not, and could not be, the characteristics of so tiny a state as Malta. The religious houses conducted an elaborate and generous charity, the Inquisitor was always present to investigate abuses and the clergy were able to live with a fair degree of comfort but without a great difference between their standard and that of their parishioners. De la Platière was emphatic on this score: "The ecclesiastics, whom I found the best instructed, the most devoted to their estate and consequently the most respected, were the *curés de campagne*. . . . Although the spirit of bigotry, so common in Italy and Sicily, does not reign in Malta, although there are not half so many Madonnas and Saints, the people there are very devout and each day an infinite number of Masses is said in the churches and in the domestic chapels. I have seen the priests in the country, dressed as peasants and carrying on their own labour, coming to say Mass in the chapels of devotion isolated in the fields."

That public charity was considered efficient is indicated by the Magistral ordinances in 1730 that forbade open begging in the streets and directed all men and women in want to apply to the Venerable Congregation of the Poor who would supply all their needs. The Church, too, lent her active patronage to many of the commercial activities of the Maltese, the various Confraternities or Guilds meeting regularly in a chapel of the church of their patron, even holding their elections there. Few enterprises were embarked upon without the blessing of the Church and little could be attempted with her disapproval.

Even the standard of behaviour, religious behaviour, was high, in marked contrast to the Continent. In fact the law had several curious provisions to uphold public morality: young people who persistently misbehaved in church, who talked through the services, ogled or leered at one another, could be given three warnings and after that arrested and punished by the civil arm. Swearers and blasphemers might be arrested and pilloried with a gag in their mouths and a placard round their necks. The sale of meat in cookhouses and taverns was forbidden by law on fast-days, and, during the Lenten sermons, taverns and wine-houses were closed in order to encourage the people to attend.

The law made very often no distinction between sin and crime. Adulterers could be separately punished until 1786 when an enlightened Grand Master confined the penalties to the man, where the woman was unmarried. If the man were unmarried too, and if she could prove that a promise of marriage had preceded seduction, the Bishop's court could compel him to make an honest woman of her. Despite various regulations to limit its scope, the government was quite unable to deal with prostitution. The Sieur du Mont in 1699 "found the courtesans here very common. Their profession has nothing disgraceful about it and when they have earned their money they can get married and are reputed honest enough women as if they had never had the slightest blemish. The harlots have established a very pleasing custom, and very convenient for the debauchees who, passing through Malta and knowing no one, will often be obliged to leave before having had an opportunity of tasting the forbidden fruit. These have only to walk through the streets of the town holding a gold sequin (a coin) in their hand so that it can be clearly seen. It is a signal that will bring out twenty gallant ambassadresses in less than an hour." Thomas Walsh, Captain in H.M. 93rd Regiment of Foot, just a hundred years later passed through Malta on his way to Egypt. "Prostitutes of all ages, from the lively girl of sixteen to the crazy dame of sixty, swarm through the town and their acquaintance is extremely dangerous, as few of them are free from a certain disorder of a pernicious and inveterate nature." The author of *La Nouvelle Relation* held "that there is no place in the world where the pox is more rapid or spreads more easily, since it is composed of all the poxes in the world". The international aspect of Malta, rather than medical knowledge, inspired this judgment.

For the Four Cities were dockside towns with all the flotsam of a society that earned its living from a dangerous and uncomfortable avocation—the sea. There were men from all over the Mediterranean, and though the Order tried to see that they were shipped out on board short-crewed merchantmen it was not easy to control a mixed and violent collection of men. Crimes of violence were not uncommon, and if unsolved were attributed to foreign seamen. If the offender were caught, retribution was swift and harsh. Criminals were usually hanged in the Strada San Giacomo in Valetta; if they had confederates they were strung up in other prominent places. They were just hauled up a rope with a weight tied to their feet and throttled to death. *Crimes passionels* were more lightly regarded. "The police indeed", wrote Brydone, "is very much better regulated than in neighbouring countries, and assassinations and robberies are very uncommon, the last of which crimes the Grand Master punishes with the utmost severity. But he is said, perhaps in compliance with the prejudices of his nation [Pinto was Portuguese], to be much more relax with regard to the first." The use of torture to extract confession was not abolished until the British arrived, the rack being the commonest instrument. Public whippings were used to discipline recalcitrant and impertinent citizens. The execution of a slave, if he were one who had consented to receive baptism before death, was a big affair. As his soul was destined immediately for heaven the execution was a joyful occasion, the godfathers, often Bailiffs, stood by and before a pious and edified crowd the recent criminal and neophyte was strung up nearer his destination.

The legal system of the island was not capricious, but often ineffectual. There was no trial by jury, but criminal cases were heard before three judges among whom unanimity was not required. A suspected criminal, once arrested, might be kept in prison indefinitely until the judge was ready to hear his case; prosecution witnesses were examined in private and then subjected to a rigorous cross-examination. Then only was the prisoner's advocate confronted with the testimony and the prisoner with his crime. It was then up to them to produce their own witnesses, no others for the prosecution being called, and the judge proceeded to judgment. It was not a good system, but it had redeeming points. The prosecution did not have an easy time of it, and once its case was made there was no going back on it. The accused, however, was scarcely given adequate time to make his defence. Where the system broke down was in the private examination of witnesses and the venality of the judges; habeas corpus and trial by jury were English innovations of the nineteenth century.

The maximum penalty short of death was ten years on the galleys. Capital crimes only covered a small field: homicides and their aiders and abettors, mixers, senders and deliverers of poison whose effects had been fatal, unprovoked physical assault, especially on parents or masters, and shooting at anyone with intent to kill or maim, whether he were hit or not. Compared to the list of capital crimes in England at the time it was a merciful table, suitable to a tempestuous people who were less averse to taking life than property. Torture could be ordered if one undoubted witness gave reason to think it might elicit further information; in the case of a notorious bad-hat circumstantial evidence was considered enough for a condemnation. The judges had the powers more of a colonial district administrator than of a judge as we know him today.

A profusion of lawyers is not evidence of a lawless society, but usually of an unemployable intelligentsia that has been educated beyond the provisions of the labour market. Judges had powers too little controlled by the machinery of justice: they could promote or retain cases at will, and as their income depended on the fees of a case it was in their interests to prolong it. In civil cases, the amount of documentary evidence often produced a Jarndyce *vs.* Jarndyce; the case began with an exchange of writings which were then examined by contending lawyers in the judge's private house—a process not above suspicion. Appeals from the simplest decision could be made, and from the final judgment appeal was almost invariably made to the Grand Master. In 1782 the Grand Master published the Code de Rohan, a compendium and classification of the laws of the island, which when defective fell back on the old Norman law or on the opinions of foreign jurisconsults. It was based largely on Roman law and today forms much of the civil code. It was not ideal; despite its merits, which were considerable, "it savoured much of arbitrary and despotic principles. We may hold", wrote the first Royal Commission in 1812, "its leading maxim to be *quod Principi placuit legis habet vigorem.* No definition is attempted of the authority of the Grand Master, nor is any bound or limit prescribed to it. To this omission we may trace the practice of appealing from the final decrees of the supreme tribunal to the chief of government in person, which in fact sets him above the law and virtually annihilates the powers of the courts of justice." The law's delays were so great that British traders preferred to lose 20 per cent of the value of their cargoes rather than embark on endless and more costly litigation.

Regulations covered every walk of life, none more stringently than in the matter of food distribution. The *Università*, made up of the Jurats of Valetta, was responsible for keeping a six months' supply of corn in the granaries. In order to facilitate its activities, it was given a monopoly, extending to other grains, foreign wine and spirits, oil and tobacco. It was empowered to purchase corn compulsorily in periods of grave shortage from ships in harbour at the prevailing price in Marseilles. The *Università* had quite considerable sums of money in hand and operated as a lending bank. Between 1778–88 it was the Order's creditor to the tune of over 167,000 scudi at an interest rate of 3 per cent, and in 1773 Pinto himself owed it 193,000 scudi. In that year its accounts were overhauled by the new Grand Master, who found them in chaos, and the

British wound the whole institution up shortly after arrival, as it had become riddled with monopolistic and nepotic vices.

Under the Jurats (who usually included the French and British consuls) there was a host of *cattapani* or regional headmen, who were to see that the weights and measures were accurate in the *casales* and that black markets were broken. During shortages, especially of meat, they could force tradesmen to sell at a loss. Grand Masters on accession were inclined to curry favour with the populace by reducing the price of corn; Pinto for example ordered corn to be sold at 15 scudi a *salma* (about 2s. a bushel) when it had been bought at 60 scudi. This may have been the origin of his 193,000 scudi debt. De Rohan's accession was followed by a period of cheap corn, and in the lean period between 1792–8 corn was sold at artificially low prices so that the *Università* ran up a deficit of one and a half million scudi.

Except in years of scarcity, bread was a staple of the diet; it was cheaper than elsewhere in Europe owing to the cheapness of corn and controlled distribution. "Though salted," averred de la Platière, "it is fine, white and excellent." Bakers had to draw their flour supplies daily from the Jurats and by law the day's baking had to use it all up. A loaf of coarse bread weighing $13\frac{1}{2}$ oz. cost 2 *grani*, 4 *picciolo*, a little less than a farthing. Finer bread, known as *pane del palazzo*, sold at slightly more. Where even this price was too great for the poor, the soldiers and galley slaves who received a daily ration of rye bread were permitted to sell what they did not want at a fixed price; when the practice was abused and spivs were paying in advance for this bread to ensure a quantity to sell at higher, though still infinitesimal prices, the Grand Master would put the offender into chains for a year. Dolomieu himself built improved ovens on French models which the newly instituted (1782) Paris School of Bakery was recommending. Maltese bread was superior to the Sicilian, he said, but not as good as French bread because the corn was badly ground, and it was in the texture of the flour that the excellence of bread lay.

Cheap bread, clean cities, rich churches, French fashions, bank deposits in Marseilles, Arabesque beauties and *coccagnas*, the picture of Malta in the eighteenth century is one of growing material prosperity. But along with it grew a more articulate discontent. The Order's rule was benign, it had brought law and order, security and prosperity to the Maltese. The population had increased from ten to nearly a hundred thousand in little more than two centuries; splendid buildings, a standard of living higher than anywhere else in the Mediterranean, had both served to give the Maltese a sense of national pride. But always there was a sense of caste, of frustration, of inferiority that no amount of enlightenment could eliminate. When the Knights cravenly surrendered to Bonaparte, the Maltese did not want them back. They sought instead incorporation into the Empire of Great Britain, a Protestant power it was true, but one that had a reputation for liberalism more attractive to the growing nationalism that the Knights had unconsciously promoted. As a naval power she would protect them, as a commercial power she would enrich them, as a constitutional monarchy, she would give them representative government. This was the idea behind the Declaration of Rights of the Maltese People in 1802, and in choosing the rule of Great Britain the Maltese revealed both the success and failure of the Hospitallers during their sojourn in the island of two hundred and fifty years.

Chapter VI

"WHILE I FIGHT THE THRACIANS . . ."

IN February of the year 1697 Ramon Perellos y Roccaful, Grandee of the Kingdom of Spain, Knight of the Tongue of Aragon, ascended by general vote and popular acclamation to the throne of Malta. Some six months earlier, in July 1696, after three unsuccessful attempts, a Russian army under the direction of a Swiss admiral broke through the Turkish resistance and captured the Black Sea fortress of Azov. In the triumphal procession that entered the city, the Czar Peter I marched with a pike across his shoulder in the uniform of a captain in his own navy; the fleet he had constructed some hundreds of miles up the Don floated in the bay. It was the first Russian navy. Hitherto there had been no sea for it to sail upon.

When the campaign was over, the Czar as plain Peter Mikhailoff departed for Europe and the dockyards of Deptford and Saardam with his admiral and ex-tutor Lefort. He was followed by fifty young men from the best families; fearing some might refuse to return from the fleshpots of the West, Peter sent some senior men to season the contingent. This included the general who had planned the Azov campaign.

The Boyar Boris Czeremetev was a seasoned warrior of forty-six, a veteran of many campaigns. In 1686 he had signed with the Emperor Leopold I and King John Sobieski of Poland a treaty to drive the abominable Turk out of Europe. In 1696, sobered but not deterred by the formidable task before him, he had vowed that, should he survive the siege of Azov, he would visit the tomb of the Prince of the Apostles in Rome. The campaign brought to a successful conclusion, Peter allowed him to go on condition that after Rome he should visit Malta and cast his experienced eye over the fortifications and fleet of that famous island.

He left Moscow on 22nd June 1697 and reached Syracuse on 9th May the following year. There he was met by the Captain-General on 12th May and transported to Malta with all his retinue, which included his brother. The galleys, anxious to avoid Moorish raiders out again after Ramadan, travelled so fast that most of the Russians were very seasick; they reached the island at two in the morning, while the Maltese tumbled out of bed to the sound of the cannonade to view this visitor from outer space. Perellos's gilded carriage awaited him, and, with a procession of pine torches and a platoon of guards, he was escorted to Casa Cotoner in the city of Valetta, in full view of a curious crowd.

Czeremetev stayed six days in Malta and he was not idle. On 14th May he was received with all ceremony by Perellos, and there, while the astonished court listened, the thirty-one titles of his Imperial Master were read out and Perellos heard of the Czar's proposal for a combined operation against the Turk. With the armies of Hungary probing down the Danube, with the fleets of Russia in the Black Sea, and of the Order in the Aegean all at once, Turkish power must collapse. The Grand Master listened gravely to the proposal but would not commit himself. The following days Czeremetev spent touring the island, and on the 18th, the Feast of Pentecost, he assisted at High Mass in the conventual church, sitting below the Grand Master under his baldachin. Before the sacred relic of St John the Baptist, brought on in its silver reliquary, the Boyar prostrated himself, the tears streaming down his face. Then on the 19th, in the Great Hall of the Council, he received the accolade and Gold Cross of Devotion, kneeling at his own insistence before the person of the Grand Master, and Perellos, as a special mark of distinction, granted him permission to carry the cross upon his shield or banner when fighting against the Turks. That night, escorted by two galleys, he set sail for Italy, his journey cut short at his own request so that his presence might not distract the Order from mounting its projected attack on the Morea. Before he left, he distributed costly gifts of sable furs, black fox and ermine to the Grand Master and jewelled rings to the Captain-General.

Peter's visit to Europe was cut short by the rebellion of the Strielzi, and Czeremetev had to hurry back too. For his services in the destruction of the insurgents he was made the first hereditary count of the Empire, and before he died in 1719 he was to serve in the wars against Charles XII and Turkey. His last years he spent in Moscow occupying himself in charitable work, helping the aged and sick and maintaining orphans, as befitted the first Russian Grand Cross of the Knights Hospitaller.

For many of the Knights, Czeremetev was the first Russian they had ever seen, bringing into the sophisticated society of an international order the reminder of a huge half-continent unknown. Six Russians were to follow him in July and August, young nobles from Peter's court despatched on a Grand Tour at the Czar's expense. Then the flow ceased. But Malta's name had been written in the books of the Moscow Chancellery, and from now onwards brief letters of congratulation came regularly on the assumption of a Grand Master, and routine information of the deaths and accessions of Czars and Czarinas. Peter had opened his account with Malta. It was not to be closed until His Imperial Majesty the Grand Master Paul I of Russia was dragged from dinner in the Mikhailovski palace and strangled on 23rd March 1801.

Perellos ascended the throne of Malta at a time when the Mediterranean, and Malta's place in it, were changing. The Holy War, the predominant profession of his predecessors, which had reaped its rewards in the innumerable privileges they had acquired in Europe, was no longer an universally accepted axiom of European policy. In 1697 Peter the Great had attempted unsuccessfully to re-arouse the Holy League of 1684 when Innocent XI had tried to call the monarchs of Europe about the Cross, but Perellos could not gaily join him in his projected campaign. France, in unholy alliance with the

Grand Signor, while prepared to countenance the regular forays of the Maltese fleets against the Turk, would not permit a military alliance with so imponderable a power as Russia. She was even finding it hard, as both protector of the Order and ally of the Porte, to reconcile herself to the perpetual war between Malta and Turkey.

In fact the reign of Perellos was to see the last effective expeditions that the galleys were to mount against the Ottoman. They were the culmination and conclusion of a long series of campaigns in the Levant fought with the Venetian and Roman navies. In 1685, a combined Maltese and Papal squadron under the Neapolitan commander Brancaccio had co-operated with the Venetians in the recapture of Koroni in the Morea. In 1686 they had captured Napoli in Romania and Navarino, in 1694 Chios.

But these successes were only temporary; what profits, apart from the spiritual benefits from participating in a Holy War, that the expedition made were largely in favour of the Venetians. In 1696–7 the Maltese squadrons attempted to blockade the Turks in the Dardanelles while the Venetians landed troops in the Corinth Isthmus. They were unsuccessful. The Turks slipped through and engaged the combined Venetian and Maltese flotillas off Tenedos; the battle lasted six hours and was inconclusive. The destruction of Turkish naval power eluded them and the galleys had to return in September 1697 to Malta, their strength spent.

The intervention of two wars in the western Mediterranean made it impossible for Malta to resume the offensive until 1716 when the combined Papal and Maltese fleets were entirely a Hospitallers' affair, the commanders of the individual ships and of the whole expedition being Knights. There was a battle, fought with mute bravery, but little result, save a large number of casualties and an outbreak of dysentery which prostrated the crews. Once more the fleet returned to Malta without the spectacular results Europe had come to expect of them. It was to be the last expedition against the Turks.

The real cause was not so much France's implied

discouragement as financial strain. For the fleets were ancient and the ships victims of severe mauling by both nature and man.

The 1697 campaign had done little to lengthen the life of the battleships and in February 1700 the *capitana* galley, chasing a Turkish vessel some ten miles off Corfu, rammed her in the high seas after a long and arduous chase, only for her prow to split under the concussion and for the whole ship to founder with incredible speed. Only three Knights of some twelve on board survived and hundreds of sailors perished. Then later in the same year the galley *San Paolo* went down off Cape St Vito with three Knights and over three hundred crew. They were tragic losses, but they underlined the arguments now being raised against the galleys, so perilously exposed to destruction by the elements. The Turks too were arming their ships with as many as seventy guns and committing them to sail; a general worsening of seasonal conditions had been noted over past years which made the deployment of galleys more hazardous every time.

In March 1700, accordingly, Perellos set up a commission to consider the replacement of the *capitana*, and it decided before the end of the year to reduce the galley squadron from seven to five and to build four ships of the line of fifty to sixty guns each. They were to be paid for by a general tax upon the lands of the Order and one was built and provided by the Grand Master himself. Two were to be constructed in Malta, and two, despite the fact that France was herself at war, in Toulon. The timbers of a Turkish 50-gun soltana taken off Lampedusa were to help make one of the smaller vessels. On 9th December 1704 the new squadron of men-of-war was officially inaugurated and on 1st April 1705 left Grand Harbour, saluted by the entire fortress. Louis XIV, anxious that the Algerians, with whom he was at peace, should know nothing of his assistance, had instructed the two Toulon vessels to sail to Malta with skeleton crews, flying the white flag, and to make their first cruise in the Levant. But once their commander was clear of French waters he ran up the Cross of St John and arrived, contrary to orders, with crews in which six men in every seven were French. To them there was more chance of gain with the fleet of Malta and less of destruction.

The first victim of the new squadron was a 46-gun Turkish raider, which became the fifth man-of-war, and the combined squadrons of Malta were now larger than the fleets of Naples and Sicily, larger than the galley force of the Pope and of the Duke of Tuscany. But they were enormously expensive. In the 1716 campaign, the flotillas of Malta, Rome and Venice (the Spaniards and Sicilians, also commanded by Knights, never turned up) were unwilling to seek a naval engagement with the Turks, and cruised fruitlessly along the coasts of the Morea and spent the days in visits, receptions, salutes and counter-salutes, while the Treasury watched a yawning gap in the accounts. Then, after only twelve years of life, two of the new line ships returned to be broken up as unseaworthy.

The Order was still rich, but not rich enough to carry losses like these too often. When Perellos died, he had spent 217,000 scudi from his own pocket and the Order had to raise an immediate loan of 122,000 scudi in Genoa to be met by a general tax on its lands. For what had hit Malta worst was the change which came over the western Mediterranean at the end of the seventeenth century and the difficulties the Knights Hospitaller were to experience from the dynastic wars that marked the opening of the eighteenth.

In April 1701 the Order had at once recognized Philip of Anjou as King of Spain; there was really no option. The event that was to plunge Europe into war was celebrated in Malta with fireworks and extensive junketing. The Grand Master's palace was festooned with portraits of Louis XIV and of his grandson and with banners alluding to their glory. The Inns of France, Castile and Aragon erected fountains which ran wine for three days and nights, and the celebrations concluded with a procession of "the most beautiful triumphal car, representing Hercules in the gardens of the Hesperides, with the custodian dragon lying at his feet, fleur de lys growing from every wound. The Hero was seated upon a globe, courted by Spain and Italy and the various Virtues, who hymned the glories of His Catholic Majesty to a specially composed and beautifully ingenious serenade." The German partisans of the Archduke Charles were to note that this masterpiece of carnival was lighted at night by five hundred wax candles.

Though she had recognized Philip V, Malta had an obligation to remain neutral. But that neutrality was to be sorely tested; for she was obliged to close her ports to the enemies of the new King of Sicily, yet she dared not offend the naval might of Holland and Great Britain by insisting on this too severely. As a result, both sides complained. The French claimed that Dutch ships sailed into Malta's harbours flying French flags, and the Dutch that French ships were taking prizes within Maltese waters. All supplies in Sicily were cut off because an English privateer had led its prize into Grand Harbour. The French were only restrained with difficulty from setting up magazines in the island to refurbish their privateers. The English held the Order responsible for the loss of two merchantmen that were wrecked after the Maltese had prevented them sheltering in the harbour by arbitrarily raising the port charges. Dutch prizes led into Malta were claimed by the French and vice versa. Nothing she could do was right.

Malta had her complaints too. Her ships were being depredated by both sides, and the famous French privateer L'Aigle brazenly waited in Maltese waters to seize incoming vessels. All commerce was disrupted; the Knights of those countries at war with France were in an ugly temper and British prisoners of war deposited in the island by French privateers were proving a charge upon the government and a cause of complaint with the Inquisitor, who feared their Protestant influence. Perellos bombarded the French Ministry of Marine with his cries. France received highly favourable treatment in Malta; the port was closed to her enemies, her privateers could sell their prizes, bond their merchandise and obtain running repairs. In return they behaved so badly that the Maltese were terrorized, commerce paralysed, and the fleet unable to get its provisions.

England, unaware that Malta was having her own dispute

with France, was ready enough to believe she was favouring the enemy. Informed by their consul, whom Perellos had dismissed for dishonesty, that the prisoners were being badly treated, Admiral Jennings wrote strongly to the Grand Master in threatening tones. Happily the Order was able to put itself right with the Court of St James when the line squadron off Genoa was able to assist a British man-of-war laden with treasure worth seven million pistoles and foundering in a storm.

Peace and relief came in 1713, though the French had so far listened to Perellos as to order L'Aigle away and to quash decisions in the prize-courts against Maltese ships. But the *guerres de courses* had intruded a new element into the Mediterranean. Malta's neutrality had become a political factor of the first importance and France was the first to see her value as a base half-way to the Levant. When during the War of Polish Succession, France was at war with the King of Sicily and the port was closed, Chauvelin declared to the ambassador in Paris in an outburst of indignation, "*Eh bien, vous voulez donc nous faire la guerre!*" Cardinal Fleury tried to tempt the Order with alternative supplies of corn and meat should the *tratte* be cut off, but to no avail. In future wars, Chauvelin allowed himself to remark, it would be better if Malta's ports were closed to the shipping of every nation regardless of their relations with the King of Sicily. It should be on the agenda of the next European congress.

But no European congress came to any decision, even after Malta's precarious position had been revealed when there were two Kings of Sicily. In 1718 Cardinal Alberoni landed a Spanish army in Sicily to chase out the Savoyard king that the Treaty of Utrecht had placed there. When the new Spanish viceroy called on Perellos to seize the five Savoyard galleys then in Grand Harbour, he was compelled to refuse and all trade was suspended between the islands. The destruction of the Spanish fleet by Admiral Byng off Cape Passaro forced five Spanish warships into the harbour who with their usual courtesy saluted the Grand Master's flag while one of them discharged a volley into the side of a Savoyard galley. Perellos was able to restrain Byng from sailing in to destroy them, but the admiral soon got to hear of some over-enthusiastic Maltese privateers who had bought the flag of Spain from the Spanish minister in Valetta and then turned aside from their Levantine *corso* to molest the shipping of the Triple Alliance. Byng accordingly held the Grand Master responsible for the five English ships that had been depredated and threatened to attack all Maltese shipping he met. The Spaniards in the meantime demanded the tribute falcon, upon the gift of which the Maltese would have to close their ports to the French and English, and the Spaniards would release all the sequestered goods and food supplies. It was only Alberoni's personal intervention that lifted the ban, but the English were inexorable. When Alberoni fell in December 1719 and peace was signed in February 1720, the armed conflict had left the Maltese with a big bill to foot and a continued question mark over her future status as a neutral port.

The trouble with England was solved eventually when Spain decided to accept the indemnity demanded by the government. A diplomatic mission of complete futility and considerable expense was forced through its paces when the Chevalier La Val set off to London to plead the Order's case and was received courteously by George I and his Secretary of State Craggs, but at the Congress of Cambrai every attempt to get Malta's neutrality on to the agenda was elbowed out by more important issues.

For Malta possessed political privileges but no power, and her resources were not keeping pace with the changing values of money throughout Europe. Her privileges depended on the goodwill of the great powers and, tossed as she was between them, she was in danger of losing them. Barbary prizes were neither so frequent nor so valuable as before—the new fleet had done quite well, capturing eleven vessels and destroying two, including the *capitana* of Tripoli, but these scarcely met the running expenses of the squadron. In 1707 the Knights had fought their last land engagement with the Infidel.

Answering an SOS from the beleaguered garrison of Oran,

the Order despatched its line ships to the city, and put ashore
20 Knights and 315 Maltese who at once went to the front.
Through two broiling months of summer, the Maltese and the
mixed Spanish garrison of gaol-birds and Muslim renegades,
commanded by an Italian condottiere, Carafa, took the brunt
of the Algerian attacks, losing their commander in a sortie,
whose body was impaled on a forward trench and whose head
was paraded through the Muslim ranks. When the fort they
were holding was surrounded, and undermined, they came to
terms with the enemy, offering to surrender if granted their
freedom for an instant return to Spain. The garrison marched
out, but not to freedom. The Moors cynically disregarded the
terms and threw three Knights and a Servant-at-Arms into the
Bagno as common slaves and enslaved sixteen Maltese aboard
the flagship. The intervention of the French consul obtained
gentlemanly conditions for the noble prisoners, but de Langon,
cruising in search of the flagship, attacked it with such ferocity
that 115 of the crew of 400 were killed, the sixteen Maltese
liberated and himself killed. The Algerian Bey, in fury,
clapped the captive Knights into irons and set them to heavy
work, chained to cartloads of stone for the walls of Algiers.
When they attempted to escape on board a French cutter, the
Bey threatened to fire the consul out of a cannon and kept the
Knights in chains until 1717.

Their release was made conditional upon the return of all
the captives from the flagship. Perellos, unable to accept these
terms, and unable by the statutes to ransom Knights, was
powerless, and it was only in 1717 that the Regent Orleans,
anxious to have his bastard admitted to the Order, prevailed
on the Redemptionist Orders of Mercy and the Mathurins to
add 24,000 livres to what the prisoners' families had raised.

The relief of Oran had coincided with rumours of a vast
armada preparing in Constantinople to reduce Malta. Large
and expensive supplies of powder, mortars and bombs were
hastily laid in from Civitavecchia; but the threat passed. The
bill, however, did not, and the Order was in serious financial
difficulty. Responsions from France and Spain had been

interrupted; in 1710, from France alone, 150,000 livres in paper money lay in the coffers of the Receivers, redeemable at a loss of 40 per cent. The Lascaris Fund, invested in Sicilian property for the upkeep of the Magistral galley, was paying no interest because the Viceroy was dissatisfied at the conduct of the Order. The Treasury was supporting Knights whose commanderies had been engulfed by war. To crown these troubles, another scare came from Turkey in 1714, of another huge naval conglomeration, thirty *soltanas*, seventeen Barbary men-of-war, twenty galleys and forty galliots, preparing for an attack on Malta. All the able-bodied Knights were summoned to its defence, but only a tithe bothered to respond, confident that France would avert disaster by diplomatic means. Two battalions of French marines and four companies of French infantry reached Malta only to be sent home again.

In addition to the costly expenses incurred throughout his long reign, Perellos saw the schemes of Law collapse and all the bullion in the *caisses* of the Receivers seized for nearly worthless *billets de liquidation*. Again France rescued her from disastrous loss, but when the Grand Master died, eighty-four years old, on 10th January 1720, after eighteen months in a semi-paralysed condition, the last of the fabulously rich Grand Masters had reigned. He had lent the Treasury his money, he had given two ships to the fleet, he had presented a superb set of tapestries to the conventual church, woven in Brussels to designs by Rubens, Poussin and Matia Preti. He had procured the priceless Gobelins for the Council Chamber figuring the animals of the four continents designed by Henry of Nassau. He had found the Order great and striven to leave it greater. But the cracks were already visible. Good farmer though he was, he could not see that new methods, not continued subsidies, alone could save it. On the gates of the Porte des Bombes at Floriana, erected also at his expense, he inscribed the words: *Dum Thraces ubique pugno in sede sic tuta consto*. It was still possible to fight the Thracian, but even that privilege was to be increasingly denied the Order over which he had ruled for so long.

Chapter VII

NEW GIDEONS

THE first Italian for thirty years ascended the throne on 14th January 1720. Marc 'Antonio Zondadari was a Sienese, with a reputation for severity. "The people", wrote a contemporary diarist, "were ill content with his election, fearing much from his command, but he was a lover of the Maltese and honoured their country with many liberal arts and sciences, loving Justice and Charity." He was an ex-Captain-General, and it was hoped that his high connections in Rome—he was a nephew of the late Pope Alexander VII and of Cardinal Zondadari, a revered dynast in the Papal court—would help to smooth out the disputes that were slowly suppurating between the two courts, disputes that involved the *Corso* and the meddling of the Inquisitor in the tribunals of the island.

The *Corso* in the Levant had already been slain by French objections, and Rome appeared to be knocking in the coffin nails by her repeated support of Greek claims. The Maltese too were not confident that France, who was so anxious to keep the Maltese out of Turkish waters, would exert herself to the same extent to keep the Turks out of Maltese waters. They were worried about their defences. It was at this time, with rumours of attack from Turkey almost annual, that the Inquisitor tried to hold that his patents conferred immunity from military call-up, and when in 1721 Zondadari tried to call out all available forces, many chose to flaunt their patents in the faces of the recruiting officers. The Inquisitor, too, refused to hold that the Greek community was a political fifth column to be shipped off should an emergency occur and was supported in his stand by the Secretary of State.

Zondadari was unable to do anything before he was suddenly struck down by an intestinal disease and died on 16th June 1722, aged sixty-three. His successor was a very popular choice, the Bailiff of Acre, Manuel de Vilhena, Zondadari's most zealous partisan and a cousin of the King of Portugal. Vilhena ascended the throne at a moment of crisis. For on 7th March 1722 a report reached Malta that six Algerian *soltanas* were sailing for the island and had joined thirteen Turkish warships somewhere off Crete. The galleys *en course* were recalled, but on 28th June only five *soltanas* were sighted off the island. They were commanded by the Aga Abdi, who did not actually launch an attack but merely sent a letter to the Grand Master by the hand of a French merchantman ordering him in the name of the Grand Signor to release all slaves in his possession, and sailed away.

Vilhena was not dismayed. The defences were manned and the Grand Master himself made tours of inspection, while a general evacuation of the old and disabled was ordered from Gozo, on which, reports indicated, the Algerians were planning a raid. But when the Algerians did not return, Vilhena replied to the Aga's letter. Seeing a possible opening for negotiations he wrote direct to Constantinople. The fleets of Malta, he said, were not for hunting slaves, but for protecting commerce. If they met with those who intended to impede it or to make slaves of Christians, then they attacked them and took prisoners in a just and legitimate war. He would always consider ransom or exchange of slaves: but as the Moslems held far more Christian slaves than the Maltese held Moslem, he would never consent to release his prisoners unconditionally.

The only response was the reappearance of the five *soltanas* in battle line flying the colours of war. They fired a volley at the defences of Grand Harbour and then sailed away again. But rumours from the east continued to be alarming. A large fleet of fifty battleships were gathering in Constantinople, commanded by an ex-slave of Malta who would know the lie of the land. The Sultan had ordered reinforcements and men from the Regencies and had written to France and the Empire warning them not to assist the Maltese.

The ambassador in Paris at once contracted a 400,000-franc debt to purchase munitions, much to Cardinal Dubois' annoyance, for Versailles pooh-poohed the threat to Malta. Vilhena wrote a long memoire to Pope Innocent XIII asking for aid and chilling his spine with reports of increased pirate activity off the Italian coast should the Maltese fleet be laid up for lack of funds. But the Pope was as little concerned as the French. He did, however, appeal to the Sacred College for contributions and himself gave 30,000 scudi. But the Cardinals held back. Cardinal Scoti presented a bill for 500 scudi and Cardinal Salerno gave a diamond cross which he said was worth 12,000 scudi, but which turned out to be worth only a quarter of that sum. But the Cardinal Secretary of State, Sant' Agnese, would not commit Papal funds, and the Cardinals who lived without paying their responsions off commanderies in the Priory of Rome contributed nothing.

Only Spain offered to help. If the Emperor would permit them to shelter in Sicilian waters, she would send four men-of-war. The Imperial ministers were at once suspicious, and believed that the Spaniards and Turks were in league together and under cover of attacking and defending Malta would land troops in South Italy to oust the Imperialists, while France opened war on the Flanders front. So no agreement was reached between Spain and the Empire as to the extent of the aid each would offer—a combined Hispano-Imperial army of six thousand troops at one time was to descend on Malta, a prospect almost worse than that of a Turkish attack. As the year passed, so the hopes of aid evaporated along with the threat of attack. Vilhena tried one more source of subsidy. He despatched the Bailiff von Schade to the Rhenish electors and Prince Archbishops cap in hand. One and all they made excuse: the Archbishop of Mainz was building fortifications for his own city, the Elector Palatine was heavily in debt, the Elector of Bavaria had spent too much money promoting his candidate for the Electoral Bishopric of Cologne. In June

1724, the Elector of Trier, Grand Master of the Teutonic Knights, was ready to make a contribution as from one military order to another, but nothing prompted him actually to make it. Only an order from the Emperor himself would move them. And the Emperor did not give one.

Bitterly, the Grand Master realized that alone of European powers Spain believed in the Holy War, subject to the considerations of national politics. Rome was indifferent, France incredulous. No one believed that a few ships could do much harm to the extensive fortifications towards the construction of which every monarch and prince in the past had been pressed to contribute. The impregnable fortress was Malta's boast, but Vilhena was now preoccupied by considerations of practical defence that had never bothered the extravagant Cotoners. There were quite simply neither enough men nor enough money to go round.

When in April 1723 the French Ambassador in Constantinople wrote to the Grand Master to report his conversation with the Grand Vizier about a mutual cessation of raiding and an exchange of prisoners, Vilhena was ready to listen. A truce with the Porte would release the fleet for action against the Regencies; the *Corso* in the Levant was virtually suspended and the results of the general summonses had been so poor that, if Turkey wished, she could launch an attack before enough Knights could reach the island to defend it. A truce with Turkey that exempted the Regencies could be only to Malta's advantage.

Vilhena consulted the protecting powers. Rome was cajoled with the theory that if Malta no longer remained the ostensible object of Turkish war preparations, it would be easier to discover her real intentions. France was well disposed as long as the fleets were not allowed to decline. But nothing came of the truce, for the Grand Vizier's unofficial conversations were never resumed, but in effect from that date Malta's war against Turkey was over. Henceforward the waters of the western Mediterranean were to be a hunting ground for Barbary vessels only.

And successes against these were legion. In 1723 Jacques de Chambrai, the most resourceful ands killed sailor to have served the Order, captured the Tripoli Vice-Admiral's flagship, a ship of 56 to his 52 guns, with a crew of 400 to his 300, in a bitter running combat of two and a half hours in which he fired 328 salvoes of cannon. A hundred *Tripolini* lay dead, 270 were captured and thirty-three Christians freed. It was the most overwhelming victory for a quarter-century. Many lesser vessels were his victims in succeeding years; by 1732 he had taken six Barbary corsairs and eight hundred slaves; then while cruising off Damietta he sighted the flagship of the Turkish Counter-Admiral. Though this was a Turkish warship it was too big a prize to miss, and after a stiff fight, the Admiral struck, with 73 dead and 117 prisoners. Throughout Vilhena's reign and that of his successor, between 1722–41, the Order's line ships accounted for fifteen Barbary vessels and one Turkish, with a total of 1,455 slaves. The galleys were less successful, but added five ships, all from Tripoli. That city did not recover for many years, and the virtual destruction of her fleet led to what nearly passed as friendly relations between the Karamanli Beys and the rulers of Malta.

The spirit of the fleet was at its highest; the Algerian caravels were armed with 80 guns, but these did not deter the lighter-armed Maltese. In 1716 the four line ships had turned out to chase twenty-four Algerian corsairs at war with Holland and in 1725 they searched for four Turkish *soltanas* sent to Algiers to reclaim for the Emperor a ship of the Ostend Company depredated in the English channel. The Algerians were the toughest assignment, being commanded by Turks and the most heavily armed. But a Barbary vessel was a prize to be captured to men like Chambrai. When he once heard that a squadron of nine ships trying to slip back to Algiers had put in at Tunis and that their captains were arranging for their crews to be taken home on board European ships, he proposed to stop every ship leaving Tunis and to remove the Algerians. Only a direct order from the Grand Master restrained him. The Barbary corsairs had a healthy respect for his reputation.

The galleys were now almost superseded, and no more were built; as they were laid up, their timbers were used to construct new frigates. The men-of-war did not have to keep a slave force of three to four hundred men, and were cheaper. Slaves, too, were becoming scarcer and the Grand Masters were increasingly hard put to it to meet requests from European monarchs, including one from the Sergeant King of Prussia, who wanted some slaves of suitable size for his new troop of giants.

The reign of Vilhena was remarkable for the resurrection of an ancient Papal gift. Chambrai's success, growing Maltese exasperation with the tergiversations of Rome over depredated Greeks, the virtual end of the war against Turkey, remorse over the meanness of the Papal court in 1722, all inspired Benedict XIII to present the Grand Master with the Stock and Pilier. The Stock was a naked sword with a pommel ornamented for this occasion with a device of ships, galleys, crossed palms and the Cross of St John, the Pilier a casque of violet velvet like a morion, with the dove-like symbol of the Holy Ghost in gold and a brim of damascened gold and silver. The Republic of Lucca had been the first to receive them in 1306, and over the centuries the gift had been repeated thirty times to those warrior kings, soldiers of Christ, who had needed reminding of, or rewarding for their services to the Church.

The conferment was made on Vilhena in the conventual church by the Pope's legate, on the Feast of the Invention of the Cross, 3rd May, 1724. Vilhena in his encomium was reminded of Judas Maccabeus, who had restored the courage of his men by relating to them the dream wherein he had seen a sword, an undoubted sign from heaven of aid from God and a symbol for coming victory. A new Gideon, Vilhena would go forth to greater victories over the *Barbare genti*.

The ceremonies and gifts cost the Grand Master a pretty penny but they gave at least a moral assurance that Rome could never entirely neglect the recipient of so high a reward. Vilhena lived twelve more years, to die at last on 12th December 1736, at the age of seventy-three. He had been a great builder: largely from his own purse he had built a fort on the island in Marsamuscetto harbour to protect the Lazaretto and the inlying creeks. The theatre in Valetta, a new palace for the Jurats of Notabile, a seminary and hospital for invalid soldiers and incurables of both sexes in Floriana, which came to be known as Borgo Vilhena, were all his legacies. His face, for the first time among Grand Masters, had appeared on a new issue of gold sequins and silver scudi. He died in the fullness of age and popularity, known affectionately to his people as plain Manoel.

His successor was a gaunt Majorcan, Ramon Despuig, Velhena's seneschal, and a veteran in positions of responsibility short of the Grand Mastership. Almost at once he received an appeal for help from the Bey of Tunis, who had been chased off his throne by an insurrection of the principal corsairs of his realm, disgusted at his truces with France and England and his mealy-mouthed prepossession with trade, and anxious to return to the remunerative days of freebooting. Blockaded in Susa, the Bey rallied his forces and, offering the Knights commercial privileges and a free market for foodstuffs in return for assistance, he begged the Grand Master to recall his humanity towards Christian slaves. The two squadrons were sent off to Lampedusa, and since French traders had been putting back into Malta for fear of the blockading ships, Despuig was able to reconcile assistance to the Moslem with his duties as a protector of Christian shipping. Treaties with the Turk in Rhodian days were not unprecedented and a Bey devoted to trade was preferable to a junta bent on piracy. The galleys sailed into the Gulf of Susa, drove a 16-gun tartan ashore and broke the blockade. The recapture of Tunis was not long delayed, and the Order took advantage of the good relations established to collect a cargo of meat at reasonable prices in default of supplies from Sicily. For some years Tunis remained an unofficially friendly state. The Bey's son in 1740 visited Malta flying the Tunisian flag, to be received with all ceremony, and there was an exchange of slaves.

If Tripoli and Tunis were changing their spots, Malta would have to follow suit. Piracy could no longer support the rapidly growing population: a new era was beginning, and when on 15th January 1741 Despuig died, it was ushered in by the flamboyant and masterful spirit of the Portuguese Emmanuel Pinto de Fonseca.

Chapter VIII

PINTO MAJESTAS

THE new Grand Master was a remarkable man in many ways, not least in his longevity. He reigned thirty years, and remained throughout in full possession of his faculties. Brydone in 1770 met him when he was ninety and found him in excellent shape. "He has no minister, but manages everything himself and has immediate information of the most minute occurrences. He walks up and down stairs and even to church without assistance, and has the appearance as if he would live for many years." This perpetual agility, this apparent indestructibility was at once the marvel and exasperation of the convent. For thirty years ambitious men saw the greatest prize of all denied them by an immortal. Pinto was amused at and tolerant of their mystification: in 1758, at the age of seventy-seven, he read his own obituary notice in a French paper. "Aha," he exclaimed in delight, "it is the shadow of Pinto, not Pinto, who rules in Malta", and proved his corporeal nature by walking the length of the harbour to the mosque at Marsa, some three or four miles away, watching his attendant Bailiffs fall out and call for their chairs. "We are old," he said to one of his cronies, "but we're killing off the younger men."

Few Grand Masters aroused such violent feelings among their subjects. The Maltese found him severe but practical; his rule inaugurated a period of prosperity; he was careful to see that corn was cheap from the *Università*, loans easy from the *Monte di Pietà*, the funds of both of which he assisted from his own pocket. He built warehouses for the accommodation of merchants and stimulated the growing of cotton and silk. He fixed the value of foreign exchange artificially high against the scudo and seized every opportunity to promote the increasing standard of living by declaring a *scala franca*. But he was haughty, severe and implacable: punishments ran their full term, executions were remorseless, sentences to the galleys inexorable. His lion of the throne, Judge Cumbo, was typical of his temper: as chief judge in the Criminal Court he sent 120 men to the gallows and, like Pinto himself, held office until past his ninetieth year.

The Order, too, found him an uncomfortable head. He made no pretence of wanting to shed the trappings of constitutionalism that limited his power. He intended to rule as a benevolent despot, and hoped to circumvent the irritating claims to feudal sovereignty now being raised again by Charles VII of Naples and to escape the equally irritating claims to dominance from Rome. In all Councils he jealously guarded his right to propose the agenda, and threatened anyone who should attempt to move a motion without prior consultation with him with imprisonment in St Elmo as a "criminal of the first order". He never abandoned this control, and when he died, all the troubles of the Order were to be laid at his door. Within five years of his death, a French visitor, de la Platière, wrote of him as a man "without good habits, without decency, who held nothing in veneration; he upset the affairs of the Order, ruined the Treasury of the *Università* and authorized all sorts of pillage, debauchery and brigandage". When the final disaster overtook the Knights Pinto became the scapegoat. Doublet accused him of sexual excesses, and of dying, like Attila the Hun, *in flagrante delicto*. His shocking example was followed only too willingly by members of the Order in all grades. "The depravity of manners," he wrote, "the irreligion of the Knights and of the other classes of the Order, the entire relaxation of the ancient discipline had never reached such a pitch as it did during the reign of this dissolute Grand Master."

The truth, as is so often the case, is otherwise. Pinto was not sexually lax at all, and his severity on young Knights caught out in misdemeanours was well known during his long reign and a cause of constant complaint. He professed a stark, orthodox piety, conducting a purge of Jansenists throughout his commanderies. He was punctilious in his religious observances, once standing at the age of eighty-four throughout the entire length of the Palm Sunday Passion. If he had a major vice, it seems to have been a gross *joie-de-vivre* at the table. He was, of course, ambitious, and his ambition was not in the best interests of the Order, as it was too personal. He would be royal. His portraits show us a face of immense length, with thin, sallow lips and close-set eyes. The high range of his forehead is covered by a special wig fringing the acid severity of his mouth and chin; his nose, slightly aquiline, is humourless and dominant, though he does not seem to have lacked humour. He was a man of caprice, of steady intelligence mixed with cunning. As his reign progressed, his portrait became more flamboyant. Favray, in a symphony of red and black, showed him standing against a cascade of scarlet velvet in full habit, pointing with magisterial gesture at a crown, closed and royal for the first time, leaving in no doubt the change that had come over the Order on his succession. Pomp and circumstance, such as had not been seen since the days of the Cotoners, ruled in the Palace, court punctilio was reaffirmed; in his movements the Grand Master showed either an orgy of public pomp or a royal condescension, moving freely on foot about the city, paying sudden visits where he was least expected. The Canons of St John's, sleeping through their Office, were startled early in the morning by the apparition of the Grand Master, who reported them to the Grand Prior. His great age added to his mystery.

He was not, as a result of his ambition, immune from the fancies of his day, and like many another princeling he pursued the search for the philosopher's stone, in which, according to Doublet, "he dissipated immense sums", and for which he constructed a laboratory in the Palace. Appropriately enough, he may have received assistance in his researches from no less a man than Cagliostro himself, for, in 1786, the famous charlatan, on trial for complicity in the fraud of the Queen's necklace, claimed that he had come to Malta in 1766 from Rhodes where he assumed his name for the first time, put on European clothes and was lodged in the Palace. With Pinto he had discussed his childhood in Medina, his visits to Mecca, his supposed origin from Trebisond, and the Grand Master had offered him every advancement should he become a Knight of Malta.

There is nothing inherently improbable that Joseph Balsamo, *detto* Cagliostro, came to Malta after his flight from Palermo in the 'sixties. A visit to Malta lent colour to his story. But if Pinto did patronize Cagliostro, he would have been surprised, perhaps shocked, perhaps not, had he been told that after he was safely dead Cagliostro would claim that the parents who had abandoned him at the age of three months were Pinto himself and the Princess of Trebisond. This hapless lady, captured on board a Turkish pleasure-boat by the galleys of St John, had been sent home to her family by the amorous Grand Master, when she had borne him a son who was at once whisked off by her outraged parents to the palace of the Muphti of Medina. Cagliostro, visit to Malta or no, was in touch later in his story with many Knights in Italy and returns to play an embarrassing part at a critical moment in the Order's history.

Pinto's researches into the secrets of alchemy failed, and his hopes of rescuing the island's economy by a spectacular discovery of the philosopher's stone were thwarted. Malta was now too small to support so large a population and some other source of income was desirable. Two prospects that offered proved tantalizingly inaccessible.

In the reign of Vilhena a proposal had reached Malta for the foundation of an Ethiopian Company under the patronage of the Knights. The fountain head of this curious project was a Franciscan missionary, Francesco Rivarolo, Prefect of the Missions in Egypt, who in 1735 returned from a long series of adventures in Egypt, Ethiopia and Goa. In the course of them he had received an invitation to proceed secretly to Gondar and to see the Emperor Bakaffa. The object of Bakaffa's summons was to resurrect the project of Louis XIV that had foundered at the turn of the century, an alliance between a Christian power and the Ethiopians to help clear the Arab slavers from the Red Sea ports. In return he would give commercial advantages and admit missionaries. Rivarolo, impressed by Bakaffa's professed adherence to the Council of Chalcedon's decision on the dual nature of Christ, had returned to Portugal full of enthusiasm for the alliance, but the Portuguese, hard put to it to defend what they still held, turned the proposal down. Rivarolo however made one convert—the Danish émigré Count d'Esneval, Director-General of Artillery Manufacture at Lisbon.

One of the conditions Bakaffa had made was that he could enter into no alliance with a power which had relations with the Moslem. France, Britain and the Empire were out and their influence alone would prevent Spain or Portugal from taking action in the Red Sea. D'Esneval saw the only solution in a merchant company which should finance an expedition. The Pope was the obvious patron, as the trading nations could not suspect him of territorial ambitions in Africa. The Pope, however, who received Rivarolo in 1735, was interested but not ready to give his flag to an expedition that might get involved with the British East India Company. Instead he passed the proposal on to Malta and d'Esneval, now a General in the Papal armies, came in 1740 to plead his case. With the loan of a 40-gun frigate, then lying idle, and two hundred men, he would sweep up the Red Sea, clear Massawa of Arabs and destroy the slave traders whose dhows would be no match for a Maltese corsair. Merchants in Leghorn, Pisa and Venice were ready to put up the money, and such a *Corso* would reap rich rewards. The Order's patronage would prevent the expedition from appearing as an undignified scramble for money, which would only arouse the hostility of Great Britain, and would dignify it with the name of a Crusade. But Despuig, though dazzled by the glittering prospect of cornering a market in gold, myrrh, ambergris, senna, cassia, ebony, ivory, coffee and spices, did not succumb. He had a healthy respect for the

English and for the turbulent and unscrupulous seamanship of that rapidly growing commercial empire. Though d'Esneval said that Maria Theresa had personally guaranteed the expenses of the missionaries, that the slaves made at Massawa would alone cover the costs of the expedition, that a Knight of the Priory of Brandenburg had already offered his services and that others were interested, the Grand Master refused to commit himself. Malta's relations with France and England were too delicate. The project was finally shelved by Pinto. In 1752 the Franciscans made a private attempt to penetrate to the court of Bakaffa's son but the hostility of the Coptic hierarchy was so fierce that they had to be smuggled out. It was the last Catholic attempt to secure a freehold in the Black Empire for nearly a century. It is doubtful if d'Esneval's expedition would have rounded the Cape, but in the caution of the Grand Masters we can see the demise of that folly from which the grandest projects are conceived and despite which success and grandeur are so often gained. In the century of Clive, d'Esneval's idea was not so impossible.

The Ethiopian project was rejected because it was too distant. Corsica, on the other hand, was conveniently near. The revolutions in that island in 1763 awoke in the Grand Master's mind the idea that a possible solution to her troubled past and uncertain future would lie in her incorporation into the possessions of the Order of St John. The Bailiff de Froullay, Ambassador in Paris, was instructed to consult Choiseul and to reveal that ever since the island had been under the Genoese she had shown distinct inclination for the "political domination of the Order of Malta". Instances in 1559, 1567 and 1667 were to be cited when the Order had unsuccessfully negotiated the issue at the request of the Corsicans. Possession by a neutral power would protect the south coast of France from Barbary raids in peace time and from Christian privateers in time of war. Above all, it would render the island of Malta independent of Sicily for foodstuffs. Choiseul had, however, other designs for Corsica and in 1769 Pinto was laconically informed by Paris that the island was a French possession and that any Corsican ships still at sea were pirates to be arrested as enemies of a friendly power.

If Malta were quite unable to act against the wishes of the great powers, Pinto had every intention of setting up shop as independent of the smaller ones as he could. Independence of Sicily had been a dream of previous Grand Masters and Corsica would have provided it. But the accession to the throne of Naples in 1735 of the Bourbon Charles VII, son of Philip V and Elizabeth Farnese, had given the Neapolitan kingdom a new injection of life. Charles soon showed that he was nobody's stooge. A peace with Turkey and a truce with the Barbary Regencies alarmed Malta, who feared that Moorish raiders would take refuge in Sicilian waters; and disgusted the Pope. The Holy War was dying on its feet, if fewer European powers paid it lip service, how long could Malta continue? Spain with her inner resources, her easy suspension of the vigour which had made her great, could continue in her ancient ways unruffled by the changing world, but Malta, so dependent on her neighbours, could not. Pope Benedict XIV, then, in an effort to keep the crusade alive issued in January 1743, his Crusade Bull for Malta. Anyone who served a year in the Order's ships against the Infidel, however humbly, or who appointed and maintained a deputy, qualified for a plenary indulgence. To all who fought or served, and to those women who visited shrines, permission was granted to eat meat, butter and eggs during Lent. It was a great concession to an island which took its religious duties seriously and performed prodigies of spiritual valour in the penitential season. Malta was still a dearly beloved child of Benedict XIV; the rulers of Naples were consequently determined to pull his beard.

The Concordat of 1741 which Charles eventually signed with Rome achieved what Pinto was to battle for all his reign, a limitation of clergy in the country as well as an agreement on contributions. Originally Charles had intended to consider the Knights as clergy liable to ecclesiastical contributions like the rest. When Pinto objected, the King's attention was drawn to the position of his neighbour. Malta was, after all, his fee, and though Feudalism was not a concept that appealed to Charles's modern mind, the feudal umbilicism binding Malta to Sicily might be tweaked once or twice for the malicious delight of watching the embarrassment of the over-confident minuscule that was the Grand Master's court.

The first canter began in 1753, when the Prior of a Carmelite convent in Notabile quarrelled with the Visitor of his Provincial in Sicily. Until Malta became an ecclesiastical province of her own she was dependent on the *Regio Monarchia* or ecclesiastical appeal court in Palermo for decisions in ecclesiastical disputes. Charles VII advertised his intention of sending an Ecclesiastical Visitor to enquire into the state of the Church in Malta and to intervene in the dispute. Pinto most vigorously protested. He was the sovereign of Malta and was quite capable of co-operating with the Inquisitor to settle church disputes in the island. The Visitor could not be received: the Donation of Charles V made no provision for such a thing. In a conflict of this nature Malta needed support and her ambassadors at once canvassed among her protecting powers, even approaching Lord Albemarle, the British Ambassador in Paris. To support their pleas, the Forty Hours devotion was ordered in Malta against a visit by a priest.

But when the secretary to the Bishop of Syracuse, the King's Visitor, was turned away at Valetta (as Pinto said to forestall threats of manhandling by zealous French Knights) Charles disregarded the cautions of Spain and France and banned all commerce with the island, stopped the *tratte* and sequestered the commanderies of all Knights that were not Neapolitans. For eleven months Charles held out against all the efforts of the Pope, while the French, unwilling to antagonize the future King of Spain, held aloof. Supplies had to be obtained from North Africa and Pinto warned the European powers that he might have to come to terms with Barbary. Louis XV on being told, considered that this would be a very desirable thing, but was persuaded to make the necessary diplomatic intervention. Charles relented on 28th December 1754, worried at last by what looked like a flirtation between the Order and the King of Sardinia who had suggested a sequestration of commanderies in his Kingdom held by Neapolitans. He reserved the right to send a Visitor, but did not send one; he received the Captain-General as an ambassador with great cordiality, and the *tratte* were released.

Pinto knew that small powers survive by playing off one great power against another, and realized that France's assistance in the end would always be decisive. The independence of the island was vital to her interests. But where Malta felt her dependence most was in respect of Rome, and despite Pinto's protestations to Charles that he and the Inquisitor were perfectly capable of minding the ecclesiastical affairs of the island, for the greater part of his reign the two were at loggerheads both with one another and with the Bishop. They quarrelled mostly over patentees. In 1755 the Grand Master reckoned that there were 6,000 men with patents in the island, either from the Bishop or from the Inquisitor; the latter alone, allowed merely twelve officers and twenty *familiari*, had between 150 and 200. It was impossible to tell how many there were as lists were never published and though there had been a ruling that no cleric should wear peruke and sword it was, since 1716, being openly flouted. The Bishop, a decrepit and infirm old man dominated by his Curia, was granting patents to all applicants, one of whom, tonsured at 11, but never wearing clerical dress, savagely butchered two old women in 1766. For two years the Grand Master and Bishop wrangled over which should try him and Pinto lost. It was only in 1761, after repeated representations, that the right of sanctuary had been restricted to parish churches, after it had been revealed that gangs of footpads were using the wayside chapels as safe hide-outs and that even a prostitute had used one as a brothel. The Church was reluctant to surrender its power to the sovereign will of the Grand Master and the dual system, while irritating and anachronistic, did prevent too great a concentration of power in too small a place.

But Pinto did win one notable victory. When the Bourbon Kings expelled the Society of Jesus from their lands and

Naples in 1768 called on Malta as a feudal vassal to follow suit, the Grand Master, with rather too much compliance considering his earlier denial of Naples's feudal powers, declared that the Jesuits, who had maintained a house of studies since 1592, should leave the island forthwith. He justified himself to Rome saying that he could not risk another ban from Naples, and once the order had been given, he seized their house and property and lands, and informed the Inquisitor curtly, who claimed them in the name of the Church, that they belonged to him as Prince and Master of the Isle, and that he intended to set up a University from the revenues that had formerly been those of the Society. He was supported in this by the Neapolitan Tanucci, though it was remarked by his enemies that he had behaved in a most arbitrary manner. It was all very well to call Rome in to defend Malta from the pretensions of Naples, but now he was reversing the process. Pinto, however, anxious to get his way, was prepared to accept the support of the Neapolitan court which held that he was acting in his sovereign capacity; Tanucci claimed that, even though this sovereignty derived from the feudal overlordship of Naples, the Grand Master was acting within his rights. Pinto warned Rome that she must either accept his disposition of the Society's goods or watch him incur the wrath of Naples that had declared the sequestered property was not to return to the Church. To steel the Grand Master's resolve, Tanucci held up the corn supplies, and Rome capitulated.

Pinto got his University by which he wanted to crown his reign with a glory that could not be obtained by arms. The Neapolitans grumbled that it needed a Papal brief to establish it, but had to accept that the only alternative was a Chapter General. Pinto had learned that he could never act on his own; he could play Rome off against Naples but resist neither. It disappointed him.

The University was not a great success. Its first Rector was sacked soon after his appointment, and it was soon in financial difficulties despite the revenues of Pinto's warehouses that were made over to it. In the end all foreign professors were replaced by lower paid Maltese and De Rohan got his Chapter General to make it the concern of the Treasury.

Pinto's desire for a University was not only for prestige. If the local clergy could be persuaded to follow their higher studies in Malta, it would keep them from Rome. "The priests of this diocese," he wrote in 1769, "are fed and nourished with a spirit of fanaticism for their personal immunity and, furthermore, educated with the maxim of servile dependence on the Court of Rome and upon the Inquisitor." The period of honeymoon with Benedict XIV as Pope turned sourer with Clement XIII, less willing to listen to the Grand Master on all occasions. The state of undeclared war between the Order and the clergy continued unabated and in the reign of Pinto's successor was to erupt in a startling conflagration.

But Pinto had other preoccupations than a cold war with the Inquisitor and Tanucci. His reign was not to remain untroubled for many years at a time and, not unexpectedly, his worst anxieties were to come from the high seas.

Chapter IX

ENGLISHMEN AND TURKS

T HE question of Malta's neutrality had not been solved at any of the Congresses that followed European wars in the eighteenth century and it was to be revived with unwelcome complications in the reign of Pinto. During the War of Austrian Succession, with the Kingdom of Naples equivocally supporting the enemies of Maria Theresa, there had been no problem. French privateers were admitted freely to lodge their prizes in the Lazaretto, to take on provisions and water and to sally out refreshed in search of further prey. The English, secure in Port Mahon, avoided the island. But the Seven Years War was different: in that Naples was neutral, and Great Britain lost Minorca.

The development of Malta both as a French trading post and as an asylum for war-weary vessels was not lost on the British consul. In 1749 Pinto had appointed to this post a Leghorn-born Englishman who had served before the mast on both English and Dutch vessels in the wars that had ushered in the century. He had settled in Malta and married the daughter of the then British Consul, Alexander Young, whom he now succeeded. His name was John Dodsworth. The Consulate was a family affair—Young had taken it on from his own father-in-law in 1713—and as so few British merchantmen used the harbour that they were unable to live off the consulage dues, the Consuls usually indulged in a little private trading of their own. Dodsworth had bought a prize off an English captain in the Austrian Succession War and with a special pass from the British consul in Barbary he now had a prosperous little business with Tripoli. The sea was his métier; his own son in the fullness of time was to serve on board a

British man-of-war. He liked and understood sailors and had a sailor's temper and a sailor's eye.

His one overriding passion, however, was Francophobia. In a community largely French in sympathy he felt very acutely his position as the representative of the greatest naval power in the world and was irked at the way the French used the island shamelessly as a French naval base. According to him, when decisions in the *Consolato* went against the British, it was the result of Maltese favouritism towards their enemies. On several occasions he had comported himself in a manner lacking in proper dignity towards the Grand Master, the Inquisitor and the Judges of the island's tribunals, and complaints to London through the ambassador in Paris earned him a rebuke from the Secretary of State for Southern Affairs. He wrote back that it was time British men-of-war appeared in Maltese waters "to inculcate that respect which is due to our colours and for want thereof is much diminished."

As a result of London's coolness Dodsworth determined to wage his own war against French influence, as he saw it, in the island. He had two good reasons; one was a genuine if boastful pride in the power of his country, the second was his determination to get a proper patent out of London which would give him immunity from the tribunals of the island. This he needed, for the conduct of his business was beginning to attract suspicious attention. The outbreak of the Seven Years War gave him his chance. In Grand Harbour there were two merchantmen which had sailed in before war was declared and who had both begun to arm themselves as privateers, the Frenchman, a larger vessel, having a start on the Englishman and arming more heavily. But as soon as the news of the capture of Port Mahon arrived, the Venerable Council ordered both ships to disarm. The Frenchman agreed, but the English captain, prompted by Dodsworth, refused. The French captain, he said, was only pretending to disarm and was going to wait off the island to gobble him up when he sailed out. The Council reluctantly applied sanctions; he was denied supplies, declared a prisoner in his own ship, and had his rudder removed. The captain, Robert Miller, wrote to Pinto himself in exasperation: "The rigours of this government are enough to make all Englishmen mad and all Frenchmen to laugh—as they are paid such compliments by distressing their enemies the English."

Dodsworth hoped to prove to London the perfidy of the French and of the government and thus to secure his patent. In October 1756 he found an unexpected ally in the person of Fortunatus Wright, one of the most successful privateers in the Mediterranean, who sailed in with two French prizes. Wright was a redoubtable man, had taken six prizes already and sailed with a price of £200 on his head. He readily believed what Miller and Dodsworth told him and they plotted a way of circumventing the blockade of Miller's ship. Contrary to all regulations, Wright took Miller's crew on board, and between them they tried unsuccessfully to slip a letter out to the British Commander in Chief inviting him to sink all Maltese ships when he found them. But Wright could not stay for ever and, as the Council proved obdurate, he sailed off. In December, Captain Burnaby of H.M.S. *Jersey*, watering in Malta, heard the same catalogue of woes and wrote personally to Pinto demanding that Miller be released or he would find himself "extremely distressed to have to treat the flag of the Order rather differently from what has so far been experienced from us." The Council was unmoved; it knew that Dodsworth was carrying on a lurid correspondence with London, but also that London had so far failed to respond. In the end, Miller capitulated. He disarmed, received back his rudder and was allowed to depart. Dodsworth, disgusted at such base surrender, could not complain. The news of an illegal transaction in which he had been engaged with Wright and Miller had reached the authorities. He had bought a brigantine off an impoverished Englishman whose crew had mutinied and he had intended, until the captain blabbed, to fit it out as a privateer. He had to lie low.

He lay low until 1758 when in July Captain Augustus Hervey of H.M.S. *Monmouth*, the future third Earl of Bristol,

Casanova of the Sea and one of the glamorous captains of his day, appeared off Malta in pursuit of a French frigate and her prize. Disregarding warning shots from the shore-forts, he closed on the frigate, whose prize had slipped into harbour, and until it blew up he fired at it with such disregard for the neighbouring coast that his cannon balls were found on the esplanade. Hervey was no stranger to Malta. He had visited the island in 1755 when some of his prizes had been unsuccessfully claimed by the French *chargé d'affaires* as having been taken within Maltese waters. Though he had won his case, he had thought less of the Portuguese Grand Master who should have been more pro-British and held that "the Maltese are all governed by French Consuls." When on this occasion the Guardian of the Port came to protest, he dismissed him airily: "Having had the honour to see His Eminence the Grand Master on his balcony, I could not do otherwise than salute him with a cannonade of joy." He would lie off shore and if they wanted to shoot at him they could, but if they did he would sail off at once to destroy their galleys loading corn at Augusta in Sicily.

The French minister then asked Pinto's permission for the escaped prize, the *Tiger*, to be fitted out as a privateer with men and guns brought from Toulon. The Council refused, but Dodsworth wrote to tell Hervey that the *Tiger* was being set up as a raider, and the captain came back post-haste. Though assured that nothing further than purely legitimate repairs had been undertaken, he chose to believe that the Guardian of the Port was lying. He challenged the prize to single combat with one of his frigates, H.M.S. *Lyme*, and then announced that he would sail away to return in a fortnight. If in the meantime the *Tiger* had sailed out, he would attack every Maltese ship he met. He toyed with the idea of sailing in and sinking her where she lay in harbour, but deciding that such an action might not be supported in London, he contented himself with informing the Grand Master that he would chase Frenchmen into Maltese waters whenever he thought fit, and in a whirl of righteous indignation and defiance, he sailed off—but he failed Dodsworth, for he never returned.

The Council was alarmed. Dodsworth was put under strict watch and regulations were made limiting admission to Grand Harbour to four ships of a belligerent nation at a time, whatever their relations with the King of Sicily. The regulations were only to be acted on twice: against the Russians in 1770 and against Napoleon in 1798. Another opportunity was not to offer itself.

The English retired from the war in 1762, but English privateers bought the Prussian flag from the Prussian minister in Naples and continued their depredations. Taking up with one of them, Captain James Merryfield, Dodsworth used his warehouses to lodge the depredated goods and began to sell them freely. Unluckily for him one of these depredations was questioned before the Prussian minister in Naples, and an order was given for Merryfield to deliver an account of his prize. The goods were no longer in Dodsworth's possession and both men had been guilty of disposing of goods that had not been declared lawful in a prize court. Pinto accordingly ordered the consul to give up the keys of his warehouses and to produce his books. He refused to do either. Then, taking a calculated risk, he put over his doorway a plaque showing the arms of His Britannic Majesty. This was a crime of *lèse-majesté* which no Grand Master could tolerate. No royal insignias were allowed in the island. In an international community protected immunity gave too much scope for the interference of foreign governments. It was the policy of the Order never openly to give preferential treatment to one nation over another and never to make invidious distinctions between Catholic and Protestant powers. The corps of the Grand Master's guards rounded up a band of young French Knights who had declared their intention of shooting the Lion and the Unicorn down with musket fire, a guard was placed on the Consul's house and he was suspended from his consular duties.

But offence could not be given to a power whose sea captains appeared so hectoring and trigger happy. The Chevalier

Valperga di Masino was therefore sent to London to complain of Dodsworth's intrigues and insubordinations; he arrived to find that Frederick II had personally requested that the consul be made to disgorge his spoils. Seeing that Dodsworth's position was unlikely to be supported, Pinto ordered his arrest. On 3rd February 1763 the arms of George III were solemnly taken down, covered reverentially with a white cloth and removed to the Grand Master's palace. Dodsworth himself was placed in St Elmo, whence he ceaselessly protested against his treatment. He was allowed only two scudi a day, he wrote to London, for the upkeep of his whole family and a slave. His children had been denied water during a fever, his wife had been lodged in a house for penitent harlots; antelopes belonging to the Bailiff de Tencin, a sworn enemy of England —had he not assisted Bonny Prince Charlie's escape from Rome in 1745?—had been put in a room adjacent to his as an insult, and his dogs had been forbidden to run about in case they disturbed them. But Dodsworth's frenzied grievances could not disguise that it was a strange persecution which allowed him a slave, his dogs and three rooms with an excellent view and a whole length of bastion on which to exercise themselves, all in a castle reserved for prisoners of noble extraction.

At first the Secretary of State was inclined to accept Dodsworth's assertion that he was a protected person with consular immunity, but the list of his debts, the catalogue of his illegal transactions, the news of the manner in which he had abused his position turned him against him. A mission was sent to Malta to settle his problem, headed by Captain Harrison of H.M.S. *Jersey*, and it found Dodsworth persistent in his refusal to accept the jurisdiction of the Maltese courts. He was a protected person. Pinto informed Harrison that unless the Prussian court was satisfied, the King might sequestrate the commanderies in Silesia. The English captain had to tell his compatriot that London would protect his person but would not protect him from the legal consequences of his malversations.

Dodsworth held out for another two and a half years before allowing the case against him to be prepared. He was now bankrupt. In return for a sentence of five years' imprisonment, to run from the moment of his arrest, the Prussian court paid the compensation it had demanded from Dodsworth. In 1767, his debts unpaid but his sentence completed, the British Consul was shipped off with his family to Alicante in an English trader, whence he made his way home. In his pocket he had £35 to cover his travelling expenses. They were a gift from the Treasury. The Knights were nothing if not magnanimous.

The whole incident had been puffed out to international proportions. Masino had proceeded to London via Naples, Turin, Versailles and the Hague to pick up letters of recommendation. Pinto had behaved with scrupulous correctness— the French accused him of favouring the English. Yet Dodsworth, rash, arrogant and tactless, had seen into the future. He had aroused but a faint flicker of interest in London, but he and Hervey had with some justice referred to the island as a French arsenal. They had noted the predominant influence of French sympathies and interest, which were to grow no weaker as the century progressed. The loss of Port Mahon for a few years had underlined England's perilous dependency upon Gibraltar in the Mediterranean, but no attempt was made from London to make the English connection with Malta any closer. When in 1789 de Rohan was to request the Court of St James to recognize his appointment of a new British consul, it took the Secretary of State four years to reply!

Regular readers in England, if there were any, of the Gazettes and *Relazioni* printed in Paris and Rome could have read for themselves of the imponderable influence of France in the affairs of the Order. On two particular occasions in Pinto's reign this was to stand out in special relief. The first occasion occurred in 1748. On the night of 10th January the Turkish crew of a Rhodian galley returning from Anatolia, whither they had conveyed the deposed Vizier Osman Pasha, was surprised by an attack from the Christian slaves on board, who with fists full of shot, marline spikes and axes made a well-planned sortie from below deck. It was so sudden and so fierce that out of a crew of 130, 110 escaped only by jumping overboard. The chief passenger, none other than the Pasha Mustapha of Rhodes himself, was secured in his cabin, and the mutineers set sail for Malta. Evading the coastal batteries of Rhodes, and battling with contrary winds the ship only made the island on 1st February, bringing in with them their own prize, a small Candean caique with a crew of seven. The public sensation was enormous. Among the Christians, who were mostly Greek and Georgian buonavoglie, were some Venetians and seventeen Maltese, and Pinto himself lodged them at his own expense and provided them with free passages to wherever they wanted to go.

The problem was now what to do with the Pasha. At one time such a prisoner would have been a priceless bargaining counter, but now he was a high-ranking officer of a power in friendly relations with France. The French court at once interested itself in his fate. Though he had a reputation for harshness and an implacable hatred for all Christians, he was lodged in the best apartments of the Lazaretto with all his retinue. Quarantine over, he was transferred to St Elmo where he found himself the flattering cynosure of the Knights who hastened to pay their court to him. He was even taken to the Palace to be presented to Pinto. But Mustapha was not the genial Pasha of a Rossini opera. Though his stay in Malta was made as pleasant as possible, he was consumed by the indignity of being a prisoner and by the fear that his misfortunes would alienate him for ever from his royal master. He was rude and unappreciative during his many receptions and showed quite openly that he was consumed by chagrin. It was not difficult for the Cadis and other leaders of the Muslim slaves to put an idea in his head: it was no less a project than the rising of the slaves, the overthrow of the Order and the delivery of the island to the Turkish fleet. What finer way to gain the eternal gratitude of the Sultan? The plot was laid on horrible oaths of secrecy. On the Feast of SS. Peter and Paul, when all Valetta would attend the celebrations at Notabile and the

Grand Master would retire after lunch to sleep, his *valet de chambre* would murder him. The success of the assassination signalled by a vase thrown from his window to the courtyard below, all Christians in the Palace were to meet the same fate, the armoury was to be looted, the *Corpo di Guardia* overwhelmed and an attack made on St Elmo, which the Pasha would lead from within. St Elmo seized, they would then attack Sant' Angelo and seize the arsenal.

On 5th May 1749, however, while plans were still incomplete, the Bailiff de Bocage announced that the good offices of the French court had obtained the Pasha's freedom and his liberty to return at once to Turkey. This was awkward. Playing for time, Mustapha replied that he had been unjustly detained all along and to accept liberty just like that would be to admit that he had been a slave; this he would not admit, since he had not been taken by a proper enemy in a proper battle. He would stay where he was in St Elmo until he received orders from Constantinople. But to allay suspicion he accepted as his residence a house in Floriana and from there he wrote letters to the Pasha of Morea and to the Regencies under his own seal. These were not tampered with. He was given to believe that ships would be forthcoming, that the Turks would be ready to take over the island. A few days before the feast of St Peter and Paul he would find something wrong with the air at Floriana and request his removal to St Elmo.

But three weeks before the conspiracy was due to occur, in the tavern of a Christian Jew near the lower *baracca*, a negro and an Armenian slave, both in the plot, quarrelled. The negro drew a knife on the Armenian and when he was disarmed by the taverner, the Armenian told him all. The Jew at once revealed the plot to the Grand Master himself. Pinto was aghast. The negro was arrested and submitted to continual torture until he gave up the names of the ringleaders and that of Mustapha himself. As soon as the Pasha heard that all was up, he fled to the house of the Bailiff de Bocage and begged sanctuary, swearing his innocence upon the Qur'an. Pinto ordered the Bailiff to hand him over before the mob broke into his house and murdered him, and to the execrations of the people he was taken under heavy escort to St Elmo.

As the feast day approached, all preparations were made to receive the enemy. The Turkish flag was hoisted from St Elmo and the beacons were lit. But no one sailed into the trap. The Pasha had been deserted by his own. As a protégé of the French, however, he was untouchable. His chief accomplices, one tied to a St Andrew's cross, the other rigged to a spiked horse, were paraded round the town and afterwards quartered by four caiques in Grand Harbour. One of them called on baptism at the last and died an exemplary death crying to Our Lady; their remains were exposed about the island. Another twenty slaves died, some on the wheel, some by hanging, some by decapitation, their bodies burned and their heads exposed. Six of them accepted baptism at the end, comforted with the promise of immediate access to the Kingdom of Heaven and sponsored by the men they had sworn to destroy, while the crowd was moved to prayers and tears. Another slave died after thirty-six hours on the rack; *Te Deums* were sung for a safe delivery from peril. For a few weeks the customary benignity of Malta was turned to a savage and vengeful holocaust; through the welter of blood the Pasha remained untouched.

France's immediate concern upon hearing of the Pasha's capture had been to obtain his release before reprisals were taken by the Turks against French merchants in the Levant. The Grand Vizier who considered Malta an appanage of the French crown was annoyed at the time it took for the French court to secure his freedom. The revelation of his complicity in the plot proved further embarrassing. The Grand Master demanded the right to try and to execute the Pasha; the Bailiff de Bocage, now a vigorous octogenarian, stoutly resisted the attempt to confront Mustapha with his accomplices and threw over him the mantle of French protection. The French court received repeated demands for his release from Turkey, for his execution from Malta; all they could do was to play for time, requesting a full account of the conspiracy, claiming a period for the French ambassador to convince the Grand Vizier of the enormity of the Pasha's crime. Puyssieulx, the French foreign minister, knew that the Pasha would have to be released and hoped the Order would be satisfied by a guarantee of his trial in Constantinople. This hollow prevarication roused the disgust of the Grand Master, but France was all-powerful. On 19th March 1751 the Pasha left after two years of debate; he returned to Turkey on a French martingale and no guarantee had ever been given that he would stand trial for his crimes.

France was torn between her duties to an ally, and to a protectorate; as usual decisions of state decided for the ally. Yet within a few years of this event, another occurred not unlike it. In September 1760 the Christian crew of a 78-gun Turkish *soltana*, the *Ottoman Crown* rose against their captors in the Levant. Seventy-one strong they overwhelmed a crew of 350, many of whom again escaped overboard. Pursued by coastal craft the *soltana* set her sails for Malta and reached the island on 6th October. Like their predecessors the mutineers had stopped to make their own prize, which turned out to be a Leghorn martingale. They took off the Turkish crew in case they gave the alarum. These they released as promised on arrival in Malta.

Pinto was again delighted, and rechristened the battleship *Il Santissimo Salvatore* and gave it the flag of the Lieutenant General. But his joy turned to concern when he learned that the Sultan was resolved to get his vessel back. The usual preparations for a siege were made, lines of defence at Naxxar dug, the protecting powers asked for men and munitions, corn laid in and the younger Knights summoned to Malta. But the Grand Master had cried "Wolf" once too often. The Knights mostly refused to come, the great powers offered many courteous words but the Republic of Lucca alone 30,000 lbs of gunpowder. Then, once again, the French court stepped in. To avoid the evil consequences of war, not only to Malta but to His Most Christian Majesty's subjects in the Levant, Louis XV offered to purchase the vessel and to hand it back to the Sultan. It cost him 834,800 livres, but he considered it cheap at the price.

There were two legacies of this unsatisfactory state of affairs, apart from the fact that the obsolescent machinery of defence had once more been denied a trial of its real strength. The first was a sum of 1,661,400 scudi to be raised from somewhere to pay for everything. The second was a tardy, almost shame-faced, recognition in Paris that Malta's dependence on France needed some mitigation. By an order from Versailles in 1765 all Maltese were granted rights before French civil, criminal and commercial tribunals as if they were Frenchmen. From the first legacy Malta never properly recovered. From the second she began to realize that short of incorporating the island into his empire, the French king could do no more for her.

Chapter X

POLES AND RUSSIANS

THERE was in Europe, strangely enough, one Catholic country that provided a proportion of recruits to the Order far below what her population or history would have suggested. In the Priory of Bohemia were two Polish commanderies, of Posen and Stolowitz, the last the *ius patronatus* of the powerful Radziwill family. In 1609 a wealthy magnate had attempted to remedy the position: Prince Janus of Ostrog, owner of a vast estate in Volhynia, made his will, leaving his lands as an entity to his own male heirs succeeding, to the male heirs of his brother-in-law if the line died out, and if they failed to the Order of Malta in the person of a Knight to be elected by a majority of the ecclesiastical and noble vote in the Diet. Should this eventuality occur, the estate of Ostrog would be obliged to contribute a force of 300 foot and 300 horse to the Polish army on the occasion of war with Turkey.

In 1672, the event for which Janus had provided occurred, and in accordance with the will, Prince Jerome Lubomirski, Grand Marshal of Poland and Knight of Malta, became the ordinat of Ostrog. He had, however, obtained a dispensation to marry and on his death the lands had passed into the administration of his widow until her death in 1701. Perellos had tried to get another Knight appointed but the estates of Ostrog were too rich a legacy, and greedy claimants determined to see that the operative clause of Janus's will was set aside. With the tacit support of the Saxon Elector, then King of Poland, Prince Sanguszko moved in with the dubious claim that his wife was the sole survivor of the family of Janus's brother-in-law.

Sanguszko had married a Lubomirski and between them

the two families were the props of the Saxon kings. Nothing therefore could dislodge them and, despite the letters and blandishments of Perellos, the illegal possession of the goods of Ostrog persisted. But the Grand Masters were not going to lose the inheritance without a fight and in 1719 they found a powerful backer in Prince Augustus Czartoryski, a Knight of Malta in the German Tongue, and the Affair of Ostrog, as it was called, became a *cause célèbre* in Polish politics. Czartoryski, who had acquired an immense fortune at his marriage, was at once a dominating political force and the obvious champion of the Ostrog claims. Vilhena had already sweetened King Augustus II by receiving his bastard, the Prince of Teschen, as a Knight, and Augustus Czartoryski was instructed to dislodge the Sanguszkos. But it proved impossible. Sanguszko with his powerful connections broke up Diet after Diet before it could discuss Ostrog, and Czartoryski's political ambitions made him a suspect champion. For the Family, as the Czartoryskis were called, were known to be seeking power for its own sake and when in 1725 the succession problem came once more to the front, an anti-Saxon party led by the Potocki clan began to scheme with Rome for the return of Stanislas Leczynski. The Czartoryskis inclined in favour of the Saxons from whose absolutism alone any reform could come and so Polish politics were divided between the Czartoryskis and the Potockis—whose annual revenues exceeded the entire army budget by four million zlotis. Strong in support of the Potockis were the Sanguszkos and Radziwills, with the Lubomirskis tied by family to the illegitimate holder of Ostrog. For thirty years the Czartoryskis and Potockis manœuvred, the one to obtain, the other to retain control of the army. As a *hetman's* baton could only be conferred by a Diet, the Potockis saw to it that the Diet never met and the claims of Malta went unheard.

In 1753, however, the Sanguszko ordinat suddenly declared his intention of retiring to a monastery. In an attempt to conciliate his enemies, he made a testamentary division of the estates of Ostrog, leaving the two largest portions to the

Lubomirskis and, surprisingly, to Augustus Czartoryski, and smaller settlements in favour of nine other families including the Potocki. The annual revenues of the entire ordination were estimated variously from nine million Polish florins to three hundred thousand. They were never exactly known. But the magnates who were not beneficiaries moved at once. Under the leadership of the *hetman* Branicki, they asked Sanguszko to reconsider his decision, stating they were only concerned about the 600 men that the Estates contributed to the army, but really determined to queer what they feared was a reconciliation between the Czartoryskis and Lubomirskis. Branicki quoted Janus's will. The Order of Malta was the proper Ordinat, and acting on what he conceived to be his duty, he established a military occupation of the Duchy.

The whole issue was re-opened. Augustus Czartoryski found himself isolated in the Diet and broke it up. Pinto, however, seeing a ray of hope in the action of the Commander-in-Chief, despatched the Grand Prior of Bohemia, Emmanuel von Kollowrat, to Warsaw in the role of Plenipotentiary to see what he could do. He found the situation in a terrible muddle and was inclined to accuse the Czartoryskis of sacrificing the Order to their own ambitions, and when the King had set up a commission to investigate the affair of Ostrog, the Czartoryskis threatened to set up a confederation against it. But Kollowrat did the family an injustice. Aware that the future stability of the Kingdom depended on a strong monarch they had decided to break the Saxon hold on the succession and to obtain a Polish King at the next election. The Potockis were already scheming for a French claimant, the Prince de Conti, Grand Prior of the Tongue of France, but not for all that likely to be particularly vehement in the interests of the Order. The agreement the Czartoryskis had made with the Sanguszkos to divide the Ostrog Duchy among themselves, the Lubomirskis, the holder's principal creditors, and the Potockis, had been an attempt to divide the aristocratic opposition. Branicki, however, had recently gone over to the Saxon party and intended to spike the Czartoryskis' guns. The

King's Commissioners were all from the anti-Russian group, of which the Czartoryskis were now the leaders.

Kollowrat, despite the surprise his sumptuous embassy had caused, found it difficult to convince the Poles that the Order would make the best Ordinat. They feared an *imperium in imperio*, a drain of money to Malta, a foreigner. But the best solution began to advertise itself. If the Duchy were converted into a Priory with its own commanderies, for Polish Knights only, there would be no danger of the lands falling into the hands of an overmighty subject. Kollowrat found himself besieged by Bishops and magnates for Crosses of Devotion, but he was not deceived. Poland was "an anarchy that calls itself a Republic," and the magnates were not won over yet.

Augustus Czartoryski, isolated and temporarily out-manœuvred, left Poland for Russia and took with him Stanislas Poniatowski, himself a beneficiary of Sanguszko's disposition. But despite a sprinkling of Gold Crosses on Polish Bishops, Kollowrat was able to obtain nothing. The Royal Commission came to no decision and for seventeen years other troubles and divisions ensured that Malta's claim was forgotten. But when the Czartoryskis went to Russia, it was certain that the future destinies of Poland could not be reckoned without the participation of the Russian court. If Malta had a stake in Poland, whom better to cultivate than the Czarina?

Pinto by rare good fortune was able to call on one Knight who knew Catherine the Great. The Veronese Michele Sagromoso was one of the most widely travelled men in Europe and had actually lived in Constantinople, attached to the French Embassy. He was a friend of Frederick the Great, of the Kings of Denmark and Sweden, of the great Linnaeus, of George II—who had made him a Gentleman of the Bedchamber—of Tiepolo and of Goldoni. He had been an amateur mineralogist and botanist with Linnaeus in Sweden, an amateur philosopher on the shore of Lake Geneva, and a gentleman farmer near Verona, whose agricultural academy, the first in Italy, he had helped to found. And in 1748 he had gone to St Petersburg where he had made a great hit with the Czarina

Elizabeth and a greater hit with the Grand Duchess Catherine to whom he brought secret letters from her mother. Catherine never forgot the friend who had talked to her of her family in the jealous and faction ridden Court in which she was feeling so lonely and insecure. In 1769 she was delighted to welcome Sagramoso once more to the Russian capital where she now ruled. He had come as the unofficial envoy of both the Grand Master and the Pope, with instructions from the one to discuss the affair of Ostrog and from the other the establishment of a Catholic hierarchy.

He arrived at an auspicious moment. Catherine was already preparing for a great campaign against the Turks, which she planned as the first stage of that reconstruction of the ancient Byzantine Empire for which she was to christen her grandson Constantine. A crushing victory over the Porte would at once capture the Crimea and render her ex-lover King Stanislas of Poland further dependent upon her. She was perfectly prepared to assist the Maltese in their claims on the Polish Republic and even to ask their assistance in her campaign against Turkey. To solicit the latter she despatched to Malta an Italian noble-man, the *soi-disant* Marquis di Cavalcabo.

With the arrival of Cavalcabo a new and sinister element intrudes itself into the story. Little is known about him save that he was born in Cremona. In 1764 Boswell met him at the Court of Brunswick and discussed with him their stomachs, women and a method for making ice that Cavalcabo claimed to have invented. Sagramoso, however, in St Petersburg knew that he was an adventurer and warned Pinto.

Cavalcabo arrived without warning on board an English ship on 11th January 1770. He had left Admiral Orlov's Russian armada at Port Mahon in order to bring Catherine's letter in advance. This was presented at once to Pinto, who discovered that Catherine wanted permission for the fleet to enter Grand Harbour and for Cavalcabo to remain in the island as her *chargé d'affaires*.

Both were impossible. Only Knights of Catholic powers could be *chargés d'affaires* and France quickly instructed

The inner part of Grand Harbour, showing Valletta on the right and Senglea on the left. *(From a watercolour by Brocktorff)*

The 'Gran Galeone' of Grand Master de Rohan. *(Courtesy National Library)*

Monument of Grand Master Ramon Perellos y Roccaful. (1697-1720)

Monument of Grand Master Manoel Pinto de Fonçeca   in St. John's
Co-Cathedral, Valletta. (1741-1773)

A seventeenth century painting of *Piazza San Giorgio* (now Republic Square) showing the Palace of the Grand Masters on the left, with Verdala's column and Wignacourt's fountain on the right.

Piazza San Giorgio. and the Grand Masters' Palace at the beginning of the British connection. *(A Brocktorff watercolour)*

Grand Master Ferdinand von Hompesch. (1797-1798)

Portrait of Grand Master de Rohan Polduc. (1775-1797)

Portrait of Grand Master Ximenes de Texada. (1773-1775)

Interior of St. John's Co-Cathedral in Valletta. *(From a Brocktorff watercolour)*

Wedding scenes at the beginning of the eighteenth century.
(From the frescos at Villa d'Aurel, Malta, the country residence of Baron Trapani Galea Feriol, by whose courtesy they are reproduced)

Bronze statue of Grand Master Manoel de Vilhena. (1722-1736)

Portraits in oil of Grand Masters Pinto and Ximenes *(top)* and de Rohan and Hompesch *(bottom)*.

General Bonaparte lands at the Dogana, in Valletta, in June 1798

Pinto to refuse admission to the fleet. Orlov was informed accordingly of the ordinance, passed at the time of Lord Hervey's filibustering in 1758, but the Russian admiral passed on, and did nothing more than send back ships from the Aegean for repairs. In November Orlov inflicted a crushing defeat on the Turkish fleet at Tchesmé and sent back seventy Algerians and twenty-two Maltese he had taken. The French, however, claimed the Algerians who they said had formed part of the crew of a French polacca depredated illegally by the over-enthusiastic Russians.

Cavalcabo, whom Boswell had found "very knowing and extremely clever", at once set about ingratiating himself with the octogenarian Grand Master, He made a ceremonial entry into the city aboard the *San Gioachino*, and Pinto, though he refused to recognize his official capacity, came to meet him on his state barge. The Marquis presented the Grand Master with a portrait of his Imperial mistress and on 11th March he watched the island's defences alerted in case her fleet made an attempt to enter the harbour. On 1st May he ordered the Greek Papas to sing a *Te Deum* for the Russian victories in the East and on the thirteenth anniversary of Pinto's accession, his house was illuminated with candles that lit up a portrait of His Eminence and a representation of Malta surrounded by Russian ships.

Pinto was flattered and intrigued. Indulging a foible he put his *corpo di guardia* in Muscovite uniforms for the Corpus Christi procession and ordered them to beat the retreat *alla Moscovita* more than once. But Pinto was eighty-nine and could not last long. Cavalcabo had other fish to fry, and his secretive nose had soon discovered that the island was seething with discontent.

Though the Grand Master was mentally alert, an air of decrepitude hung over the Palace, and among both Knights and Maltese restiveness at the abuses of government was growing. It was to be set off by a trivial affair. On the night of 6th February 1771 the Chevalier de Pins, a notorious badhat, was arrested by the Captain of the *Castellania*. On this occasion, however, de Pins had done nothing and on release he at once complained to his fellows that violent hands had been laid on him, a Knight, by a Maltese. The younger French Knights then met in a very excited frame of mind in the Upper Baracca, resolved to demand the most condign punishment for the offending official and marched noisily to the Palace threatening to burn it down if their demands were not met. Inside the Palace, the seven Piliers, also deeply moved, were in conclave with the Grand Master. Pinto bowed before the storm: the unhappy captain was flogged and sent to the galleys. Though six of the Piliers were not in favour of it, two French Bailiffs and the Hospitaller proceeded to demand the punishment of the Fiscal as the officer responsible for the order of arrest, and called for the convention of the Complete Council to examine the case. Pinto refused this, but allowed the Piliers to examine the Fiscal whom they found guiltless. The two Bailiffs then, joined by the Grand Priors of Germany and Navarre provoked another tumult, presenting "the ridiculous and scandalous picture of two Grand Crosses parading the walls of the city, demanding the convention of the Council."

Pinto was too canny not to see the hand of a trouble-maker. He knew that Cavalcabo had been closeted with the two Bailiffs, and at once ordered them out of the island. Cavalcabo took fright, came immediately to the Palace to implore Pinto's pardon, leaving his two accomplices to make their own peace with the Grand Master.

In the course of this brouhaha, the malcontents had laid a list of their grievances before the Inquisitor. Direct insurrection had failed, it was now time to see what Rome could do. Foremost among the complaints was the Grand Master's persistent refusal to employ the consultative machinery of the Councils. As a result, the enforcement of military and religious duties had become slack, the Grand Master had not presented an account of expenses incurred by a small syndicate of bureaucrats working in secret, money had run short and prices had risen. Last, he had permitted the arrest of a Knight by common soldiers. Pinto at once justified his actions to the Pope who ordered the offending Bailiffs to apologize. This they did, but Pinto ruefully remarked that what they said to the Inquisitor behind his back bore no relation to their humility in his presence. But, he told Choiseul in Paris, as he hoped to live out his life at peace with all men, he would readmit the Bailiffs to his favour.

Cavalcabo's part in all this was, we must assume, dictated by his orders to ingratiate himself with the rising French party in the island, especially as the French government was unhappy about his presence there. It was now only a question of time before Pinto died, and at his death there would be changes. It was up to him to be in at the kill. But Pinto was a tough old hanger-on to life, and when the end came in 1773, in his ninety-first year, he was over a month a-dying. As the conventual bells tolled out the *Agonia*, an era was ending. A King, not a Grand Master, was dying. Towards the end of his reign, financial shortage had impelled him to appropriate funds of the Confraternity of the Holy Souls in Purgatory. "I am very old," he said to the administrator who told him that the Holy Souls would suffer, "very soon I shall be joining them and shall put everything right." On 24th January he went to square his account. He died unlamented; he had become cantankerous of late and his hand had always been hard. Besides, an event he had always tried to avoid had occurred in the island—there was a shortage of corn.

In the last year of Pinto's reign, the Knights had witnessed the rising star of an energetic, critical Frenchman, who with a colleague of his own age, the Bailiff de Belmont, had fallen foul of Pinto over the arrest of de Pins. Emmanuel de Rohan was a cadet of a famous family. His father had been exiled to Spain in 1720 after the conspiracy of the *Gentilshommes Bretons* against Louis XV, and Emmanuel was born in Mancha of a Spanish mother in 1725. He had become the First Gentleman of the Bedchamber to Don Philip, the younger brother of Charles VIIth of Naples, and had accompanied him to Italy in search of a throne. When Don Philip was established at Parma, de Rohan was his Master of Hunting, and his representative at

Vienna. On the death of his father, he had gone to Paris to clear his name and at 26 became a Knight of Malta. Promotion was rapid. In 1755 within the statutory ten years, he had become Captain-General, after seeing service with the Bailiff de Suffren in the Indies, and Louis XV himself was prepared to subsidise him in his new capacity. But Louis wanted him as a sailor, not as the Order's Ambassador in Paris. When Pinto appointed him to that position in 1766, he was declared *persona non grata*.

This check did not upset de Rohan, and as one of the leading Frenchmen in Malta he became the spokesman of the French faction that now desired, after so long an interregnum, the election of a French Grand Master. But their claims were not yet paramount. Despite an election campaign by the Bailiff de Saint-Simon, which cost him 15,000 scudi, the election went to the sexagenarian Navarrese Ximenes di Texada.

Chapter XI

TURBULENT PRIESTS

THE election was clearly a stop-gap; the change, any change was welcome, and Ximenes, according to de la Platière, was "haughty, not particularly spiritual, but an honest man for all that, though he put nothing right and left everything to carry on as before". Clement XIV at once despatched the Stock and Pilier—which Pinto had also received—now a mark of mere politeness.

Ximenes was aware of the deep currents of unrest against the long hand of Pinto within the Order itself. He must also have been aware that similar unrest had affected the Maltese, particularly the clergy. As the largest educated minority in the island, the Maltese clergy resented the manner in which the Order emphasized its distinction, only recognizing socially those clergy who were Conventual Chaplains. The new Grand Master, with either superb disdain or ignorance, at once proceeded to upset them further by issuing a ban on hunting. It was obvious that if there were to be any game at all, it had to be preserved, but indiscriminate slaughter by priests and clerics attached to the Bishop's household had so weakened the stock that Ximenes forbade all shooting for six months. Normally such a ban would have caused no trouble, but hunting was among the pastimes to which the local clergy were most passionately addicted, and it came at a time when relations between the Order and the Bishop were at their worst.

In August 1772, while Pinto was alive, a steward of the Bishop's household started a quarrel with the sailors of the Magistral galley. The irascible captain at once gave orders for any of His Lordship's officials found lurking in the area to be seized and bastinadoed; when one of them foolhardily defied the crew to carry out this threat, they were only too ready to do so. The Bishop accordingly ordered the arrest of two of the non-commissioned officers, who were taken at night while off duty and lodged in the Bishop's prison in Vittoriosa. Thence they were rescued by a party of young Knights who broke in the doors; Pinto had promptly complained to Rome about the behaviour of the Bishop's men. The local clergy, sensible of the insult to their spiritual head, rallied round His Lordship, and in a large "spontaneous" demonstration outside his Palace at Notabile demanded the convocation of a Chapter General. The Bishop shrewdly knew that this cry would find a ready echo among the Hospitallers themselves. But His Lordship had not reckoned on the presence in Rome of two ex-Inquisitors, Cardinals Serbelloni and Stoppani, who, while they had had their bitter disputes with the Grand Masters of their time, had had no less bitter quarrels with the Bishops. Pope Pius VI summoned the Bishop to Rome to answer for his actions.

The Maltese clergy saw him go with black feelings against the Order, and these were mollified in no way when on 17th August 1775 the new Inquisitor, recently arrived from Rome, admonished them to keep the laws of their rightful sovereign, to dress modestly, to refrain from launching excommunications against members of the Order without prior consultation with Rome *and* to abstain from hunting in the off-season.

But among the clergy, disappointment had distilled a dangerous spirit. At the time of the bishop's recall in 1772, Joseph Zahra, a priest of Floriana and instructor in Mathematics to the Grand Master's pages, had become the leader of a small conclave of rebellious-minded priests. Zahra, who was not himself in favour of direct action, was soon displaced by a disappointed and unbalanced priest called Gaetano Mannarino. Mannarino had already been rejected as a missionary by the Bishop and suspended from preaching because of the highly coloured content of his sermons. He felt that he had been passed over and denied. The malcontents then entered into a conspiracy, the objects of which were nationalistic in that their declared aim was to force the observance of the ancient privileges of the Maltese, including the summons of a Popular Council, and to demand a reduction in the price of corn. Apart from Mannarino, there were ten others, but when Pinto died and the price of corn fell, they found that the immediate causes of rebellion had been removed. But by 1775 they had been renewed.

Cavalcabo in the meantime had not been idle. Having failed to build up a party among the younger Knights, he turned now to the Maltese. He represented to the ringleaders that they could count on the assistance of the Czarina in any rebellion they might foment. At one time he seems to have obtained their consent to hand over the island, once they had seized it, to the Russian fleet. But the Russian agent did not promote the insurrection when it came. During that summer the harvest failed in Sicily, prices rocketed and misery was everywhere. Libels appeared on the Palace walls promising a Maltese Vespers, but no precautions were taken. The Maltese were esteemed "a very quiet people".

In September the combined fleets of Malta put to sea to assist the Spanish squadrons in a punitive expedition against Algiers. The greater part of the available defence force was accordingly absent from the island. At 2.0 a.m. on 9th September, with the aid of a disaffected corporal, a small troop composed largely of priests entered St Elmo, overpowered the meagre garrison and shut the Commandant in one of the dungeons. The drawbridge was then lowered to admit a motley crew of rebels. At the same time a watch-tower on the St James's Cavalier, by the Inn of Castile, was entered with adulterine keys, and from both places was run up a flag, half-red, half-white, the colours, according to tradition, granted by Count Roger d'Hauteville, liberator of Malta from the Saracens, to the Commune of the island in the eleventh century. This triumphant gesture to the ancient identity of the Maltese people was accompanied by a discharge of cannon.

The alarum once given, the Grand Master did not lose his

head. French traders in harbour at once offered a hundred men between them to help recover St Elmo, and the aristocracy of the island, anxious for their privileges, hastened to offer their services. De Rohan was put in charge of operations and a hundred men attacked the occupied watch-tower with the loss of one Knight, killed perhaps accidentally by one of his own side in the mêlée. The walls were scaled and, to everyone's astonishment, only four men were found inside. The rest had left earlier to rouse up their friends.

St Elmo on the other hand kept up a desultory fire and succeeded in scoring one direct hit on the Palace itself. The Vicar-General was able to negotiate a cease-fire for a time, but not a surrender, and it was not until 6.0 a.m. the following morning that the insurgents offered to surrender if they were promised personal immunity and "the observance of the privileges of the nation". The Venerable Council offered both, unable to understand the second, if the insurgents sent out twelve hostages and laid down their arms at once. But at 8.0 a.m. only six hostages emerged with a message from those inside that unless they were given bread they would blow the castle sky-high. There was no talk of surrender, and the Vicar General was still inside. It was obvious that they were waiting for something—either the local insurrection they had expected or the arrival of the Russian fleet. That night the Commandant and two soldiers broke out of their confinement, released the garrison, mastered the gun-galleys and began to round up the rebels. By 5.30 a.m. on the 11th all was over. In the surprise and confusion many ran away and it was never known how many rebels there were. Ximenes had three of the defenders of the watch-tower hanged, the fourth was an imbecile; the defenders of St Elmo were largely clerics and though they had not kept the terms of the amnesty the Grand Master was disposed to be merciful. With the approval of the Pope, the leaders, Mannarino and Joseph Dimech, were imprisoned for life, Mannarino to emerge in 1798 a bewildered captive released by Bonaparte to find himself a national hero. Five more were exiled for life. Everyone else was pardoned.

What was remarkable about this rising was not its failure but its comparative success. The guards at St Elmo had been unbelievably lax—proof of the accusation that under Pinto the whole machinery of defence had run down with disuse.

Cavalcabo's implication was revealed by the confession that Mannarino at once made. The Russian agent had been an accomplice of Zahra's in 1772 and the whole rising was not an amateur's idea. Someone "very knowing and extremely clever" alone could have suggested the seizure simultaneously of both St Elmo and a watch-tower on St James's Cavalier, both at commanding ends of the city. Cavalcabo therefore lay doggo until a general amnesty was published; when on 16th September he was emboldened enough to complain to the Council in person about the unworthy suspicions entertained of him, de Rohan tartly warned him to watch his step as too much was known about him already.

It was only a question of time before the Order seized an excuse to get rid of Cavalcabo. But he had one champion. This was the Chevalier Valperga di Masino who had taken Pinto's griefs against John Dodsworth to London in 1762. Masino while engaged on that mission had heard from the Russian ambassador in Paris that Catherine wanted a Knight of Malta to command her galley fleet and had considered himself just the man for the job. Pinto, however, had thought otherwise, and was not in favour of meeting Catherine's request. Instead he had received six chosen officers from the St Petersburg Naval Academy, who came in 1766, served for three years aboard the galleys and slipped off in 1769 to join Orlov's armada. Masino, pretending that he had business in Italy, went with them—"*Voici un chevalier*", Catherine remarked, "*qui a pris le mord aux dents*"—and returning from the Aegean expedition, he openly bragged of his services to the Czarina and swore to uphold Cavalcabo's innocence with the sword. He might have saved his breath and reputation: de Rohan had once conspired with Cavalcabo, and the worst thing to befall an intriguer is for him to see an old accomplice come to power.

For Ximenes did not live out the year. He was never again at ease, saw plots and conspiracies all round him, and went nowhere without a bodyguard. Doubting the reliability of the Maltese he organized the recruitment of a special Regiment, a thousand strong, from abroad. On 9th November 1775 he died. Three days later the Bailiff de Rohan was elected Grand Master. His first action was to get rid of Cavalcabo. With the excuse that a murderer had been seen escaping into the Russian's house in Floriana, the police entered and searched it. As they expected they found in the cellar a great cache of arms. Cavalcabo was put under arrest, a courier was sent to St Petersburg, and the Russian agent was recalled immediately. He left the island in disgrace with his sovereign and died not long after in France dodging the police who wanted him on various charges of fraud.

Catherine's purpose in appointing a man like Cavalcabo is still obscure. Her policy would seem to have been to edge onto the list of powers that "protected" Malta, and to build up there the sort of faction that the French could command. Cavalcabo, once he had failed, was discarded without a second thought. But when in 1774 the treaty of Kutchuk-Kainadji had established Russia as a potential Mediterranean power, her interest in and importance to Malta became more obvious. And Catherine knew that she could always do the Order a good turn in Poland.

Chapter XII

MAL FRANÇAIS

SAGRAMOSO had arrived in Warsaw, armed with the promise of the Czarina's diplomatic support and that of Frederick the Great, at the very moment of Pinto's death. The Polish government, embarrassed by his powerful friends, declined to recognize him until new credentials had arrived. This was not until May 1773. But Sagramoso had not been idle. He had persuaded the King to set up a delegation to examine the Order's claims to the Ostrog estates and had induced Prince Adam Poninski, Marshal of the Confederation of the Crown and one of the possessors of the lands shared out by Janus Sanguszko, to found a commandery from his share.

When Sagramoso at last met the delegation on 18th January 1774, he was able to announce that Poninski had consented to found a commandery to be held by his family in perpetuity by his male heirs, with the right of nomination. It was worth 300,000 Polish florins and enjoyed an annual revenue of 15,000, and Poninski was the first Knight on whom Sagramoso had conferred the Cross of Devotion with a dispensation from the vow of celibacy. Sagramoso had given up any hope that the Estates would be recovered in their entirety, but hoped that Poninski's example would be followed.

The King's delegation still prevaricated, hoping that the Diet would throw out the Order's case. But Sagramoso had a trump card. He informed the assembled delegates that he was empowered to offer the Order's pretensions to the Prussian minister, and though Frederick the Great had renounced all claims on the Republic by the treaty that concluded the first partition in 1772, his brother Ferdinand, whose claims had not been renounced, was Prior of Brandenburg. This Lutheran

Priory, that had existed entire in its dignities and structure since the Reformation in a state of schism, had already in 1763 through its Prior sought reintegration into the ancient Catholic order and the Brandenburg Knights were already paying responsions to Malta. Now Ferdinand was prepared to bring the pressure of the Prussian court to bear upon the dilatory Poles. "That which is denied to my modest and pacific overtures," Sagramoso warned the delegates, "will then be given over to the authority of force." The force with which Sagramoso chose to threaten was Russian. But his connection with the Czarina was well known and the Poles had an uneasy feeling that the affair of Ostrog could easily lead to a renewed intervention from both Prussia and Russia.

Opposition crumbled. Unwilling to make the Ostrog issue an international one, the holders of the estates agreed to found a Priory with six commanderies. Its capital value of 120,000 Polish florins would bring in an annual revenue of 42,000. The first Knights Commander, dispensed from celibacy, were to be chosen from the illegal holders themselves, but their successors were to keep all the rules of the Order. Eight other families proceeded to found commanderies in *ius patronatus*; when the final papers were signed, their total endowment amounted to 1,440,000 florins, and the revenue to 87,000. Responsions to the Order for the Priory would total 24,000, from the Family commanderies 8,200. There would be fifteen Knights in the country, while the 600 soldiers, for which Janus of Ostrog's will had made provision, would be paid for by a special foundation.

Sagramoso had done better than he had dared hope: but it was a long way short of the annual nine million Polish florins the estates were said to be worth. It was, however, a diplomatic triumph. "It is not by money that he buys his creatures," wrote one admiring witness, "but by a black ribbon with a little cross. Indeed I admire the Knight who finds it possible to satisfy the greed and vanity of those people he needs at virtually no cost to his Order."

The Poles, whose natural pride was too easily dissipated in

empty shows, were happy enough to wear the Cross of Malta and to have avoided an imbroglio with Prussia and Russia. The Diet did not actually sign the Declaration until 18th October 1776, though the preliminaries had been signed two years earlier. But the interference of foreign powers represented one more irritating indignity and the Priory was unsatisfactory from the start. The Polish Knights proved less eager to pay their dues than to wear the cross. A quittance fee of 4,000 florins was never paid, and the receipts from Warsaw were always in arrears. Indeed, the whole foundation had a flimsy and tenuous look about it, as if doomed to die young. In no place in the negotiations were the Czartoryskis mentioned.

Sagramoso returned to St Petersburg to thank the Czarina for the support of her ambassador early in 1775 and was pressed to remain at the Russian capital. But his health had never been good, he was tired out, and so he returned by easy stages to Malta and the court of the new Grand Master. Catherine did not take Cavalcabo's expulsion at all amiss and still hoped for good relations with de Rohan. But France was suspicious, and France had now acquired a new interest in Malta, for, after a gap of thirty years, the new ruler was a Frenchman.

De Rohan's election had been almost a foregone conclusion. He had a reputation as a reformer and he was, while not rich, known to be generous. Above all he was French, and sluggish support during the reign of Pinto from the Court of Versailles, the Order's "polar star", as de Rohan called it, had convinced the Knights that it must be quickened into taking a livelier interest. But the election of a Frenchman caused considerable dismay to the Spaniards who had grown accustomed to the Grand Mastership being vested in an Iberian, and the island was filled with rumours of a Spanish plot to poison the new Grand Master. The Spaniards apart, however, his election was popular, and de Rohan's public appearances were greeted with demonstrations of joy such as had not been witnessed for fifty years. The Maltese knew of his opposition to Pinto and did not hold against him his part in suppressing the priests' revolt.

"The spirit of intrigue," as the Abbé Boyer wrote in the last months of Ximenes' reign, "has as much influence here as pretty women once had in the affairs of France under Louis XV." A strong section of the Order looked to the Grand Master to rise above it and to do something to assert the independence and majesty of the Order without the bravado and bluff of a Pinto. Unhappily de Rohan had been tarred by the brush of intrigue himself, and the reformers, such as they were, were loath to abandon it themselves.

Ximenes had intended to summon a Chapter General, the first since 1631. Only by a meeting of the supreme legislative corps of the Order could any measures be taken to arrest the constant drain on the Treasury and to bring the entire system of government under review. But Ximenes died before he had done more than obtain from Rome a bull forbidding any discussion on the pre-eminence of the Grand Master. It was only with this card up his sleeve that he felt he could face the Chapter General. De Rohan inherited it.

The need for overhaul was apparent as soon as the accounts of the Treasury were presented. The Order was now in debt to the tune of 1,813,456 scudi, and the annual interest alone amounted to 51,157 scudi. There was an annual deficit accordingly of 120,098 scudi. So far the Order had met it by the wholesale felling of trees in the woods of the French commanderies, but trees were not an indefinite source of revenue. The responsions would have to be raised and the Chapter General alone could raise them.

But almost as soon as the summons was made the inherent conflicts of the future began to emerge. De Rohan, who believed in reform from the top, merely wanted money to stabilize the finances of the Treasury; the reformers wanted the comprehensive overhaul of the machinery of government. As it was obvious that the Pope's bull ruled out any review of the Grand Master's power, they hit on a method with which to break his spirit. They would not help to implement a new consultative machinery, but insist on the absolute and meticulous adherence to the ancient statutes which, they claimed, were being constantly overridden. But de Rohan, though he had conspired against Pinto, now that he occupied his place, was soon convinced that the old man, though overbearing in his manner, had had the right idea. A small council, called a Congregation of State, chosen by himself, had come to be responsible for the day to day administration of the Order and for decisions of policy. The Grand Master was thus spared the more cumbersome process of the Councils where faction was allowed full play. The reformers, on the other hand, wanted the old Councils restored to their full powers, but during the discussion on the agenda for the Chapter General de Rohan came to the conclusion that its more determined supporters were secretly hoping that the major item—the increase in responsions—would be voted out. The old men did not fancy a decrease in their incomes, the young men who still expected promotion to richer commanderies felt that their expectations were being reduced. What they wanted was power, not increased taxation. They claimed that proper administration would render the existing revenues sufficient and decided to call for enquiries into corrupt practices.

It was no surprise to de Rohan then, when the Chapter of the Grand Priory of France, headed by the Grand Prior himself, the Prince de Conti, refused to pay its share of a temporary imposition that the Grand Master had laid upon all commanderies to tide the Treasury over until the new taxes were voted. Its example was quickly followed by the Priories of Toulouse and St Gilles. But de Rohan, confident of the support of the French court, did not take it too seriously. Then Frederick the Great, who had for thirty years been ruler of Silesia, decided not to allow the Silesian Knights to attend the deliberations of the Priory of Bohemia to which they belonged, and refused also to admit the imposition. Frederick had persistently declined to allow money to leave the Kingdom from Silesia, pleading the poverty of the commanderies as a result of two wars, but he had not been above laying a tax of 40 per cent on their revenues. The Silesian Knights, who were quite happy about this decision, were, however, shamed by the Protestant Priory of Brandenburg, whose Prior, Prince Ferdinand, signified its readiness to accept both the imposition and any new taxes the Chapter General might impose. Brandenburg deputies would attend its deliberations as observers.

It was a discouraging start. In the meantime, the Bailiffs from France began to arrive, the French rearguard, de Bon, Mirabeau, des Barres, Tudest and de Brillane reaching Malta in September 1776, and de Brillane came with a special request from Marie-Antoinette that he be appointed Captain-General. De Rohan knew that they hoped to fight the rise in responsions and received them coldly, sadly discountenancing de Brillane who saw his Captain-Generalcy evaporate before his eyes. Mirabeau and Des Barres came into the open immediately: no Servants-at-Arms or Conventual Chaplains should be allowed to vote; the lower orders would undoubtedly vote on measures put before them by a popular Grand Master and so provide an automatic majority. They began canvassing at once by holding nightly receptions and converted to their standard a young Knight of distinction and formidable abilities, the thirty-three-year-old Auvergnat, Bosredon de Ransijat, whose significant career had now begun.

In November the elections for the Sixteen began—two representatives, a Bailiff and a Knight for each Tongue. The representatives for the defunct Tongue of England were in de Rohan's nomination and this was at once challenged as unstatutory by de Ransijat with commendable forensic art. One of the elected deputies for Champagne then fell ill and was replaced without a vote of the now disbanded Prioral chapter to save time. De Ransijat again objected. When his friend and crony, des Pennes, who had not gone to Communion as the statutes demanded at the opening of the Chapter General, was rejected accordingly as the representative for Provence by the fifteen elected deputies of which he was to be the sixteenth, de Ransijat drew up a lengthy protest and put it in the hands of the Inquisitor, stating that as a deputy of the Tongue of Auvergne, he would hold as null and void all decisions of the

Chapter General on account of the refusal of the authorities to acknowledge the sovereignty of that same Chapter.

De Ransijat owed his escape from censure to the fact that de Bon, Mirabeau and des Barres also filed their protests and de Rohan thought he was their dupe. The Auvergnat Club— the Knights were all Auvergnats—were furious that their demand for the disenfranchisement of the Servants-at-Arms and Conventual Chaplains had not been accepted. With their vote, the composition of the Sixteen was such that it was able to decide on the Grand Master's proposals.

They agreed, without undue debate, to raise the responsions to provide another half million scudi a year. The medieval punishments of septaine and quarantaine were replaced by terms of simple imprisonment, and the penalties for gambling were increased. It was also decided that a Knight once deprived of his habit could never be re-integrated and Knights cashiered in foreign service were to be deprived of a voice in the Councils of the Order. It was also decided that for certain capital crimes a Knight could be both despoiled and handed over to the secular arm for execution. The rigorists had their way but no major reforms were promulgated. But de Rohan with prophetic insight summed the whole thing up at the end: "Where interest clashes with pride, and authority with liberty, there will always be storms. The juniors, enlightened on the subject of their natural rights, wish to retain them, and the seniors, hardened by custom and precedent, believe that authority alone can uphold the state and that liberty will degenerate into licence, to produce anarchy and destruction. Public spirit is lost among the factions and what corruption and flattery began, thoughtlessness and error conclude. It remains only for the faithful to wrap themselves in their virtue and to weep over the ruins of Jerusalem." Certainly there had been storms and they were to blow for the rest of de Rohan's reign, at the end of which de Ransijat and des Pennes were to preside at the virtual dissolution of their Order. The last years of the Hospitallers were to be racked and torn by the dissensions that were so assiduously aired in the Chapter General of 1776.

De Ransijat later claimed that the reforms for which the Chapter General was called had been thwarted by a Machiavellian ruse on the part of the Grand Master, but he had not behaved in 1776 as their champion. Rather, in common with many of the Knights, he disliked the change that had come over the Order in the last decade and resented the way de Rohan seemed to cosset the Maltese, making himself available to hear complaints and receiving those from the better families who were not received by the Piliers and Bailiffs.

The Chapter General broke up early in 1777 and the Priories of Germany and Bohemia announced that they would not pay the new responsions, persuading Joseph II to protest to Rome about them. It was an act of deliberate disobedience, supported in Vienna by the Order's Minister, and in Valetta by the Imperial *chargé d'Affaires*, Ferdinand von Hompesch. De Rohan, anxious to avoid a direct clash with the Emperor, decided that von Hompesch was being suborned by a factious Conventual Chaplain, the Abbé Boyer, now his secretary, and had him arrested for questioning. Von Hompesch protested that the Imperial protection had been violated and Joseph II, always ready to harry religious orders, sequestered all the commanderies in his dominions. In order to avoid the Imperial wrath, de Rohan had to accept a compromise: von Hompesch was promoted, Boyer released and pensioned and the Grand Master agreed that the Germans should pay only half the extra responsions voted by the Chapter General. It was a sorry business, but the Grand Master was powerless to discipline his subordinates against the wishes of their sovereign and in their own way these assisted at the decline and fall of the Hospital.

The picture in Poland was equally dismal. Von Hompesch led a successful opposition to admitting the Poles into the German Tongue; the various Knights Commanders tried to get their dispensations from celibacy to apply to their own sons whom they wished to instal in the commanderies. Poninski's private affairs had become so muddled that he had no time for the business of the Priory of which he was Grand Prior. The banker de Rohan had appointed in Warsaw to collect the responsions found his job so difficult that he wanted to resign and the arrears were growing. In 1788 only 535 florins reached the Receiver in Venice, out of a total due of 48,000. The receipts scarcely covered the expenses incurred in setting up the Priory—all the Order had gained was a membership of dilatory Knights, amounting with the Knights of Devotion to twenty-two, and endless worry.

Then in 1783 Catherine II informed the Grand Master by the most devious way that she had appointed a successor to Cavalcabo. The news reached de Rohan from Vienna where the Russian minister had mentioned it casually to the Maltese. De Rohan, who could never accept an official agent, was unanxious to offend the Czarina, but he did not want another Cavalcabo. He would prefer to have the appointment rescinded. But Catherine's envoy was already on his way, his credentials in his pocket; he left St Petersburg in June 1783 and then disappeared. It was a peculiar business, quite in keeping with the peculiarity of Catherine's appointments, for the new agent was a Greek, the Chevalier Antonio Psaro, a Captain (2nd class) in the Russian navy, who had been decorated with the Cross of St George (4th class), hence his title, for services rendered in the 1770–4 war. Despite letters to the Russian minister Razumovsky, at Naples, de Rohan could not get his point home to the Czarina, and when on 13th April 1784 Psaro suddenly arrived, he had to receive him.

Psaro was met by the Bailiff Vice-Chancellor, who was surprised to find him "*sans épée et dans le negligée le moins présentable.*" He explained that he had delayed his arrival because he had been told that his reception would be frosty, an illusion the Chancellor endeavoured to dispel by pointing out that the Ambassador of the Emperor of Morocco had recently been received in the island with all honour. It was true that Psaro could not be received in any official capacity; the statutes forbade it. The Greek, rallying his pride, treated the Chancellor to a diatribe against the machinations of France, Spain and the Empire who obviously dictated Maltese policy and warned him that the Czarina was not a person to be crossed.

The English had had experience of her temper in the last war when she had raised up the Armed Neutrality against them. This declaration made, Psaro became quite reasonable: he accepted a compromise whereby he called himself a *chargé d'affaires* without being one; he was received by de Rohan in a private capacity and impressed the Grand Master as a likeable, modest man, with whom he soon struck up relations that were almost intimate.

Psaro, however, was not far wrong when he claimed that France dictated policy. It was true that with a war on its hands, the French court had refused to ruffle the Czarina by demanding his recall, but now the war was over, it viewed his presence with great suspicion. And, as if to underline it, that very year, while Joseph II was visiting his brother-in-law of Naples, the news burst on its astonished ears that a secret arrangement had been made between Naples and Russia, to which the Order was party, wherein Naples abandoned to the Czarina the sovereign rights that her kings had sometimes claimed over the island of Malta. De Rohan indignantly denied it, but Paris was alarmed and Naples annoyed. Just how it had begun no one rightly knew, but the origin seems to have been in one of the Knights of the Auvergne Tongue who aimed at embarrassing the Grand Master. This Knight was Déodat de Dolomieu.

Chapter XIII

THE UGLY COMMANDER

THE Commander Dieudonné Sylvain Guy Tancred de Gratet de Dolomieu was a young man of brilliant parts, one of the great names in eighteenth-century science. He was also a prickly, hot-tempered and troublesome Knight. He had entered the Order at two, done his first caravan at sixteen and killed a fellow Knight in a duel at Gaeta when he was only eighteen. Pinto had condemned him to loss of his habit and perpetual imprisonment, but the Duke de Choiseul, speaking for Louis XV, and Cardinal Torriggiani for Clement XIII, had obtained his release and reinstatement. At twenty-one, Dolomieu, an officer with the Carabineers at Metz, began to study chemistry and physics in the military hospital. But it was the Duke de Rochefoucauld, Colonel of the Sarre Regiment, who opened his eyes to the wonders of mineralogy, and introduced him to the *salon* of the Duchess d'Enville, where he met Condorcet and Turgot. From that moment, Dolomieu launched himself so enthusiastically into his studies that he was soon an authority known to the *cognoscenti* of Europe who corresponded with him regularly. In 1780 he became the Commander Dolomieu, and in 1783 was appointed the Lieutenant of the Marshal, the Pilier of Auvergne, and, as the Marshal was permanently absent, he found himself the officer responsible for the troops of Malta. He took his duties very seriously but found that he was not expected to do much. He accordingly began to throw his weight about and soon quarrelled with the Colonel of the Regiment.

This was the force that Ximenes had decided to raise after the priests' revolt, but it was never more than a comic opera troop. The only recruits were largely riff-raff and beggars from

169

the Papal states, and these so frequently deserted that it was difficult to keep it up to strength. The men were badly disciplined, but understood the persuasion of a rifle and in a very short time they had become a sort of legalized banditti, who carried the officers with them. De Rohán tried to do something about this by appointing as Colonel a martinet who was later to become the Captain-General, the Chevalier de Freslon. De Freslon after trying unsuccessfully to discipline his officers, and fighting two duels, was forced to sack them all, and clearing out the worst elements among the soldiery began once more to recruit Maltese. He was an enlightened commander, he saw that the soldiery were taught to read and write and even apprenticed to a trade. But the Regiment, ironically, did their best service in Egypt whither Bonaparte took them in 1798; they did not fight the French when they arrived.

Dolomieu chose unwisely to espouse the cause of the insubordinate officers, claiming that he alone had the authority to confer or cancel commissions. When the Congregation of War upheld de Freslon, he resigned in pique. "I have had to fight against the authority of the Grand Master," he wrote in 1783, "to defend the rights of my position and to put some bounds to the power he wants to arrogate to himself. . . . I have sounded the tocsin against the abuse of magistral power."

And Dolomieu continued to fight the authority of the Grand Master to the bitter end. He soon became the most active of the Auvergnat Club. Though he indignantly denied that he was the source of the Russian rumour—he said it had been well known in Versailles for a year that something was afoot—he had undoubtedly helped to spread it in Naples where he was engaged on a study of Vesuvius. He was at once banned the kingdom, before he had concluded his researches, and had one more grievance in his cap. To get his revenge, he decided to foment trouble for the newly founded Priory of Bavaria.

In 1782, Charles Theodore, the eccentric and religious Elector of Bavaria, had achieved what successive electors had

dreamed of—a Bavarian Priory. Endowed with the funds of
the sequestered Jesuits about whose expulsion the Elector had
never been happy, twenty-eight commanderies had been set
up, four of them for Conventual Chaplains. The total revenues,
after deducting the pensions of the Jesuit fathers, were not
marvellous, a bare 50,000 scudi a year, but the prestige and
protection of the Electorate was a welcome asset to Malta.
Charles Theodore wanted the Priory to have the status of a
Tongue; George III having graciously given his consent, the
defunct English Tongue was accordingly transformed into the
Anglo-Bavarian, to which was added the Polish Priory.
Everyone was satisfied—the negotiations, initiated by Sagramoso on his return from Russia, had been conducted at the
Elector's expense, who had in return obtained the unique
privilege of interchange between the Cross of St John and the
Cross of St George—his own exclusive chivalric order. The
Auvergnats however noticed two things: an Alsatian Knight,
the Bailiff de Flachslanden, who had played a considerable
part in the negotiations, had landed a pension of twelve
thousand livres a year, and an obscure priest, the Abbé
Hoefflin, later to be Bishop of Chersonese, had landed another,
for services rendered that were not wholly clear. Then the
first Grand Prior was no other than one of the bastards of
Charles Theodore, who when he married later continued to
occupy the dignity. Had not too much principle been sacrificed
for insufficient gain?

For the annual responsions scarcely amounted to 4,000
scudi, and when in 1783 a Bavarian Knight was appointed to
the traditional office of the Pilier of England, that of Turcopilier, the Auvergnat Club determined to make trouble for
the Grand Master and his new creation. The Turcopilier's
ancient command had been of the light infantry used for
fighting off marauding Arabs, known as the Turcopoles. Since
1540 the post had been in the nomination of the Grand Master
and it had customarily been held by a Provençal, responsible
for setting the watches and reviewing the guards. At once the
Lieutenant of the Pilier of Provence, also the *chargé d'affaires*

of the French court, protested. He was the Bailiff des Pennes, the man who had failed to secure a seat on the Sixteen in the Chapter General, seven years earlier. His protest, however, took the form of a public demonstration on the part of the Provençal Knights. Backing des Pennes were Dolomieu and, more discreetly, de Ransijat, but the Provençals were forced to come to heel by a direct order from the Count de Vergennes, French foreign minister.

Des Pennes took his defeat hard and from then on openly espoused the Auvergnat Club who were the main malcontents. It was no longer exclusively composed of Auvergnats and soon the Tongue was to be itself in schism. For de Rohan's French secretary was an Auvergnat, the Chevalier de Loras, who had already been used on a number of ticklish diplomatic assignments and had deserved a reward, which de Rohan made in the form of a pension. The Grand Master, in fact, had six pensions to provide, one for de Flachslanden, another for Sagramoso, two for the prelates who had brought the Stoc and Pilier to Ximenes, one for the Abbé Boyer, and now one for de Loras. After prior consultation with the Chapter of the Priory of Toulouse, he decided to meet them out of a small tax on its commanderies. But moved by des Pennes, and by Dolomieu who disliked de Loras, the commanders were persuaded to object to the Chapter that they were the victims of a despotic levy from the Grand Master, and unwilling to run the risk of an adverse decision by invoking the *sguardio*, they asked des Pennes to present a memoire of their grievances to the Pope. Dolomieu, who had received no change from Rome in his own quarrel of 1783 over the Regiment, was only too ready to espouse the quarrels of other Frenchmen and he at once posted to Rome to inform de Brillane, who had recently been appointed ambassador at the insistent request of Marie-Antoinette, that the Grand Master was building up a clique of yes-men by creating subservient Bailiffs and that it was in the interests of the Order to see that no more briefs for the conferment of a Grand Cross were given to Frenchmen, who might form one more tame vote in the Councils. De Brillane, therefore, persuaded Cardinal Buoncompagno, the Secretary of State, to hold up the brief for the Chevalier de Foresta, the Receiver in Marseilles. De Rohan, in an attempt to see that the Cardinal de Bernis, the French ambassador in Rome, was ordered by Vergennes to cease aiding and abetting de Brillane, instructed the old sea-dog, de Suffren, to take the case up to the highest level.

But Vergennes declined to act. Indeed he implicitly accused the Grand Master of nepotism and of seeking to avoid the summons of another Chapter General which should by the Statutes have been summoned in 1786. Rome, meanwhile, instructed the Inquisitor to look into the case of the Toulouse Priory. This was not conducive to peace, good order and discipline. "I would consent to convene a Chapter General far more readily than the general capitulants themselves," de Rohan wrote to de Suffren, and a new tax which he would order would soon silence the clamour against the Treasury which had retrenched valiantly on its expenses. Des Pennes had now shifted his ground. As Lieutenant of the Grand Conservator, the Pilier of Provence, he was *ex officio* the senior officer in the Treasury and he turned to attack the methods being introduced there. He complained that the incorporation of the Order of St Anthony, decreed by the Chapter General, would place too great a strain on the Treasury—in which he was quite right—but he took to filibustering in the Council meetings so much that de Rohan declared the Committee of the Treasury a Congregation of State and removed its sessions to the Palace. Des Pennes, thus excluded, launched an attack on Congregations of State. He had the support of the Statutes as they were an innovation, a streamlined version of the Sacred Council, against which de Rohan, in his own time, had protested. Its duties were purely administrative—it could make no policy decisions—but what it decided to do was final. Des Pennes appealed to Rome that the Grand Master's action was illegal—"attributing to the Pope," de Rohan wrote, "the whole government of the Order both religious and political." But when France failed to order des Pennes a second time to back down, de Rohan was forced to allow the appeal to go through.

Tiresome, petty, nagging, but the sort of thing that was to plague the Order for the rest of its life. It was not as if des Pennes were really championing the protest of young men against the rule of old fogies, for he was himself behaving like a spoiled club member. He should have espoused better causes than this. These legal quibbles, too, were having a bad effect on the great powers. Vergennes, with more important things to see to, could not waste his time over paltry domestic squabbles in Malta. Yet viewed in Malta they were more than that: they marked the dissolution of the vow of obedience that had on the whole been observed more readily than the other two. The effect on the body politic was to weaken authority, sow discontent, born of frustration and disappointment, and to sap the morale of an Order that had up till now survived without many questions being asked.

Now, however, they were being asked. Sagramoso, some ten years earlier, had been addressed quite bluntly to the embarrassment of the other guests on the subject of the Order during a dinner given by Kaunitz in Vienna. The veteran Austrian minister said: "I recommend you to put it to the Grand Master that he should occupy himself seriously with putting his house in order by correcting those abuses and disorders that have affected the spirit and habits of his Knights —that is, if he does not want to oblige us to reform them ourselves."

In 1787 Sagramoso passed this information on to de Rohan's French secretary. The Bailiff de Loras was a diplomat, not of the quality of Sagramoso, who had had a number of quiet successes to his name. He had initiated the delicate negotiations that had led to the reshuffle of the Italian commanderies; he had in 1775 persuaded the King of Sardinia to restore to the Savoyard commanderies the privileges they had been denied for three reigns; he had presided over his Tongue during the busy Chapter meetings before the Chapter General and he had latterly persuaded the King of Sardinia to integrate the commanderies of St Anthony with those of St John and to turn down the rival claims of the Order of St Maurice—a move that had induced Vergennes to request de Rohan to grant him a Commandery of Grace and one of the vexed pensions on the Priory of Toulouse. De Loras was a zealous partisan of the Grand Master's and led the conformist section of the Auvergnat Tongue against the Club, at the head of whom was the man who detested him most. The feud between Dolomieu and de Loras was personal. Dolomieu saw his rival as a fawning sycophant—one of the Bailiff yes-men about whom he had warned de Brillane—and envied him the prospects of advancement he had gained by conforming which Dolomieu, an abler man, had forfeited by rebelling. De Loras, fearful of the power of the Auvergnat Club who could prevent him from becoming the Pilier, a position he coveted, clung to the Grand Master loyally and defended him against all attack.

"Our principles and maxims are wise," he wrote to Sagramoso, "our chiefs are impartial and just. But Rome and Naples undo the good we do by protecting trouble-makers. But despite obstacles, agriculture and commerce are on the increase, our political system is solidly and nobly united, our army, our navy, our magazines, our workshops are in better shape than our means really permit. The Treasury burdened with recurrent and extraordinary expenses . . . and ancient debts . . . is now nearly out of the wood. What then are the urgent reforms we must carry out? It is not we who must reform, it is the arbitrary jurisdiction of Rome that tyrannises over us, to whom the virulent detractors of law, order and obedience fly at the first sign of trouble."

De Loras was de Rohan's secretary until 1787; his successor, Ovide Doublet, a Donat and a Frenchman with a Maltese wife, rose on de Loras's promotion to be de Rohan's personal and confidential aide, responsible for the correspondence in cipher. When Bonaparte arrived he took service with the provisional government and was, not unnaturally, accused of treason. In justification he wrote his own account of the last days of the Order in Malta—in which, of course, he played a significant and reliable part—serving France as a Frenchman only after he could no longer serve the Order as a Donat. His is the fullest account of these times, and it makes depressing reading. "How many young people has one seen arriving from the depths of their provinces three or four days later on the galleys without having the slightest idea how to manipulate either a sword or a rifle, without knowing how to swim, much less understanding the simplest terms used in sailing or in navigation and known by the humblest sailor? What do these young men do on caravans, or between caravans but fritter away their time in the squares and cafés, playing billiards or cards, hunting loose women with whom to squander their health and money. In latter years they have seldom left port except in the summer in order to voyage with great comfort and with less danger. I have heard Captains of galleys boast that they did not want to attack Barbary corsairs . . . in order to spare themselves the expense and inconvenience of quarantine."

De Rohan had founded the Chair of Nautical Sciences at the University to remedy this ignorance, but the galleys were now obsolete. In thirty-two years, from 1764–96 only six captures or sinkings had been registered, all of smaller ships. The line ships—these Doublet ignored—were now doing the raiding, but with less and less result. There simply wasn't the game.

The quarrel between de Loras and Dolomieu—with whom Doublet sympathized—began now to infect the whole Order. De Loras bitterly and successfully opposed Dolomieu's election to the Complete Council in 1787, and Dolomieu, taking it as a personal insult, took his case to Rome complaining that he had been fraudulently deprived of his rights. De Brillane took his side and Buoncompagno was only too ready to seize on another opportunity to foster in the Pope the belief that Malta was a fief in which he could rule much as he ruled in Rome. But the statutes declared that a member of the Complete Council could only be elected by his Tongue and Dolomieu's candidacy had been turned down by thirteen votes to seven. There was nothing Rome could do, so Dolomieu took himself thence to Paris to lay his case before Vergennes. The French minister, however, had not time to listen. The Council of Notables was in session and all France was agog with the prospect of an Estates General. Malta was ignored and Dolomieu, writing to his friend de Fay, could only pour the vials of his scorn upon de Loras—"more deformed in spirit than in body, more twisted in morals than in physique, the most dangerous, the most vindictive, the most wicked person I know"—and to ascribe his failure to get redress to his enemy's influence on Vergennes.

The assiduous propaganda of the French dissidents, the lazy indifference of de Brillane, the decrepitude of the French minister, Cardinal de Bernis, and Buoncompagno's readiness to admit all direct appeals to Rome were having their effect in Malta, and in July 1788 de Rohan was defied openly and flagrantly by a mere novice. For his participation in a fracas in the theatre, the novice des Adrets was confined to his house. He refused to obey. De Rohan, thoroughly tired of angry young men with airs, offered him a reasonable alternative: he could choose to be sent home or shut up in Fort Manoel for a spell. Des Adrets at once appealed to the Inquisitor.

De Rohan thought he had acted very leniently; he felt like a headmaster whose fourth formers constantly appealed against his authority to the Board of Governors. Where would his authority be if simple acts of disobedience went unpunished? He was soon to know. Another novice, ringleader in a trouble-some circle of young Knights and novices, was ordered to leave the island on the next cruise. When he refused, he was arrested and at once appealed to the Inquisitor. It took Rome a year to decide what was to be done with des Adrets, and when it decided it ordered him to do as de Rohan had sug-gested—to return to his parents.

The Grand Master was not entirely blameless. Des Adrets should not have been living in his own house but in the novitiate. A headmaster who allows his fourth formers the latitude he allows his prefects must expect trouble. And one of the prefects was now in Rome pestering de Brillane to get a brief out of the Pope reversing the decision of the Auvergnat Chapter and promoting him to the Complete Council. "When the Grand Master is told," he wrote to de Fay, "that he is a powerful prince who commands a vast estate, and that all the courts of Europe will unite to uphold him in his independence, he is greatly deceived. It would be as easy for the Pope to snuff out the Order as it would be the Capuchins." Cardinal Buoncompagno, though, if he felt the same, dared not move too fast with the courts of France, Spain and Naples, while largely indifferent to the issue, not entirely deaf to appeals from Valetta. Dolomieu got no decision in his favour: the French court was "one week determined to let the Pope do what he likes . . . the next holding that the Grand Master is an absolute sovereign. Sometimes it admits appeals to Rome, at others it disapproves of them. The court of France suffers in this respect from a tertian ague." But on 1st August 1788 the Rota decided to summon de Loras to Rome.

De Rohan was now thoroughly disgusted. "Every pettifogging tiff, forgotten here." he wrote to de Suffren, "is published the next day in Rome where it is puffed out to all Europe as an affair of the greatest importance . . . I can see no other means of reconciliation than to resign the rights of sovereignty to the claws of the Monsignori. . . . One letter from Vergennes would put an end to all these dissentions."

De Loras hurried to Rome to court his partisans, and very soon he had found one in the person of Pinto's *soi-disant* bastard, the Comte de Cagliostro. Ever since the celebrated trial of de Rohan's uncle the Cardinal, Cagliostro's fortunes had been declining as one by one the doors of those houses that had always been open to him were closed. Not the least strange event in his strange life was the decision to tread the thorny path to Rome; it is believed that his wife, Grand Mistress of the Egyptian Lodge, whose rites Cagliostro still assiduously peddled, wanted to return to her native city. Into Papal Rome, then, defying bawdy fortune, they came, still seeking the credulous niche in which they could settle for the rest of their lives. In a society suffocatingly clerical Cagliostro's brand of mystery had a subtle allure. Among the bored and aimless nobility that he approached, he had singled out the Bailiff de Brillane.

De Brillane's habitual sloth and an inflated sense of his own importance as a protégé of Marie-Antoinette had been enough to prevent him from rashly espousing the cause either of Dolomieu or of de Loras, once they were both in the same city. He received de Loras courteously. Hoping that very soon the Embassy of Rome would be exchanged for something better, he was careful not to offend the Grand Master's favourite, and introduced him to Cagliostro. De Loras was at once captivated. Very soon he was writing to de Rohan about him: explaining that he had become his confidant and knew everything about the Lodge that Cagliostro had founded at Lyons. "It maintains a remarkable level of hospitality, gives considerable assistance to the manufacturers there and furnishes each of its members with a handsome pension all from the products of its work. This extraordinary man, tired of a vagabond life and persuaded by my suggestion, would be quite ready to settle in Malta if Your Highness deigned to promise him free asylum and the protection of Your government. No expense would be incurred on his behalf."

De Rohan expressed polite interest but no enthusiasm; Cagliostro's connections with his uncle the Cardinal had not been a happy one; if it was de Loras's belief that his much vaunted power to transmute metals would solve the economic difficulties of the Order and transform the Hospitallers into a vast mutual aid society like the Lyonnais Lodge, it was not de Rohan's. Cagliostro, however, had made a convert of de Loras and though he had failed to secure him a comfortable hide-out in Malta, the Knight was not without his uses. Then, in December 1788 tragedy occurred. The old warrior de Suffren died of apoplexy. The truth being considered somewhat tame, rumours spread through Paris and Rome that he had died in a duel with the Prince de Mirepoix, for whose relative de Suffren had refused to intercede after his dismissal from the

Navy for misconduct. Whatever the truth, the French Embassy was vacant and de Brillane was confident that he would get it.

De Loras knew what de Rohan thought of de Brillane's performance in Rome and believed that he had a chance himself. When the intervention of Marie-Antoinette secured the appointment of de Brillane, de Loras aspired to the new vacancy at Rome, but hearing that the likely candidate was the Grand Master's own nephew, Prince Camille de Rohan, ex-Captain-General and ex-Plenipotentiary Extraordinary to the Court of Lisbon, he invoked the support of his new friend Cagliostro. Cagliostro, anxious for the protection of an accredited ambassador, did what he could. Hoping that de Rohan's old ties with freemasonry—he had been admitted to a Lodge while in Parma—and the memory of the power Cagliostro had had over the Cardinal would cause him to tremble at the name of the Grand Cophta of the Egyptian Lodge, he wrote a pompous and involved instruction to the Grand Master in which he demanded the Embassy for "his legitimate son, de Loras . . . by virtue of the authority in us invested to make known to you the wishes of Eternal Providence." Prince Camille was to be told to stand down or the family of de Rohan would rue the day.

The only effect of this pathetic manifesto was to lose de Loras any slender hope he might have had of getting the job, and it seriously weakened the confidence of the Grand Master in him. A touch of insanity seemed to inflict those who went to Rome; while Dolomieu and de Loras badgered the Rota for a decision, while the Cardinal Judges fumbled over what to do with a disobedient des Adrets, while Cagliostro begged Pius VI to give his Egyptian Lodge a constitution like the Knights Hospitaller to convert Protestants "even to the shedding of blood," the command went out for the Estates General to meet at Versailles.

From that moment, though no one knew it, the days of the Order were numbered.

Chapter XIV

TIDINGS OF DOOM

IN far away Malta the internal convulsions of France were remote and shadowy; but the meeting of the Council of Notables in 1786 had first brought the Knights Hospitaller into some prominence. Were they to vote in the forthcoming elections for an Estates-General as representatives of the 1st or the 2nd Estate? De Rohan instructed de Suffren in March 1786 to emphasize that the Knights were not ecclesiastics: "our privileges, it is true, appear to unite us by analogy to the first order of the privileged, but if one considers that their exemptions are free while ours are strenuously earned, then we can conclude that we shall only lose by making common cause with them". In the end a suitable compromise was reached: the Knights voted as clergy, the unbeneficed Novices as nobles and the Servants-at-Arms as members of the *Tiers Etat*.

From the beginning de Rohan wanted to keep out of the internal affairs of France as much as possible. Malta was a sovereign state possessing lands in the country; the Knights were subjects of two states, owing allegiance to their monarch and to their Order. They should preserve perfect detachment and behave as far as in them lay rather as members of a foreign, independent state than as Frenchmen.

The death of de Suffren, however, could not have been more inopportune. Not that he was an able diplomat, but he was an honest sailor, a brave warrior and widely respected. France had few enough public heroes to dispose of in 1789, the Order only one. His replacement was a miserable choice. De Brillane was known to be a creature of the Queen, and he at once celebrated his appointment with an ostentation of wealth that the hard-pressed Paris embassy could ill afford.

Instead of allowing a decent interval to elapse after his arrival, he threw open the Temple, put all his servants into livery and gave a magnificent dinner to his fellow Knights as well as to those noblemen and their ladies who were most in favour at court. Marie-Antoinette was impressed by this show of zeal; the Bailiff de Virieu, minister in Paris for the Duke of Parma, knew that de Brillane was living beyond his means in the expectations of the next quinquennial commandery which the Queen would obtain for him.

De Rohan was kept informed from the beginning of events in the country by his Receiver in Marseilles, the Chevalier de Foresta, still a chevalier while the brief for his Grand Cross was held up in Rome. It was from him that the Grand Master learned to his annoyance that, contrary to his instructions, three Knights had been elected to the Estates General: the Bailiff de Crussol, acting Grand Prior of France in the name of the fourteen-year-old Duc de Berry, the son of Charles d'Artois, and the Chevalier d'Esclan among the 1st Estate and the Bailiff de Flachslanden, Turcopilier in the Anglo-Bavaro-Polish Tongue and member of the Sacred Council, as member for Alsace in the Third Estate.

With de Brillane opening his visitors' book in Paris and dancing attendance at court, with a vacancy in Rome, de Rohan felt diplomatically paralysed. The more sagacious of the Knights in Paris prevailed on de Virieu to be de Brillane's shadow deputy, and with the assistance of an industrious clerk-cum-secretary, Cibon, who had grown up in the Embassy where his father was also secretary, he tried to forge a policy. "It is very singular," he wrote to Valetta on 11th May, "that our Ambassador is again not here! He must find time to put himself *au courant* with our affairs. God willing, he might listen to our excellent Cibon."

He did not, however, listen to his own superiors. De Rohan's orders were that no Knight was to take any action in defiance of or protest against a decree bearing the royal seal. On the night of 4th–5th August the National Assembly in a fever of enthusiasm decreed the abolition of all feudal privileges, rights and dues. The King proceeded to put his signature to it. But de Brillane, using a blank sheet with the Grand Master's signature to it, kept in the Embassy archives for emergencies, wrote to Louis XVI demanding the revocation of the decree or, at least, its modification in favour of the Order of St John and its lands in France. This letter was sent on to the President of the National Assembly. In it de Brillane claimed that the Order, deprived of its revenues, of which the ancient feudal dues formed a large proportion, would be unable to continue its present services to France. This was true enough, but what was untrue was de Brillane's declaration: "that the Grand Master feels it his duty to himself, to the Order and to the nations that support it, to protest," and to demand that the King should "interpose his powers and stop the recent decree in respect of the Order."

The invocation of the royal veto by a foreign power, and that one which wished to establish itself as absolutely neutral, was a bad move. Though de Brillane obliged his superiors by dying unexpectedly of an apoplectic stroke shortly afterwards, the damage was done. On 30th November his letter was read to the Assembly and a deputy for Paris, a Jansenist advocate of austere piety and the future hammer of the clergy, rose to speak. "To provide a reply to this statement, I demand that the establishments of the Order of Malta in France be suppressed."

Armand-Gaston Camus moved no motion to debate this proposition, but with his prestige was able to initiate a pamphlet war against the Order. "The Order of Malta is good for nothing," ran a leaflet that appeared early in 1790. "I render homage to the courage of the Knights; on all occasions they have shown it. The memory of the Bailiff de Suffren is still green, but was it on the galleys of Malta that he earned his laurels? No! It was as a commander of our squadrons. Malta has no more infidels to fight. Nobody's head is turned today by this mania for forcibly converting them, for tearing from their profane grasp those holy places where our divine Saviour died for us. . . . It belongs to the sectaries of Mahommed to employ sword and fire to make proselytes. Religion has triumphed over her enemies. The Order of Malta, as a military force, has no further use."

In words such as these, the ancient legend of the Crusades was blown away as if it had never been. Even so, an attack based on principle was not immediately dangerous. The material services that Malta rendered France were still considerable and the defenders of the Order made great play of them. "What would be the use to France if Malta were to be cut off from the sources of her revenue?" wrote one. "She would be obliged to convoy all her merchantmen herself, which would cost twelve times what the Order costs her. She would lose all the advantages of the port. How many French vessels took refuge in her harbours during the wars with England? How many Frenchmen have been treated at the Hospital and sent back to France at the Order's expense and on the Order's ships to avoid recapture by the English? The French nation thinks now only of correcting abuses; the Order is extremely useful to her and I love my country enough to believe that she will preserve it."

Stronger still was Malta's position in international law, as it was still understood. Whatever Frenchmen thought of the Order, of its privileges, of its Republic of Aristocrats, of its services to commerce, it remained a sovereign body holding lands in France. If France wished to open all public offices to men of talent regardless of birth, the Order was not obliged to follow suit. Because the National Assembly wished to forbid men to wear foreign decorations, there was nothing to stop the Order from issuing them. While the Commanders, Bailiffs and Priors kept the laws of the land, the Order was in an unassailable position before the law.

But who was going to make the law? On 11th August the National Assembly decreed that those tithes possessed by secular and religious bodies, including the Maltese and other religions and military orders, were to be abolished. At the same time all *rentes foncières*, which were not specifically feudal in origin and implied a reciprocal service, were declared redeemable. The rents and tithes paid to the Knights as commanders came in for heated discussion and Mirabeau, no less, raising the bogey of Russian interest in the island, stoutly defended the exclusion of the Order from this decree. De Brillane's memoire was submitted posthumously on 21st August. The Order enjoyed, it read, "the most complete and authentic possession, most solemnly guaranteed, of an absolute exemption from all impositions. The revenues of the Religion cannot be diminished without its becoming a charge on the Christian powers, particularly on France." This was corroborated by the Chambers of Commerce in Marseilles, Bordeaux and Lyons, who emphasized in a specially composed memorandum the inestimable value of Malta's services to France's Levantine trade, and the danger of driving the Order to sell out to her rivals, Great Britain or Russia.

Camus did not at this stage press his point. He had not intended to "destroy the Order entire or to dethrone the Grand Master," as had been imputed to him. Was there not a difference between banishing those establishments that openly declared they would not submit to the laws of the state, and breaking with a friendly power? The Bailiff de Flachslanden, together with a Marsilian deputy, confuted his arguments in further pamphlets and stressed the need to guarantee the Order its revenues. Then, on 4th January 1790, Camus was reinforced by a petition from the inhabitants of the Commandery of Sainte Eulalie en Rouergue who "complained of the state of personal servitude under which they groaned and of the rigour with which the Commander used his exorbitant feudal rights".

Despite a message from the King in favour of the Order's exemption, the National Assembly pressed for the royal sanction to the law of 11th August, and the decree became final. The tithes were abolished; compensation was to be paid for those that were legally *rentes foncières*. In the meantime the clergy on the Order's estates were in a quandary. The National Assembly had ordered the clergy of the country to apply to the Assemblies of the different Departments for the payment of provisional salaries while the new scales were being fixed. If the Order's clergy were to do this, it would be to acknowledge their subjection to the Ordinaries and the Order's identification with the clergy as a whole. The Receiver in Paris, the Chevalier d'Estourmel, proposed then to support his clerics out of the *caisses* of the Priories. It was a considerable financial burden to take on at this juncture, for on 25th September, in response to Necker's call for a *Don Patriotique* to save the state from collapse, the Grand Priory of France and the other five Priories of the realm followed the lead of the King and the Archbishop of Paris, and offered the national exchequer a quarter of their revenues—a sum amounting to 879,391 livres. It was to be paid in three annual instalments and d'Estourmel proposed to find the money by earmarking fifty per cent of the annual responsions. For six months, therefore, Malta could expect no money from France. At the end of that time the Order's financial position might be clearer and the compensation assessed for the abolished *rentes foncières*.

In the Priory of Toulouse, d'Estourmel estimated, 36,000 out of an annual revenue of 40,000 livres had been lost in the abolition of feudal dues. But de Virieu and he could congratulate themselves on having maintained the Order's exclusive independence of the clergy which was being continually questioned by Camus. To him, the distinctions so sacred to the Order were purely academic. Did the Knights not take religious vows and owe allegiance to the Pope? Had not they on occasions become Cardinals? Was not the *Composition des Rhodiens* merely a concordat exempting the Knights from paying clerical dues to the Crown? This exemption did not prove that they were not clergy. "The Order of Malta possesses nothing in France except by permission of the King, who in granting it exercises the rights of the nation. The establishments of the Order do not form a state within a state— sovereigns in Malta, the Knights are *subjects in France*." He was prepared to suggest a compromise. The French government should offer Malta an annual subvention to compensate her for her services to France; her revenues in that country should be at once taken over and used to provide pensions for retired warriors, to finance cadetships for French officers sent to the island, to pay the *curés* the statutory 1,200 livres and to open the Order to members who qualified by desert and who should be supported financially by France. At the beginning of 1790 the inveterate enemy of the Church was disposed to be generous.

De Rohan hoped all along that the Order would be treated like those German princes who held lands in France west of the Rhine and who had so far come under the protection of the royal veto. He would order his Knights to pay the new taxes and to keep all the new laws. But he would not alter the constitution or accept indemnification raised from the ancient patrimony of the Kings and the Church of France. "Our cause is that of the King of France inasmuch as we are inclined to resist the abolition of distinctions reserved to the nobility, and to perpetuate a military order whose utility is recognized and which has always deserved well of His Majesty. We profess a perfect devotion to the sacred person of Louis XVI and our determination never to separate our interests from those of the Crown."

On 26th September 1789 the Assembly abolished all commutations from the *vingtième*. On 28th October all vows in religious houses were suspended. On 2nd November the salaries of the *curés* were statutorily fixed. On 6th November all distinctions of rank were abolished and on 28th November all those who had hitherto enjoyed exemption were to be taxed retrospectively. It was difficult to see how the Order could in honesty profess "*une obéissance scrupuleuse aux nouvelles lois de police*" without radically altering its *ancienne constitution*.

The Treasurer in Malta was none other than Bosredon de Ransijat, the trouble-maker of the Chapter General. But he was an efficient financier and had ruthlessly overhauled the accounting machinery, checked wastage, carried out a complete assessment of every source of revenue and brought out annual accounts for public scrutiny for the first time in the Order's history. In 1788 he had produced a Ten Year Balance of Accounts, based on Necker's *compte-rendu*, which showed a small surplus every year. It was not dishonest book-keeping; the surplus was there but the accounts themselves hovered perpetually on the brink of non-payment. De Ransijat greeted the convention of the Estates General with enthusiasm, and was prepared to go much further than his superiors towards placating the National Assembly. It was clear to him that the Third Estate was bidding for control and, as a gesture towards them, he was prepared to lend France ten million Turin lire to be raised on credit. This would silence hostile criticism and make it easier for the King to preserve the Order in the possession of its lands. In addition the silver in the Hospital and the chandeliers in every chapel in the conventual church should be melted down and offered to the Assembly to assist it to base the new currency on silver, which had become scarce in France. This offer would be worth 100,000 scudi and could form part of the *Don Patriotique*. De Rohan did not feel that de Ransijat's proposal was either practical or useful; he was irked by de Ransijat's memoire submitted with the proposal that the Order should follow France's example and reform itself wholesale. De Rohan was suspicious of de Ransijat, still a member of the unofficial "Auvergnat Club" and in correspondence with Dolomieu in Rome. He was well aware of the list of abuses de Ransijat produced; it had been aired extensively during the Chapter General, but he resented most the attack the Treasurer launched against the Bailiffs *de grace*, to whom he attributed all the ills of the Order. The creatures around the throne have always been the first to come under fire, but de Rohan resented the implication that his creations were bad ones. For de Ransijat was sniping at the man whom many believed de Rohan was carefully grooming to be his successor—the Bailiff *de grace* de Loras.

Towards the end of 1789 de Ransijat's distrust was almost dramatically justified. In December of that year the Papal court, alarmed at the seditious murmurings in the city and convinced that France intended to export her revolution to Rome by means of the freemasons, raided the French Academy at Santa Trinità dei Monti and unearthed a Lodge among the French students, led by a Roman painter Agostino Belli. Belli claimed that the Lodge was in direct communication with those at Liège, Lyons, Milan, Naples, Paris and Malta. On the same night, 27th–28th December, the police arrested Cagliostro. Cagliostro had been publicly prophesying that the pontificate of Pius VI was to be the last and his séances were always well-attended. More than one had been held in the Villa Malta where Cardinal de Bernis himself had watched him turn water into Falernian wine and enlarge his Cardinalatial ring and heard him foretell with dark hints the Fall of the Bastille and the September March of the Women. Present with him were the Bailiffs de Breteuil and Antinori, a sprinkling of the Roman aristocracy and a Capuchin priest who became Cagliostro's one recruit for the Egyptian Lodge. De Loras had presented the entertainment.

Cagliostro's arrest drove the terrified de Loras to the protection of de Bernis, whose surprise at Cagliostro's prophecies had turned to a suspicion that someone, probably de Loras, had been communicating to him the contents of his state papers. De Bernis refused to receive him, and the wretched Bailiff turned to the mercy of the Cardinal Secretary of State, Zelada, who advised him to retire at once from Rome. To Dolomieu's disgust, who had hoped for the disgrace and demotion of de Loras after this dramatic espósé of his disreputable acquaintances, he was neither arrested nor denied entry to the Kingdom of Naples where freemasonry was resolutely banned. The departure of de Loras however meant that there was no point in Dolomieu's waiting in Rome, and he made his way back to Paris there to breathe the free air of his liberated country and to animadvert upon the tyranny he had forsaken in Malta.

There the Order's representatives were anxiously waiting for a decision on the amount of indemnification that should be paid for the lost *rentes foncières*. D'Estourmel, wanting to force the hand of the Assembly, proposed to withhold the second instalment of the *Don Patriotique* until compensation had been agreed, and de Virieu counselled against making another loan to an insatiable Assembly. On 29th July 1790, he made an impassioned appeal for a decision: at that moment the ships of the Order were cruising off Spain and "ensuring the freedom of traders and trade from attacks by Barbary pirates".

Into this debate Camus intervened with his usual cry. "The time has come for us to decide whether the Orders of the Holy Ghost, of St Lazarus, of St Louis, of Mount Carmel and of Malta are to continue." De Virieu's memoir was sent to a Committee of the National Assembly for a decision and on 11th August the Deputies Extraordinary, representing the manufacturing and commercial interests of France, delivered a report to the Assembly embodying the conclusions of the three Chambers of Commerce. Malta's free, solvent and un-trammelled survival was, according to them, of paramount importance to France. But the decision of the all-important committee, from which de Virieu hoped for so much, was delayed by pressure of more urgent business. Time was valuable and was being lost. Already in June a decree had been passed ordering an inventory to be made of movable and immovable goods in all hospitals, factories and public establish-ments in the country, and, though the Order was at first exempted, at a later sitting it was ordered to fall into line.

From Paris the scene now shifts to Marseilles where the stalwart old Receiver, de Foresta, held the fort. But for the unseemly quarrel of 1787, when on de Brillane's instance and Dolomieu's instigation, Cardinal Buoncompagno had held up his Grand Cross, he would have been one of those Bailiffs *de grace* to whom de Ransijat objected. No man better deserved the dignity. From the beginning he had strenuously cultivated the goodwill of the Marsilian merchants, but now in the Municipality of the city a party was growing that advocated the withdrawal of all support from the Maltese and the ex-ploitation of Corsica as an alternative naval base. The con-tinued good opinion of the Marsilian notables was all important and by June 1790 de Foresta had already spent 3,000 livres in charitable works, publicly in the name of the Hospitallers. It had had a good but not lasting effect. He was embarrassed by the compromising behaviour of the Prior of St Gilles and some other Knights who had been involved in the disturbances at Avignon in a way that could adequately be constructed as "counter-revolutionary". "It is extremely unfortunate for us that the Bailiff de Villefranche and the Commander de Montauroux have been singled out by name in the official reports, the first as general, the second as an accomplice in an aristocratic plot; as such they only escaped the anger of the people by a *miraculous* flight." At least he could congratulate himself on having refused the advice of his friends to seek an "inviolable and assured" asylum in the Papal enclave. The fates however seemed destined to work against him, for an event in Malta was that year to prejudice his whole position.

Chapter XV

SENTENCE OF DEATH

On the evening of 1st March 1790, Captain Joseph Segond, commander of a Marsilian merchantman, visiting Malta where his parents had a house on the Marina, turned out for a stroll along the water's edge. As it threatened rain, he carried his umbrella under his arm, the ferrule pointing before him, and at a narrow point in the road it inadvertently struck the shoulder of a figure that stood in his way shrouded in a deep cloak. In a moment the unknown had taken offence and after an exchange of offensive remarks he drew on the captain. For a quarter of an hour the Frenchman defended himself with his umbrella, but at last received a mortal wound. His assailant escaped into the dusk. Not a single bystander had dared to intervene, as they had heard the assassin declare over his dying victim that he was a Knight of Malta.

He was soon arrested, a Neapolitan Knight with the appropriate name of Mazzacarne. At the preliminary process it turned out that both men had been suing for the favours of a lady of the town and that Mazzacarne had waylaid his rival with the intention of disposing of him. The Complete Council sentenced him on 23rd March to loss of Habit and perpetual imprisonment. The Fiscal at once appealed to the *Sguardio*, demanding the death penalty that had been provided for at the last Chapter General. The appeal was upheld.

But the sentence was obstructed by the intervention of the Neapolitan minister, the Bailiff Pignatelli, who declared that the honour of all the Italian Knights was at stake if one of them were to swing for a mere merchant captain. The King of Naples, whose name was rashly invoked, requested a stay of execution on the grounds that Mazzacarne was an officer

of the Crown and must be degraded first, and General Acton
hinted forcefully that he considered this penalty enough. De
Rohan was very angry. Good relations with Marseilles
demanded the execution of Mazzacarne who had murdered the
man who, with his brother-in-law, had first persuaded the
Marseilles Chamber of Commerce to communicate its support
to the National Assembly. The defenders of Mazzacarne held
that if the supreme penalty were meted out for a *crime passionel*,
there would be no greater penalty for the more dastardly
premeditated murders. It was a legal point de Rohan appreciated but there was a stronger argument yet. He had just
written to the Italian courts one by one enlisting the support
of their ambassadors in Paris in his attempt to get the same
treatment in France as the German princes with lands in
Alsace. He little understood the helplessness of the Royal
ministry, but the support of the Neapolitan ambassador was,
of all the Italian ambassadors, the most important. Accordingly,
on 26th June, he made a fateful decision. "In obsequious
consideration of the venerated desires of His Sicilian Majesty,"
he commuted the sentence of life imprisonment. This satisfied
the Neapolitan court which had only been drawn into this by
the intemperance of Pignatelli, but it also lent substance to
those criticisms that de Foresta reported simultaneously from
Marseilles, that the Order was *"une pepinière des nobles, un
foyer de l'aristocratie."*

By July 1790 de Foresta sensed increasing hostility, and
redoubled his efforts to counteract it. When the Municipality
set up a *Bureau de Conciliation*, a voluntary, free court of
arbitration for long and ruinous cases, he offered his home for
its meetings. "The house of the *chargé d'affaires* of the Order of
Malta is the home for charity." At the same time he refused an
order to accept only specie in discharge of bills. "It is being
rumoured that the Receivers of the Order . . . have sucked
the country dry of silver crowns." He had no alternative but
to accept assignats in ever increasing quantities. D'Estourmel
was in the same boat: in Paris the assignat lost $5\frac{1}{2}$ per cent of
its value on issue. The Treasury in Malta wanted to call in

debts quickly in Spanish pistoles. At that critical moment, de Foresta explained, it was impossible to defy the lawful currency of the land. By the end of the year de Foresta could not help remarking that the enthusiasm for Malta's services to France's Levantine trade was waning and that the merchants with business in America and the Indies viewed without dismay the prospect of a decline in the trade of their rivals. By April 1791 it was possible for a motion to be moved in the Marseilles commune that "Malta was an indifferent subject for the commerce of France." It was, however, repudiated but not by a crushing majority.

So far the Order had been able to remain tolerably detached from French politics and the Republican attacks had not made the effect the Grand Master had feared. But small disputes occurred that continually brought it into the limelight. In Aix en Provence, the churches of the Order had become the refuge of non-juring priests who were able to celebrate Mass in defiance of the Civil Constitution of the Clergy. When the Municipality of Aix closed the prioral church, the Prior obtained an order from Paris to re-open it. In Paris itself, d'Estourmel was able to prevent the closure of the Churches of St. John Lateran and the Temple on the understanding that no baptisms, weddings or burials were performed there. In Toulouse a convent of Maltese nuns was ordered to provide a man to do his turn of duty in the suburb in which they lived and two conventual chaplains were called up for guard duty. The Receiver, the Commander de Montauzet, objected to the order, claiming diplomatic immunity but to little effect. The Convent was rudely troubled by municipal officers who entered it to make an inventory of its furniture and valuables. The woods of the Priory were nightly depredated. Protests went unheeded: the "people" of France was slowly discovering its power and the weakness of its prey.

Then, during the night of 20th and 21st June, Louis XVI and his family attempted to escape from Paris, only to be stopped at Varennes. The news of his arrest and the subsequent wave of fear and confusion that swept across France caused an excitation that showed how thin monarchical prestige had become throughout the land. About the flight to Varennes, there is much mysterious, including the part d'Estourmel was reported to have taken in it. Doublet affirmed that he had lent 1,200,000 francs from the Order's funds. The Bailiff de la Tour du Pin avers that it was only 12,000 francs. Whatever the truth, the news of the King's virtual arrest set off so violent an anti-French reaction in Malta that the French traders there requested a frigate from Marseilles to protect them. The Order had so far banked on the preservation of royal power in the composition of the ministries; but it was now obvious to the wise that the King could do nothing for Malta.

On 30th July 1791 the National Assembly declared that any Frenchman belonging to an Order of Chivalry founded on distinctions of birth would lose his French citizenship. D'Estourmel believed that this meant the eventual recognition of the Order's independent existence and of its possessions in France. But the imminent dissolution of the Assembly also meant the postponement of any decision on de Virieu's motion for the payment of compensation to the Order for its loss of feudal rights, as was being paid, on paper at least, to the German princes with lands in France.

The last action of the outgoing rump of the Estates General was to dissolve the Chambers of Commerce. The deputies for the new Legislative Assembly—who had none of them sat in the old—were of a more determined stamp. In the October session, the deputy for Blois, an ex-Capuchin called Charbot, proposed that the lands of the Order should be sold to back a new issue of assignats. Far from the prospect of any decision in its favour, the future looked blacker than ever.

In Malta the financial position was critical. On 2nd September the Treasury announced that there was only enough money in the *Conservatoria* to meet current expenses for two months. The credit account with the *Università* had been swallowed up in paying for corn. In France there was, it was true, a sum of a quarter of a million scudi, but unless it could be shipped to Genoa, it was useless and, owing to the high proportion of assignats making up this sum, there would be a loss of 21 per cent on the transfer. If the Order were not to go bankrupt and if it were to keep the battleship San Zaccaria and the two frigates at sea, money would have to be raised somehow. Accordingly a loan of 200,000 scudi was resolved upon, half to be raised in Genoa and half in Malta. News from France at the time was bewildering: the moneys of the Order, one rumour had it, were to be distrained to ransom French slaves in Algiers. (Much had been expected from the sudden Algerian war of 1790 when the San Zaccaria had been able to chase raiders off a rich Marsilian merchantman. The Chamber of Commerce had gratefully acknowledged the service but it counted for little now.) Marseilles itself was in turmoil and all the employees of the Order had fled, leaving de Foresta alone. Assignats were exchanging at a loss of 38 per cent in Paris and 60 per cent in the provinces, and this made it impossible to send on anything to underwrite the loan in Genoa. On 12th March 1792 Condorcet, an old friend of Dolomieu's, deputy for Paris and President of the Assembly, moved once more that the new assignats would have to be backed by the wealth of the Order.

D'Estourmel, grasping at straws, proposed from Paris on 10th January 1792 that another Chapter General be called. "There are incalculable resources in the brotherhood that unites all members of our Republic, and it is these that I should invoke in this crisis. I have a high enough opinion of everyone to believe that it would not be in vain; this hope sustains me in the appalling struggle I have to keep up." He told de Rohan that Dolomieu supported him in this. "He is well connected here, knowing several deputies, especially those foremost among the Feuillants, who are slowly beginning to prevail over the Jacobins in the Assembly."

Dolomieu had found the atmosphere of Paris bracing after his return from Rome in 1790. "To hold despotism fully in horror," he wrote to a fellow geologist, Lapeyrouse, "one must have seen it exercised in a place as small as Malta." At one time Dolomieu's name had been canvassed as a deputy for the Legislative Assembly, but he had not accepted nomination. For all his bitterness and supposed Jacobinism, he professed in fact a liberal royalism and claimed to be a member of the '89 Club though his name is not to be found on the lists. Dolomieu did not desire the extinction of the Order; he was always short of money and lived in hopes that in time his true deserts would be recognized and he would be rewarded with a rich commandery. His younger brother, Casimir, was then in Malta doing his caravans and running up gambling debts which he was forced to pay, and his uncle, Guy-Joseph, was living out his days in a modest comfort which his nephew hoped would last his life. He was quite ready to do what he could to plead the Order's case, but before he could do so the Assembly forced the King to declare war on Prussia and the Empire.

The Order's position was now more delicate than ever. If it made one move that could be interpreted as hostile, its affairs would be brought to the fore and settled by a busy and determined Assembly. De Rohan had to tread carefully. In April, Flachslanden, now an émigré, had thrown himself wholeheartedly into the cause of the Bourbon royal princes and asked the Grand Master for ships and men to provide an expeditionary force against Provence. De Rohan refused outright, but, as Dolomieu wrote to the Chevalier de Fay in Malta on 22nd March 1792, "the role of the great number of our Knights in Germany has caused such disfavour to our cause that it will need great courage to defend it when it comes on the agenda."

The émigrés in the Rhenish principalities were loud with bitter complaints that the Grand Master's ministers in Paris were basely negotiating with the enemies of throne and altar. De Rohan showed that he was satisfied with the stand they were taking by dismissing another of Flachslanden's proposals for a Maltese attack on French Levantine shipping should the lands be lost. It was hard to refuse him so brusquely; Flachslanden had done useful service in his time but he was now an embarrassment. Another was the Commander de Maisonneuve whom de Rohan had accredited to Berlin to negotiate a more satisfactory arrangement with the Prussian court over the commanderies in Silesia and to keep a watchful eye on the affairs of the Polish Priory. But as soon as the Revolution had broken out Maisonneuve had forsaken his post and returned to France, there to contract, with Papal dispensation, an unfortunate marriage with the niece of de Rohan's old crony, the Bailiff de Belmont. Without reference to Malta he had then accepted an appointment as Louis XVI's minister to the Princes of Swabia and he had gone to take up his residence in Würtembourg—"surely," wrote Dolomieu, "the realm of intrigues." With the outbreak of war he became peripatetic and no one knew where he was. Meanwhile there was no one in Berlin.

On 20th July occurred the first attack on the Tuileries, the news of which caused even Doublet to write: "*Nous en sommes consternés, anéantis.*" But d'Estourmel still reported that they were not staring expropriation in the face; the Assembly was prepared to discuss a redistribution of commanderies into equal units among the Departments, rather like the reorganization of the bishoprics. They were also considering a new formula for admitting Knights on more democratic lines. De Rohan did not discourage this; negotiation was better than spoliation. But he was not altogether happy about what his subordinates were doing in Paris. When the German powers decided to meet at Rastadt, de Virieu, to de Rohan's displeasure, appointed the Commander d'Hauteville, an émigré, as his representative. This could be construed as an act of hostility. Besides, de Rohan had his own unofficial itinerant envoy in the Chevalier de Mayer, Baron von Knonau, an Alsatian, German-speaking member of the Tongue of France, once in the service of the Comte d'Artois. He had pamphleteered vigorously for the Order in 1790 and was believed, quite falsely, to have been responsible for convincing the National Assembly that the lands of the Order should remain inviolate. In gratitude de Rohan gave Mayer a pension of 2,000 scudi and a diamond cross. Mayer accepted both with a coolness that displeased the Grand Master, and now with letters of recommendation in his pocket, he was touring the European courts, helping himself freely from the *caisses* of the various Receivers to cover his expenses. His job was to convince the German princes and the Emperor of the reasons why Malta was unable to assist the common cause and to obtain from them the usual safeguards promising to respect the lands of the Order through which the invading armies might have to pass. De Rohan was beginning to have an uneasy suspicion that he had chosen his man badly.

In fact, at this crisis, there was no one whose judgment or integrity he could trust. The only diplomat in the Order, now that Sagramoso was dead, was in virtual hiding in the Kingdom of Naples, and the effects of diplomatic impotence were beginning to be felt outside France. In Maisonneuve's absence from Berlin, the Silesian Knights refused once again to pay their responsions and were supported in their refusal by an indulgent court. Maisonneuve himself regretted his inability to leave his post until his King commanded and de Rohan, trying to make do with the material to hand, ordered Mayer to proceed to Berlin to straighten this tangle out and then to go on to St Petersburg to see what could be done about the almost defunct Polish Priory. Though there was little enthusiasm for Russia in the Venerable Council, Mayer in his reply to this commission represented the feelings of many of the émigrés: "Russia is now our diplomatic orient, and from her comes the light, faint it is true, and false, but seeing that it has lit up the horizon we must follow where it leads." But Mayer for all his fine words did not care to brave the hazards of a journey to St Petersburg and he made no preparations to go.

From France, de Foresta, a Grand Cross at last, sent back dispiriting news. Most of the Knights in the south had fled, the commanderies in Arles had been devastated by a minor civil war and a clash had occurred in the church of St John when the Marseilles municipal officers had attempted to insert juring priests to conduct the services. The last had brought the Hospitallers into unhappy prominence. Then on 10th August a mob raised by the Paris Commune under Danton stormed the Tuileries for a second time and ransacked the Palace, while the King fled for his life to the Assembly. That night he was suspended from his functions. D'Estourmel, who had rushed sword in hand to the scene of slaughter, returned the next day in a state of nervous exhaustion. "All is lost!" he cried to the Marquis de Moleville, who met him coming back. "The King is in their hands. We shall never see him again." On the night of 14th August, after a light supper in the Hotel of the Grand Prior of France, the royal family was admitted to the tower of the Temple *enclos* whence Louis only emerged for his trial and execution. The hotel was deserted, as the Grand Prior, his father and his *locum tenens* were all émigrés. D'Estourmel protested against the violation of the Order's sovereign property but the Assembly no longer viewed it as having any.

By the end of the month de Virieu had given up. He applied for his passport as Minister for the Duke of Parma and took the émigré route for Geneva. The armies of Brunswick lumbered forward; money was desperately short. On 28th July the deputy La Croix announced that in his opinion the Order's property would underwrite an issue of three million assignats. It was only a question of time before the blow fell. It came on 19th September when the deputy Vincent moved that the Order's land and property be forfeited to the state: the motion at long last was passed. D'Estourmel was arrested, his papers seized and sealed. "It was without doubt written in the decrees of Providence," he wrote in one of his last letters to Malta, "that no ancient institution should escape the destructive system that has possessed the guiding minds of this unhappy Empire. Perhaps it is written in the sacred book that abuses now being at their height it is necessary for nothing to escape the scythe of time, so that the regeneration may be more complete." It was all the comfort he could offer: he had written to the other Receivers that they must bow to the law, but resist any attempt to make the confiscations and sequestrations retroactive.

It was a month before the decree became law and d'Estourmel had the cold comfort of knowing that the personal property of the Hospitallers was immune as long as they were not émigrés. He left Paris as soon as his papers had been sealed, for a short rest in Picardy. He returned at the end of October to supervise the execution of the decree. "The dignity with which the Order conducts itself under these vicissitudes may, it is true, diminish its resources," he wrote, "but it will gain the esteem and admiration of all Europe. We shall know how to demonstrate that, for the Knights of Malta, honour is the highest law. This will be the noblest way in which to seek revenge upon our detractors and upon the envious lovers of reform."

There was nothing else they could do.

Though the decree was final, de Rohan decided to do nothing to anger the new Republic. No official protest was made in Paris; d'Estourmel tamely capitulated, still suggesting half-heartedly that a Chapter General might find a solution to the loss of the French revenues. De Virieu, now in Vevey, near Lake Geneva, wrote to Mayer wishing him luck in St Petersburg whither Mayer had no intention of going, "I have always had a soft spot for that rare woman [the Czarina]. I don't know if she still entertains her old ideas on the assistance our island can offer her commerce and marine." His part was played. D'Estourmel was unable to stop the government seizing all the money in the coffers: he merely added to the inventory a signed statement refusing to accept the loss of the Order's rights and properties in France. He announced his intention of returning and vanished from the scene. His last action was to help out of his own pocket some distressed nuns of the Order. He was a generous man, with the true instincts of a nobleman, but he had been defeated from the start.

Cibon alone stayed at the Embassy. Upon his own initiative he kept up a correspondence with Doublet, that is now lost, and de Rohan was content that it should be so. While confiscating the Order's lands, the Republican government did not want to lose the facilities of Malta as a base—while she wanted this, there was always a chance of keeping a door open for negotiations. The Grand Master persuaded his Council not to sequestrate some French merchantmen from Smyrna then lying in Grand Harbour with cargoes valued at 50,000 francs. Frenchmen were to enjoy the same treatment in Malta that they had always received. The guns of Malta would not be turned upon her co-religionists however great the provocation.

Fortunately, just before the *Loi Spoliateur* had been gazetted, de Foresta had managed to ship 156,000 francs to Genoa. This remarkable achievement inspired the Council to send him to Paris to negotiate. He had three alternative briefs; first, he could suggest a compromise by which the Order would waive proofs and accept recommendations from the French Government of soldiers and sailors who might enjoy their commanderies as pensions, as long as they took an oath of celibacy. If that were refused, he should request a lump sum payment in recompense for the loss of the lands in return for which Malta would grant her accustomed facilities to the French. At the worst, he was to state that the Order refused to accept the *Loi Spoliateur* as contrary to the *Droits des Gens et des Nations*.

De Foresta left Marseilles in January 1793 and arrived shortly after the King's execution. Advised by Cibon to leave at once, as his life was in danger, he managed to slip out of the city but was delayed at Lyons by an insurrection. On reaching Marseilles again, he was told that his passport contained a discrepancy in the dates and was arrested as a returned émigré. He was released, however, upon the intercession of several important merchants, who had persuaded the Committee of Public Safety in the city to send him to Malta to negotiate the foundation of an *Entrepôt* where corn could be stored from the Levant to be used to offset the recurrent food shortages in France. Robespierre, on learning of the mission and believing that it was a disguised emigration, ordered de Foresta's arrest and repatriation by the French consul in Genoa. He was accordingly seized on disembarking, but saved from repatriation by the *coup d'état* of 9th Thermidor. He was stuck in Genoa for a year, unable to move, and released on parole, while the younger émigrés in Malta who knew that he had enlisted in the National Guard and thus considered him a traitor, threatened to lynch him if he ever set foot on the island.

De Rohan was now confused and uncertain. The number of destitute Knights trickling into Malta grew larger every month. "He allows himself to be eaten out of house and home," wrote his nephew, the Prince Camille, now ambassador in Rome. His salary reduced to 4,000 scudi a year, Camille had been forced to his disgust to sell all his horses, dismiss his servants and reduce himself to such poverty that he could "scarcely offer anyone a glass of water." Unable to cut the figure he wanted, the poor relation among the embassies, he had proposed raising a Regiment de Rohan to join Condé, but he had been prevented by the refusal of the Roman Government to give arms to foreigners. His uncle, however, merely ordered his household "to take care that I have one scudo a day for the expenses of my table and distribute the rest to my distressed brothers."

In order to save money, the crews of the galleys were cut down, rations reduced and clerical staff dismissed, but the deficit for 1793 was over 400,000 scudi and the *Conservatorià* had only 156,000 in hand. Work in the arsenal ceased; the Regiment was pruned. It only added to the growing number of unemployed in the island. In the Hospital free treatment for all and sundry was abandoned, diets were reduced to an earlier austerity, Alicante wine was no longer to be prescribed, malingerers were turned out. Poverty is a hard master and swept like a gale through the most hard grained benevolence.

A number of Knights whose personal fortunes had so far been unaffected lent money without interest to the tune of 80,000 scudi, to which the three convents of *Dames Maltaises* in Spain contributed 18,000. Two trusts were dissolved and released another 119,721 scudi and on 20th November, the *San Zaccaria* took the first prize for many years—a Tunisian pink with a crew of 63. To the bitter end, creaking in the timbers, the battleship and the two frigates, *Santa Elisabeta* and *Santa Maria*, the patronal galley and the four *sensile* galleys still went out to sea, but prey constantly eluded them. In 1795 two galleys had to be laid up and de Rohan purchased two papal substitutes cheaply, almost as old. But the expense was a dreadful strain. On 2nd June 1795 he raised another loan of 100,000 scudi to support the émigrés by mortgaging his magistral commanderies. In November all penions were cancelled. The silver from the Hospital and the ships, worth 28,000 scudi, was melted down; allowances to Ambassadors and Receivers were cut by half.

So much had St John depended on His Most Christian Majesty. Evil days were now upon them all.

Chapter XVI

COMMERCE WITH A CZAR

IN 1793 the Priory of Poland was almost completely disrupted by the 2nd Partition of the Republic. Hard on the disasters of the time, the imminent demise of this anaemic foundation seemed almost unimportant. De Rohan had no one to send to St Petersburg; Mayer's pension had ceased along with all the others and the angry commander had arrived in Vienna to demand that some of the Order's goods in the Empire should be sequestrated to meet it. De Rohan, bitterly disappointed in the selfish greed of his protégé, cancelled his letters of credit to Russia and appointed Maisonneuve instead. Maisonneuve had recently atoned for his offence in de Rohan's eyes by applying to the Committee of Public Safety for permission to re-enter France. It was a brave decision for an émigré, but the permit was refused, and he was instructed to go to St. Petersburg instead and to request the Czarina's protection for the remains of the Priority of Poland.

Despite Malta's refusal to receive accredited *chargés d'affaires* from the Russian Empire, Catherine still felt genially disposed towards the island and its rulers. In 1787 when Catherine and Joseph II had had their historic meeting at Kerson in the Crimea, Psaro made the long journey from Malta bearing a laurel crown with a suitable inscription from the Grand Master. Catherine acknowledged the gift by ordering it to be placed on the mizzen of the Admiral's flagship. The graceful tribute was not lost on her. The following year she sent two requests: the first reaching de Rohan by the hand of a Russian merchant captain proposed a joint attack on Turkish merchantmen. The second, coming through official diplomatic channels, requested the loan of a Knight of

Malta to help train a new galley squadron for the Baltic
fleet. De Rohan refused to grant the first, but granted the
second.

His choice fell on a twenty-five-year-old Milanese, Count
Giulio Litta, son of a Commissar-General of the Austrian
army in Lombardy, and grandson of an Imperial viceroy in
Naples. Litta's brother was a rising *monsignore*, being groomed
for the Papal diplomatic service. He himself was a handsome,
intrepid young man, one of the brightest alumni of the
Clementine College in Rome. He had been professed when
nineteen in 1782, and at 22 he was Captain of the Magistral
Galley. De Rohan had marked him out as a rising star.

Litta reached St Petersburg in 1789, and Catherine was en-
chanted by his manly beauty. Here was a second Algarotti!
He was invited, favour of favours, to form one of her party
at the theatre; he was received—significant event—with great
ado by the Czarevich Paul, and the canny Austrian minister,
Cobenzl, took him under his wing.

Litta did not disappoint his superiors. He was promoted
major-general of a light flotilla, with a special allowance to
double his pay. He was the youngest general in the Russian
service and at the Battle of Svenskund against Sweden in 1790
he saved the disorganized Russian centre by attacking the
Swedish flagship. He was promoted to Counter-Admiral and
decorated with the Order of St George (1st Class). By 1790,
pleading the extremities of the climate, he was permitted to
return to Malta where his reception was excellent. "If the
Order," Catherine wrote in January 1792, "feels an inclination for me, then truly it is not a vain one. For there is no one
who prizes more, nor loves with more passion than I those
valiant and pious Knights. Every Knight of Malta has always
been an object of worship, so that if I knew of any way in
which I might be of use to the Order, I should follow it with
all my heart." Popularly supposed to have been something
more than useful at the Court of the Semiramis of the North,
Litta was created a Bailiff in 1792—still under age for such a
decoration—and when in 1794 his brother Lorenzo was

appointed Apostolic Nuncio to Warsaw, he accompanied him
to the capital to attend his inauguration.

Maisonneuve's mission to St Petersburg never materialized.
He had temporarily disappeared and was only to make his way
to Russia later. And in Malta, so complete was her diplomatic
isolation that the first the British consul heard of France's
declaration of war on England was the reported statement of
a French merchant captain to an English: "Don't worry if we
take you prisoner, because we'll treat you well. All the humble
people are with us and we shall get them to chop your King's
head off, as we have ours."

The English consul now was called, appropriately, William
England. He had reached Malta as a youth on board a privateer
and been taken into the Grand Master's household. The aged
Consul, Angelo Rutter, Dodsworth's successor, had died in
1788, incompetent to the last and so ignorant of English that
he could not spell Stanley Porter any better than Stanier
Porten. In 1789 the Marquess of Caernavon, exercised by the
absence of a consul in an island where an increasing number
of British ships were calling, begged de Rohan to appoint one
and the Grand Master, finding England to hand, appointed
him. But London was not really interested in Malta. It took five
years for the patent, which de Rohan had decided he would
permit, to reach England, and at no time did he get the salary
he incessantly solicited. Without a monthly subvention from
de Rohan's pocket of £4, he would have starved.

In September 1793, England, now a Donat of the Order,
submitted a confidential report to Lord Grenville which was a
shrewd estimation of the results of the *Loi Spoliateur*. The loss
of the French revenues, he said, might well drive the Order
to negotiate with one or other of the great maritime powers
for protection, implying the disposal of the land and sea forces
and of the island itself by the contracting power. If that power
were France, she would be able to control the whole trade of
the Mediterranean as the Danes did of the Baltic. If it were
Russia, she would secure her commercial trade in the central
Mediterranean, find a great warehouse for her goods, and

lazarettos for her Turkey trade. In time of war the advantages of Malta were incalculable. "There's reason to think," he concluded, "that France would sooner submit to see the island in the possession of Great Britain than of Russia and that Russia would give us the same sort of preference over France."

The report was ignored, but in November H.M.S. *Captain* arrived in Malta with despatches from Admiral Hood. Needing men to man his ships while he sent his sailors ashore to hold Toulon, the Commander-in-Chief offered de Rohan His Britannic Majesty's protection in return for the loan of 1500 seamen. Simultaneously a Mediterranean convoy of 40 sail reached the island, mostly of British and Dutch vessels requiring supplies. The declaration of war on France by Naples in September had made it possible for de Rohan to refuse the French entry to the harbour and to admit allied shipping. The convoy stayed until 5th January 1794, but the laws of neutrality forbade enrolment of Maltese on board belligerent vessels. Times, however, were changed. There were three hundred sailors idle in the island; there was a strong school of thought that held that Malta was justified in taking part in the war. De Rohan, therefore, proceeded to permit the surreptitious enrolment of 414 men on H.M.S. *Aurora*, with a month's pay in advance. The party of neutrality regretted this move, for it weakened Malta's bargaining power with France should a chance of negotiation occur for a return of lands. "England," Doublet wrote to de Virieu in Lausanne on 20th August 1795, "is trying in her Machiavellian way to force us to compromise our neutrality." She was not concerned with re-establishing Louis XVIII but with destroying French naval power. Had she not shown this at Toulon when she refused the help of the émigrés under the Comte de Provence? Malta would be foolish to aid and abet her in this.

In 1795 the hopes of the peace party revived. News that Spain and Naples were withdrawing from the war and that a Conference had been called at Basle induced de Rohan to reconsider sending an official envoy to Paris. The hopes of accommodation were slender, but despite economies, the financial position only worsened from year to year. "When the five non-French Tongues prove quite insensible to the penury of the Treasury," Doublet wrote to de Virieu, "and when the Grand Master refuses to suppress institutions to economize, how can one jib at authorizing an agent to claim from France the justice that is our due?" De Rohan could make no more economies without throwing more faithful servants of the Order on the streets, and only one other Knight, the Spanish Perez de Sarrio, was prepared to beggar himself to maintain his fellows. On 13th July 1796 the Sacred Council approved the nomination of Cibon as Minister Plenipotentiary to the French Republic.

Cibon was not a member of the Order, but for four years he had stayed at his desk, for no salary at all, running the risk of arrest, to keep de Rohan, via Doublet, informed of the affairs of the capital. There was no one better qualified for the business at hand. De Foresta was suspect in Malta as a collaborator, and suspect in France as an émigré. The Bailiff de Saint-Simon who had stayed in Paris all along enjoyed ill-health. Maisonneuve was a listed émigré, de Virieu had no wish to go back. D'Estourmel was believed to have muffed his job in 1792; the Chevalier d'Hannonville, ex-Receiver in Nancy and one of the few Knights still in France, had gone to ground. De Rohan had written to both General Washington, George himself, and the U.S. minister in Paris, the future President Monroe, to ask them to do what they could now that peace-making was in the air, but in the end there was only Cibon: no doubt the ex-secretary fancied himself as an *eminence grise*, but without doubt, he more than anyone else understood the mentality of the Revolutionary government.

When Godoy, now Prince of the Peace, sent the Marques del Campo to Paris as the new Spanish Ambassador, Cibon was advised to put himself under his protection and guidance as Minister Plenipotentiary. D'Hannonville, who had suddenly come to surface as soon as he had heard he was wanted, had produced a printed address to the Council of Five Hundred on the claims of the Order. He was designated as Ambassador, but instructed to wait and see if an Ambassador Extraordinary were called for. Cibon's hands were tied by the necessity always to consult Saint-Simon, but he was to stress to the government the exemplary conduct of the Order towards France despite every inducement to behave contrarily. As the war party had suspected, the Embassy did nothing more than remind the Directorate that Malta's future had not been decided.

While this intricate and abortive manœuvre was in progress, de Rohan made a reluctant decision. In May 1794 the invasions had begun that were to wipe Poland off the map. The Estates of Ostrog became part of the Russian Empire: it was in Catherine's power to rejuvenate or extinguish for ever the dying Priory. Reluctant to part with any of the few men he trusted, de Rohan decided to send Giulio Litta back to Russia. He was conveniently near, still at his brother's Nunciature in Warsaw, so that in October, 1795, he was once again in the Russian capital. But Catherine, though pleased to see the agreeable young man, was ageing rapidly. The all-powerful Ostermann, fiercely orthodox and suspicious of Poles and Poland, made no attempt to move matters forward and when during the autumn a Maltese corsair inadvertently attacked a Turkish vessel flying the Russian flag, Catherine was glad enough to suspend all negotiations.

Then on 16th November Catherine died to be succeeded by her son the Czar Paul I. For long overshadowed by his masterful mother, his parentage impugned by the enemies of his father, Paul had waited for his turn. It had now come. Of a warm, romantic disposition, he had been shocked by the blatant cynicism of his mother and the remorseless intrigues of Russian politics. He was devout where his mother was Voltairian, he was dreamy where his mother was hard-headed. He was unimpressed by the slovenly life of greater Russia and by the tortuous mysteries performed daily at Russian altars. He was a devout member of his Church, but his travels in Europe in 1782, his audiences with the astute and courteous Pius VI, his friendly and intelligent reception by the Princes of the

Roman church, had instructed him that though the courts of Europe were materialist and the Roman church in schism, both were immeasurably more modern and gentlemanly than those of his own country. Paul was impressed, too, by the cult of the gentleman. European manners were good, its protocol restrained, its civilization at the apogee of courtliness and style. Much of his dislike for the French revolution, not untinged with reluctant admiration, was for its *sansculottisme*. As a young man he had been a devotee of the Chivalric romances: in the cult of the aristocrat, brave, chivalrous and devout, in its application to still semi-barbarous Russia, Paul could rule over a court that would be a rival to the gilded splendours he had witnessed in Europe. What more obvious model than the Knights of Malta, of whom the graceful and refined Giulio Litta was the worthy embodiment, waiting with his suit at the very doors of the council chamber! The works of Vertot had been bedside reading since earliest childhood: the sea and sailing had had a fascination for him from boyhood which had accompanied him into man's estate. As Grand Admiral of Russia, he had formed and drilled a special battalion of marines on his summer estate at Gatchina, staging mock battles on the lake, directing operations himself. An Order, at once chivalric and marine, was begging his Imperial favour.

Paul intended to shine in the brittle brilliance of his Arctic summer with a prodigal display of generosity and wealth. A new age had dawned, Kosciusko, the Polish rebel was released from prison with a pension; Stanislas Augustus was received at court with royal honours; Lorenzo Litta was summoned from Warsaw to be Apostolic Nuncio at St Petersburg and to negotiate a hierarchy for the millions of new Catholic subjects of the Liberal Czar. And on 15th January 1797 Paul put his signature to a document that was to change the destiny of his reign and to rock Europe with its echo, heard even above the orchestrated trumpets of Bonaparte. In it Paul decreed the establishment of a Russian Priory.

The Czar allotted for its revenues certain crown lands in Poland, to provide the money to maintain a Grand Prior and ten Commanders. Responsions were fixed at 41,000 florins a year. In all things the Russian priory, to be incorporated into the Anglo-Bavarian Tongue, would follow its Polish predecessor exactly, except one. The Czar, faithful to his oldest love of pageant, intended to devise a special uniform for the Russian Knights. In addition, Paul was prepared to make up all the arrears of the Polish Priory—now some 96,000 florins —and in subsequent articles he endowed three further commanderies for Conventual Chaplains and increased the responsions to a new total of 53,000 florins.

It was Litta's coup. At once a courier, the Chevalier Raczynski, was despatched to Malta for de Rohan's signature. But on setting foot in Ancona, where he was believed to be well out of range of the French army, his bags were seized and his papers searched by a flying squadron that arrived simultaneously in the city. Their contents were sent to the general in Milan, Raczynski had to return to St Petersburg for another copy, and Paul burning to set up the Priory with all pomp and circumstance was forced to wait another six months. The news was all over Paris before the courier reached Malta, but two days before he arrived, the battered and disappointed Grand Master was dead.

Chapter XVII

A GERMAN AND A SPY

DE Rohan died on 13th July 1797, overcome with fatigue, having never properly recovered from a paralytic stroke in 1791; for the last few months of his reign, the genial Belmont had ruled as his Lieutenant. The Prince de Rohan died a poor man. He had a few creditors and a multitude of debtors, among whom were d'Estourmel, de Freslon, de Suffren—now dead— de Ransijat, Litta and von Hompesch, who alone owed him 21,000 scudi. Friends and enemies alike had benefited from his generosity. The source of his wealth had been stopped by the Revolution and he had had to raise credits from the *Douane*. He had continued to appoint Knights to commanderies that no longer existed in order to give the men who had borrowed money from him an honourable basis to their pledges of repayment. By the revolutionary government this sweet tact was called an act of provocation. He left a little to private charities and to Masses for his soul. In haste and penury the masons in the conventual church tried to give him a mausoleum worthy of his name, but the bronze bust was roughly cast and the tomb of the noblest of the Grand Masters is among the poorest in the church.

De Rohan's reign had ranged from grandeur to poverty. He had aspired to a dignity that had turned to wormwood. He had inherited the machinery of Pinto and learned that, in a period of declining resources and enforced inactivity, discipline alone could keep the Order together. Authority had robbed him of his friends and thrown him on to the support of men like de Loras who were prepared to defend the establishment but not revivify it. He was the last Grand Master to reign and before his death the temporal power of Malta had become a cypher: the opposition of Rome, the interference of Naples, the abandonment by France had defeated him. The times were against him, and he was too good-natured, too meticulously honest to set them right. Selfishness, greed, sycophancy and intrigue thrived on inertia and by 1797 he had known that it was only a question of time before one of the protecting powers revoked the tolerance of two centuries and a half and took the island for her own use.

On 26th May, a few weeks before de Rohan's final agony, Bonaparte wrote to the Directors in Paris proposing that, as a German was almost certain to be his successor, 500,000 to 600,000 francs should be spent on securing a Spaniard. Godoy, the Prince of the Peace, might fancy the post. "Valetta has 37,000 inhabitants extremely well disposed towards the French —there are no more English in the Mediterranean," he wrote. "Why should not our fleet (or that of Spain) on its way to the Atlantic pass in that direction and capture it. . . . This small island is priceless to us."

Godoy could not be persuaded to abandon his vaster ambitions for a title without power and a vow of celibacy, however nominal. But the withdrawal of the British fleet from the Mediterranean in November 1796 laid Malta open to assault. In a last desperate move the electors voted without dissension for the Bailiff of Brandenburg, Ferdinand von Hompesch.

Von Hompesch was not a negligible person, but he had, as the Emperor's minister, interpreted the unwillingness of the German priories to co-operate with the Grand Masters. He had supported them in their refusal to pay the increased responsions voted by the Chapter General; he had stoutly refused to consider incorporating the Polish Priory into the German Tongue. In 1793 only one German Knight had responded to the request for help from the Treasury and he was Count von Thurn, Lieutenant of the Grand Bailiff, who contributed 1000 scudi. Von Hompesch gave nothing, yet he was receiving in addition to his commanderies a handsome pension granted him by de Rohan.

The election of von Hompesch, the only German Grand Master, was in default of alternative candidates. He had been a liberal Bailiff and had founded from his own pocket—or de Rohan's loans—a *casale* which bears his name to this day despite the almost universal contempt in which the modern Maltese hold him. And he spent freely while the election was in doubt. William England reported to Grenville on 20th July 1797 that the Maltese had proclaimed him Grand Master before de Rohan's death and that a revolution must have followed had he not been elected. Certainly von Hompesch entered upon the magistracy considerably in debt: he was accustomed to live on credit and owed 12,000 scudi alone to the *Monte di Pietà*. He made much of being the Emperor's protegé, and the egregious Bishop of Chersonnese, the Abbé Hoeffln, one of the secret architects of the Bavarian priory, led a large number of Bavarian Knights to Malta when it was known that de Rohan would not live. On the *Bavière*, the Inn of their Tongue, the outraged Bailiff de la Tour du Pin saw among the triumphant illuminations, the signs and symbols of the masonic brotherhood. The Bailiff firmly believed that von Hompesch abandoned Malta because he had been so instructed by the German lodges.

Von Hompesch was only fifty-four, comparatively young. Immediately upon his election his portrait was painted, elegantly attired in a suit of armour, with his lithe, athletic body poised gracefully in a skin tight corselet and greaves. His first action was to communicate the news of his election in most respectful terms to "the Citizen Directors" recommending to their attention his *chargé d'affaires*, Cibon. But he received no reply, only a disquieting rumour from Vienna that Napoleon had informed Talleyrand that Malta should be occupied by the French.

Talleyrand, impressed by his exile in the United States that France's greatest failure in the eighteenth century had been the loss of her American colonies, was now advancing a project of his own, i.e. the seizure of Egypt. Von Hompesch's election, arguing Austrian designs on Malta, made it imperative to seize the island as a prologue. Vienna had bargained at Campo

Formio for Venetia and she had seized Ragusa. Her influence in Naples was paramount. If she were in possession of Malta, her proposed partition of the Balkans with Russia would be greatly facilitated. Talleyrand saw the ghost of Czeremetev rising mist-like from the grave and Perellos' successor in Malta—unless France acted soon—would be the young Emperor, Francis II.

Talleyrand's skilful mind weaved a web from rumours and intrigue. Malta, he told Bonaparte on 27th September, was a hive of Austrian, Russian and English spies. The General was empowered to instruct Admiral de Brueys to forestall the Austrians and to seize the island. But de Brueys was in Corfu, refurbishing the recently acquired Venetian battlefleet, and could do nothing until the Spring. So Bonaparte decided to spy out the land.

He used as his agents a Maltese and a Frenchman. The Maltese, Vincenzo Barbara, had in April 1797 been involved in an obscure plot to steal firearms and powder from the arsenal in Casal Pinto. His accomplice was none other than the Oriental scholar and incumbent of the University Chair, Antonio Vassalli. Vassalli had disappeared into a dungeon in Fort Ricasoli, Barbara and eight others into exile for life. Von Hompesch, who appreciated Vassalli's researches into the Maltese he himself spoke so well, had exchanged his durance vile for a more comfortable room. But the farmers, who had been implicated as a body in the plot, were murmuring among themselves that they were being paid in debased coinage for their compulsory deliveries of foodstuffs; the new Grand Master set about appeasing the countryside. In the meantime Barbara had made his way to Milan and been ushered into the presence of Bonaparte. When the two frigates, *L'Artemis* and *La Justice*, called in on Malta on their way to Corfu on 27th December, Barbara was landed by night and the French agent, officially, by day. He was none other than the cousin of the Guardian of the Port himself, who shared the same name, Poussielgue. As First Secretary of the French Legation at Genoa he had written *The History of the Revolution in Genoa* and was now on an "official" mission to inspect the sea-ports of the Levant; his unofficial mission was to make contact with the disaffected Knights whose names Barbara had given Bonaparte. The list included de Ransijat, de Fay, a Spaniard Bardonenche, St Priest, all Knights, and Toussard, a Servant-at-Arms. Of the French "colony" he was instructed to sound out Caruson, an ex-clerk of the office promoted when the *chargé d'affaires* refused to serve the regicides, Eynaud, an ex-Royalist who had first come to Malta as a purveyor for His Most Christian Majesty's ships, Poussielgue, the Guardian of the Port, and Doublet himself.

Poussielgue stayed four months and reported by letter to Bonaparte on 24th February 1798. He told him how he had been received amiably by the Grand Master but had failed to penetrate his reserve. Von Hompesch was undeniably popular and he had behaved discreetly to all and sundry, particularly to the French émigrés, whom he had arranged to keep as had de Rohan. He had gone to great lengths to revive the pomps and ceremonies of an earlier epoch now fallen into desuetude, "which by their puerility have astonished even the Knights of the Order." Of the three or four hundred French Knights in Malta only a score seemed at all favourably disposed towards the Republic. The Grand Master, if the island were attacked, would rely on the émigrés to defend it, knowing that they had nothing to hope for from France. It was different for the more prosperous of the Maltese; they had nothing more to hope for from the Knights. A surprise attack, however, was out of the question; a diplomatic coup might do the trick. Spain might be persuaded to sequester all the commanderies in her realm and the Pope, now an ailing prisoner in Florence, be induced to suppress the Order and allot its lands to the monarchs of Europe who would be glad of them. Von Hompesch could then be offered a pension or a principality and the payment of his debts which were considerable. The French Knights would have to be accommodated or they would fight to the last. But he was convinced that they would rather lose the island to the French than to the English.

Von Hompesch, according to Poussielgue, was behaving with considerable skill. In reality—and this was what Poussielgue did not see—he was living in cloud cuckoo land, spending money that was not his, hoping by a show of confidence and serenity to stave off the evil day. He had some grounds for optimism. Russian protection was assured as soon as Raczynski reached St Petersburg with von Hompesch's signature to the foundation deed of the Russian Priory. With him he carried two of the most treasured relics of the Order, the silver crosses of de l'Isle Adam and la Valette which had hitherto lain in the chapel of Our Lady of Philermos in the conventual church. With these Litta was to decorate the Czar and Czarina, when as Ambassador Extraordinary he waited upon their Imperial Majesties with a message of thanks.

But Paul had not saved the Order; he had merely replaced a moribund Priory by a more lively one. Von Hompesch hoped to survive under Russian protection. In December, Litta presented the Crosses to a delighted Czar. "This august symbol, this revered mark of our Order, the memory of our ancestors, the example and valour of the Knights of Malta will, Sire, excite among the illustrious, brave and faithful nobility to your Empire an emulation and enthusiasm worthy of the greatest centuries of chivalry." Before the entire diplomatic corps of the capital, the Czar bestowed upon his wife, his sons and his chief ministers Crosses of Devotion with his own hands. It was an augury for the future.

Paul's nominee for the Grand Priory arrived in November. He was a figure well known in Europe, detested by the revolutionaries, admired by the émigrés, an exile of the exiles, warrior of the warriors, Knight of the Knights, Louis Joseph de Bourbon, the Prince de Condé. Condé's army had already had a chequered career, and he himself had passed from English to Austrian pay and from Austrian to Russian. He had been disappointed, disillusioned and unsuccessful, for his fate was to fight against his countrymen for whomever would employ him. To Paul, this weary and disgusted soldier was the Bayard to command his new Priory and to inspire in his subjects those qualities of loyalty and service to their monarch that Condé had shown to his. He was not a member of the Order until Litta decorated him with the Grand Cross. He accepted the dignity because it made him recruiting colonel in a new regiment.

Condé's priory had a mixed crew of commanders. The Polish family commanderies of the Radziwills, Platers, and Lopots were members along with Prince Adam Czartoryski, the confidant of the Czarevitch Alexander, Calixtus Poninski, Michael Radziwill, Litta himself, four other Poles, a German and the French émigré the Chevalier St Priest, then in Malta. It was later to include five further Knights of Justice nominated by the Czar, among them another émigré, the Count de Choiseul and three further Polish family Commanders created in January 1798. Paul, at the height of his Polish enthusiasm, made Stanislas Poniatowsky a *Chevalier Honoraire*.

The Litta brothers were very satisfied. Paul wore the soubrevest of the Hospitallers daily and above all his other decorations the cross of La Valette. Lorenzo Litta, writing to Cardinal Doria in November 1787, applauded the intentions of the Czar. As a means of keeping alive the maxims of religion and the sentiments of honour in a topsy-turvy world "he proposes with his new establishment to consolidate ever more in the nobility of his Empire that love of glory and that elevation of spirit which is more productive of the greatest actions."

On 24th February 1798 de Brueys at last set sail from Corfu, for Toulon. He reached Malta on 3rd March. Uncertain of the intentions of the fleet, von Hompesch ordered a general alert, and noticed that the muster of men amounted to little more than a third of what was considered necessary to defend the island. De Brueys, however, had no order to attack the island and set about allaying the fears of the garrison. He merely requested some repairs for an ex-Venetian battleship while he waited offshore. It was beautiful March weather, and the curious watchers from the roof-tops of the old city of Notabile could see and admire the entire flotilla of seventeen warships anchored a mile out to sea. On 11th March de Brueys wrote to

Bonaparte, "My appearance has calmed the apprehensions of the Knights; it has convinced me that our partisans are numerous, and I am certain that France can become mistress of this port if the Directors intend to take it."

He picked up Poussielgue by day and Barbara by night, having taken soundings off the north-east coast. When he reached Toulon in April de Brueys learned that the Army of England was destined for Egypt and that orders had been given for the reduction of Malta.

Chapter XVIII

MALTA VICTA

THE three months that elapsed between the visit of de Brueys and the arrival of the Napoleonic fleet were days of almost total inactivity in Malta. Poussielgue, who had estimated the Order's human resources at some two thousand regulars and ten thousand irregulars, believed that the backbone of resistance would come from the three hundred or so French Knights in the island. There were in fact only two hundred. The fortifications were impregnable if adequately defended but it had become plain to von Hompesch that there were insufficient tried men, particularly artillery-men. Yet von Hompesch made no attempt to remedy the deficiencies that had become apparent in March. It was obvious that he relied on the support of Russia and Austria, neither of whom would allow Malta to be attacked. Already Prussia and Austria, with the imponderable power of Russia in support, had prevented the proposal of the French plenipotentiaries to the Congress of Rastadt, that the Order should be wound up, from being put on the agenda. Paul had informed the German princes that support for and favour to the Knights would be considered as marks of respect to himself and the commanderies that had not yet fallen to France were not sequestered.

But with the establishment of the Roman Republic, Catuson had been ordered to summon the Inquisitor, Citizen Giulio Carpegna, to deposit an inventory of his properties, now the property of the Republic, in the French consulate, and all indications were that the island itself was in danger. It seems certain that von Hompesch knew of an impending attack. Lomellini, ex-Receiver in Genoa, is believed to have informed him of the destination of the Toulon armada. The Bailiff de la

Tour du Pin said he had received a letter from Poussielgue, trying to enlist him as a fifth columnist, which he had shown to the Grand Master. Doublet avers that von Hompesch received a courier from Rastadt on 4th June who told him that the French delegates were talking openly of the reduction of Malta. However this may be—and officially the destination of the Toulon fleet was a closed secret known to very few—von Hompesch did nothing. If he were relying on instant aid from Russia and Austria, he was unnaturally complacent about his ability to hold out till it came. But then everybody, friends and enemies alike had always said that Malta was impregnable.

According to Doublet, who is our sole source on these last months but whose information is suspect as being a justification of his future actions, a proposal was put to von Hompesch to bring in the collected harvest, the cattle, the women and children, the men both active and inactive and to concentrate them behind the walls of Valetta and the Three Cities. Von Hompesch would not listen. He was convinced the Maltese would not defend the walls; he hated the prospect of having to make a decision. The words "assault" and "bombardment" upset him. "Let us pray to God that we shall not be attacked."

Von Hompesch was defeated before anything started. He was fully aware that any defence was likely to be bloody and useless. Bonaparte's reputation was at its height; the Maltese, ready enough to cheer a generous Grand Master, were not ready to die for him and the Knights and soldiers, for so long unused to the exaltation of gun fire or the glory of fighting, were a force likely to protest much and do little. It was futile to quote the example of La Valette; von Hompesch, despite his *soigné* suit of armour, was not convinced that heaven or glory were the alternative results of a siege. If he did not already know that the French force numbered 29,000 men, he acted as if he did.

Bonaparte received final sanction to his plans on 12th April. The French Republic considered that the government of Malta had put itself in a state of hostility towards France since the opening of the war in 1793, as witness its assistance to the

British ships in 1794, its assistance to the armed sovereigns against liberty, and its reception of émigrés who had been appointed to high positions in the state. As it now seemed prepared to deliver the island to a power at war with France, General Bonaparte was empowered to reduce it, if he could do so without prejudicing the other aims of the campaign.

A rapid reduction was essential. Had von Hompesch known that a resistance of a fortnight would have changed the history of the world, he might have acted differently. But he put his confidence in his star, which had made him popular, had made him Grand Master and could not desert him now. It was all he had while he was uncertain of the movements of the British Mediterranean fleet: Nelson and St Vincent could not keep up an incessant watch on Toulon and the armada slipped out while Nelson was watering off Sardinia. By the time Nelson had reached his station off Toulon again, de Brueys and Bonaparte were heading for Sicily. On 7th June Troubridge joined Nelson off Cape Sicie with 8 line ships. On 9th June, the van of the French armada had reached Malta.

"Never had Malta seen such a numberless fleet in her waters," wrote Doublet. "The sea was covered for miles with ships of all sizes whose masts resembled a huge forest." At four o'clock in the afternoon, a launch from Bonaparte's flagship *L'Orient* entered Grand Harbour with a message for Caruson. The Grand Master was to be asked to admit the fleet for water. Von Hompesch convened the Council for six o'clock. With one dissentient voice, the Spaniard de Vargas, who remarked that as France was an ally of Spain the fleet should be admitted, they urged von Hompesch to enforce the regulation of 1756, that four ships alone could enter at once. Caruson took the message back to the Commander-in-Chief; von Hompesch was too lazy to send a courteous refusal.

"They have denied us water," Bonaparte said when he received the message. "Then we shall take it." In the early hours of the 10th June, he dictated his reply. "The Commander-in-Chief is indignant to learn that you will not grant permission (to water) except to four vessels at a time—what length of time would be required therefore to water and victual 500–600 sail? This refusal has surprised General Bonaparte, all the more as he is aware of the favours shown to the British. . . . General Bonaparte is resolved to obtain by force what ought to have been accorded by virtue of that hospitality which is the fundamental rule of your Order."

The plans were then set in motion for the attack on Malta.

The defence of the island had creaked into position on 6th June, when two frigates had appeared off Gozo. Of the 200 French, 90 Italian, 25 Spanish, 8 Portuguese, 5 Bavarian and 4 German Knights, 50 were either too ill or too old to fight. The ancient guns, repeatedly painted up to look like new, but unused for nearly 100 years except for ceremonial purposes, were wheeled out. The powder was found to be rotten, the shot defective. The urban militia, drilled on Sunday afternoons by officers too lazy to learn the language, ill-disciplined, given over to obstinate stupidity and malingering, shuffled into place terrified at the prospect of fighting the French. "If they were Turks, we should have no fear, but we've always been told that the French are devils. How then can we be unafraid?" As if in a trance the ancient dispositions for defence, drawn up in 1716 and again in 1761, were carried out. The Marshal was now de Loras, rescued from obscurity by sheer seniority, who assumed command in Valetta. Camille de Rohan, evacuated from Rome, was Seneschal and took charge of the Militia. Floriana was put under Belmont, Senglea under de Suffren's younger brother; the Bailiff de la Tour du Pin commanded the Cotoner lines and the Bailiffs de Clugny and Tommasi entered the Naxxar lines to repel any landing at St Julian's and St George's Bays.

Bonaparte on his side put Berthier in charge of operations, and Berthier divided the island between Vaubois, Reynier and Baraguey-Hilliers. Vaubois, with Marmont and Lannes as his two brigade commanders, landed at dawn with five battalions of infantry in St Julian's Bay. They were opposed by desultory fire from the Malta Regiment that quickly retreated into Valetta—Doublet says they ran, hurling their arms away in order to run faster. Desaix came ashore at Marsa Scirocco un-opposed. He and Marmont made straight for Wignacourt's aqueduct which they cleared of sharpshooters quickly. The retreat of the defenders was skilful and rapid, but two dozen were taken and a standard. Marmont then approached the walls of Floriana to be met by a large body of Maltese soldiers behind the earth ramparts outside the gates. Momentarily checked, the French withdrew and from over the drawbridge of the Portes de Bombes an Auvergnat Knight led a sally. It was lured into the cross fire of the 2nd Battalion of the 19th Line Regiment which caught them in an ambuscade and drove them back into Floriana, Vaubois himself capturing the standard of the Order.

Reynier, detailed to reduce Gozo, landed at Ramla Bay under heavy fire from the hill. By the end of the day, however, he had captured Fort Chambrai and the citadel. He alone had been resisted but sweet words, in which he promised the Gozitans no harm and their personal and religious liberty, had drawn their sting. Baraguey-Hilliers came ashore at St Paul's Bay. By the evening he had killed one Knight, and one Maltese, and captured three Knights and 150 Maltese. These he dis-armed and released on parole to bruit abroad the clemency of the French. "The Maltese," he reported officially, "defended themselves as far as lay in their power, but all had to give way before the audacity and intelligence of the attack."

The landing at St Julian's was not wholly unopposed. The Chevalier de Soubiras sallied out in a galley with two galliots to attack the landing boats, sinking one, under covering fire from Fort Tigné. But he was forced back into harbour. Barbara had called successfully on the Jurats of Notabile to surrender the city, and in the evening of the 10th Vaubois landed artillery and set it up against Fort Tigné. Save for the Four Cities and Floriana, Malta was in the hands of the French.

Inside the city fortress there was bewilderment and panic. "One could hear from every porch," wrote Doublet, "the women groaning in their houses, cursing the French and the Grand Master at once, and imploring all their tutelary saints to preserve the island." The statue of St Paul was paraded through the streets. Von Hompesch and his Council were in perpetual session, stunned by the message they had received that morning from de Ransijat. Having contracted no military obligations beyond that of fighting the Turks, he could not contemplate turning his arms against Frenchmen. "Finding myself in this critical and painful dilemma, for on whichever side I declare myself I shall be considered at fault by the other, I beg Your Highness not to take it amiss if I observe the strictest neutrality." He offered to deliver up the keys of the Treasury and to accept whatever residence the Grand Master might assign him. Von Hompesch consigned him at once to Sant' Angelo. De Ransijat had betrayed him; who else was there suborned by the crafty wiles of Caruson and Poussielgue?

In the course of the night of the 10th–11th events moved rapidly. The Maltese, bewildered at the speed of the French operation, saw the refusal of the Order to admit the French fleet as the reason why the *carmagnoles* were at the gates, threatening them all with death and ruin. In the palace of the *Università*, the Jurats met the leading bourgeoisie and nobles to decide on what to do. They had no confidence in the Order's power to defend them and resolved to call on the Grand Master to come to terms with Bonaparte. They were admitted to the Council chamber late at night and appealed to von Hompesch to ask for an armistice. They had taken particular glory fighting for the Order against the Muslim, but they could not understand why they were now threatened by a large Christian army with which they had no quarrel.

The Council was thunderstruck. "If I were Grand Master, stormed the Bailiff Caravaglio, "I would see you hanged." "One hangs robbers and murderers," was the reply, "but one listens to the deputies of a nation which like ours has everything to lose and nothing to gain from this war."

Von Hompesch dismissed the deputation with vague promises. Having always courted popularity, this ugly turn of sentiment unnerved him. And reports of violence from within the city were coming in hourly. On the morning of the

10th two Frenchmen had been slaughtered by a frightened harbour patrol—the purveyor Eynaud, who tried to resist the search of his house for arms and was bludgeoned to insensibility, and a hatter, Damas, who was sabred while trying to defend him. Eynaud's inert body had been taken to the Hospital where a frightened Infirmarian had clapped it into chains as that of a French agent. There he had died. A scuffle on a Greek vessel, which was believed to be full of arms hidden under its bales of corn for distribution to the mob, had resulted in twenty dead. Patrols, convinced the French had penetrated the walls, began sniping at one another. From the Cotoner lines a report told how the militiamen had risen against their officers and killed two Knights—Bonaparte's ADC Sulkowski avers that it was because they had cravenly deserted their posts at the first fusillade. Whatever the truth, the Maltese were shortly afterwards deserted by their officers and left the walls unguarded.

Roving bands of soldiers, now without officers, began to stream into Valetta, with stories that the Knights had surrendered the island to the French. The Irish exile, O'Hara, now Russian minister, on rushing into a crowd of them with orders to turn and fight, was stabbed in the arm with a bayonet and only rescued by the Knights in the nearby Inn of Castile. Individual Knights were attacked by frightened squads of armed men and in the confusion created by conflicting report and rumour, four were killed, three dangerously wounded and three more winged by musket shot.

Von Hompesch all this time sat and did nothing. The Council advised against a personal appearance; had he gone out, as de Boisgelin wanted it, in the armour of La Valette, he might have steadied the situation for a short time—assuming that he could have fitted into it—but it was soon clear that there was no fight in him. Reports of desertion and disobedience came in from every officer who returned from his post, where he should have stayed. The Maltese leaders, who von Hompesch was convinced were in collusion with the enemy, wanted a truce and after an hour and a half's wrangling in the early hours of the morning, with all the older Bailiffs gone to bed, the Council decided to request one. At 9 o'clock in the morning of the 11th a French émigré, Melan, designated for the occasion as Chancellor of the Consulate of the Dutch Republic, clambered on board *L'Orient* with a message for Bonaparte and a letter for Dolomieu.

Since the dissolution of the Feuillant Club, Dolomieu's political significance had faded. He had already had one near escape from the "people" whose liberation he had so much applauded, when the Duke de Rochefoucauld, President of the Department of the Seine, was butchered in his coach while on his way to stand trial before the Committee of Public Safety. Dolomieu, accompanying the Duke's sisters in the next coach, had sat by, a helpless witness. The spoliation of the Order, from which he had persistently expected justice and advancement at a time when he alone of Frenchmen was up to date in his responsions, had diluted his bitterness and turned him by contrast almost to think nostalgically of the little island he had been glad to leave "for ever" in 1791. He had accepted his position on the expedition as a geologist, ignorant of its designs on Malta. "I protested loudly," he wrote afterwards, "reproaching those who had, with rather more urgency than was necessary, urged me to associate myself with an enterprise designed to destroy a government of which I had once been a member."

The letter, addressed to him in the hand of the Chevalier Miari, von Hompesch's Italian secretary, begged him in the name of "that affection he once entertained for the Order" to use what influence he had upon Bonaparte. The General, who opened the letter himself, appointed him one of his emissaries; the others were the brigade commander Junot and Poussielgue, now chief of the Commissariat. As the white flags were raised over St Elmo and Fort Ricasoli, von Hompesch, des Pennes and Tommasi prepared to receive them in the Council Chamber. When they arrived, von Hompesch embraced Dolomieu and his old crony des Pennes busied himself with fetching chairs for the rest of the party. Without the waste of many words, a twenty-four-hour truce was signed on condition that the Grand Master should send his plenipotentiaries to negotiate the surrender of the city.

Von Hompesch had already drawn up his list. It contained four Maltese who asked to be represented—the Baron Maria Testaferrata, Dr Niccolo Muscat, the Grand Master's auditor, the advocate Benedetto Schembri and Bonanni, the councillor of the *Università*. The Order was represented by the Neapolitan Bailiff Frisani, and de Ransijat, released that morning from Sant' Angelo and included because his actions of the day before might impress the French commander. With them went Doublet as secretary and the Chevalier de Amati, representing the King of Spain as a friendly power, The three-mile journey to *L'Orient* by launch was so choppy that they were most of them seasick and did not reach the flagship until midnight. Bonaparte, already in bed, had to be woken up, and ordered rum to restore their drooping spirits. Then, with de Brueys and Berthier, he personally drafted the clauses of the capitulation, that *"par ménagement pour l'honneur chevaleresque"* he called a Convention.

Of the Maltese negotiators de Ransijat alone kept his end up. Frisani whose French was poor was dumb throughout, but before signing inserted a note reserving the rights of his sovereign, the King of Naples. "You may make what reservations you like," Bonaparte told him good-humouredly, "for if need be we can cancel them with a few cannon shots." Malta, its forts and harbours, and the sovereignty enjoyed by the Order now passed to the French Republic. The Grand Master should, if French influence prevailed at the Congress of Rastadt, be given a principality in Germany equal to the one he now lost, and in the meantime the Republic would pay him a pension of 300,000 francs a year. After an acrimonious exchange between Bonaparte and de Ransijat it was agreed that the French Knights actually in Malta would be received without prejudice in France and her satellite Republics, only if they had not borne arms against her in foreign armies. They would receive an annual pension of 700 francs (de Ransijat had raised this from 600) if they were under 60, otherwise they would receive 1,000. There were minor clauses promising France's good offices with other powers to preserve the privileges, possessions and immunities of those Knights that were not French, promising freedom to the Catholic Church in Malta and guaranteeing the property and privileges of the Maltese.

The reign of the Knights Hospitaller was over. Though von Hompesch was advised by some to renounce the Convention, such an act of shallow heroics was beyond one who had shown no decision or steadfastness throughout the crisis. Inevitably cries of treason were raised and Bonaparte implicitly supported them. When on 13th June he decreed the expulsion of the Knights, he excluded those by name who had either furnished him with useful notes during the last six months or had made particular contributions towards the expedition against England. De Ransijat figured prominently on the list. It included de Fay, the Commissary for Fortifications, Royer, von Hompesch's chief equerry, Doublet, Greicher, von Hompesch's chamberlain, six French Conventual Chaplains, five Knights, two of them Italians, and the Servant-at-Arms, Toussard, an artillery engineer.

On the expedition itself were the ex-chevalier Picault de Mornas, and Dolomieu himself. Picault had served under Toussard in Malta. Dolomieu, despite the later accusations of Maisonneuve, did not act traitorously. His letters to de Ransijat, said to have been received on 6th June and categorically stating that Malta was in no danger of attack, have never been found. There is no reason why we should not accept his protestations of innocence. Maisonneuve, who wrote a highly charged account of the fall of Malta, at which he was not present, adds that the Spanish artillery commander, Bardonenche, had deliberately reduced the issue of cartridges and failed to charge the cannon. The Bailiff de la Tour du Pin, who was present, accused Toussard of withdrawing the men of the Malta Regiment from the Naxxar lines and leaving them in the charge of 400 raw militiamen. To him de Ransijat was the chief traitor, who had held a Rebels' Club in his rooms in the Treasury every Monday morning at 11 o'clock. The Congregation of War, too, had consisted of three traitors, Toussard, Bardonenche and Fay, to whom were added by von Hompesch himself, he remarked significantly, three ancient Bailiffs as soon as the attack developed. None of these had ever seen any fighting. The Spanish minister, too, had called off all the Spanish Knights in the name of His Catholic Majesty—a fact to which O'Hara owed his life, as they were all confined to the Inn of Castile. De Amati himself dined Vaubois, Marmont and Lannes in his house at Zurrieq on the 10th. But von Hompesch himself was at fault; he had never once left the Palace and his public appearances as Grand Master had been at festas and parties, never once at a drill or an inspection.

The heroes of Maisonneuve's tale were de la Tour du Pin himself, who with sixteen other Knights had personally lumped supplies of powder with their own hands along the Cotoner lines when the Maltese deserted, de Loras who, he said, had organized the sole sally against the landing craft, Tommasi who had tried to hold the Naxxar lines with unarmed men, and the 80-year-old Bailiff de Tigné who was carried out on to the ramparts by his servants in order to be where an officer ought to be, leading his men. The other Bailiffs Maisonneuve congratulates ironically for not putting their names to the capitulation. De Suffren cravenly forsook Senglea and withdrew with the officers of the line ships into Valetta. As von Hompesch did not meet Junot in full council, the absent councillors he said pointedly "were at their posts which they proposed to defend until death." It seems they could not be found.

Bonaparte in his memoirs wrote: "Malta could not withstand a bombardment of 24 hours; the place certainly possessed immense physical means of resistance, but no moral strength whatever. The Knights did nothing shameful; nobody is obliged to perform impossibilities." But at the time he was well aware that the gates had been virtually opened. Mayer, who hastened to von Hompesch's defence, put the blame on the

Maltese. "Victuals and munitions were not short, but were pillaged by armed rebels. Desertion became general. The feebleness of certain commanders did not permit adequate measures to be taken. The air rang to cries of blood; the crowd which had got into the Palace spread throughout the rooms clamouring for surrender. The militiamen insulted their commanders. . . . 'We began by killing your countrymen. We'll end up by killing you.' One Knight was chased from his post near Zabbar; another was wounded. Townsmen made themselves adjutants-general and began to give orders saying they had no further faith in the Knights. . . . The Chevalier de Chateauneuf, major in the *Cacciatori*, entering the Palace to deliver his report, was seized by the hair and thrown down the main stairs. The Marshal, de Loras, trying to open the main doors to introduce reinforcements, was disobeyed, and would have been murdered had he persisted."

Mayer picked up his information from the demoralized Knights who trickled into Trieste with von Hompesch. Doublet, whom Mayer had accused of treason, wrote, long after, the fullest and most detailed account of those confused days. He had his honour to vindicate. The Maltese, according to him, wanted to fight but their officers ran away. A Knight, accused of spiking the guns at Marsa Scirocco, was dragged under the Grand Master's own balcony and would have been slaughtered but for the intercession of the *Maestro Scudiere*. Eventually, when the Convention was signed, only a personal intervention from the Bishop could convince the men of Cospicua that resistance was futile and that they should disperse. Had not Doublet himself urged von Hompesch to active defence? Had he not advised him to tear up the Convention and to put himself at the head of the brave Maltese and hold out until Nelson arrived? We have only his word for it; his wife was Maltese.

The chaos of conflicting reports makes it hard to discover what exactly happened, but through them all von Hompesch presides, languid, defeated, unhappy, unnerved by the clamour and the torrent of advice. The French disembarked with precision and discipline, quietly mopping up the countryside, Knights and Bailiffs alike waiting for orders that never came, the soldiers and peasants unwilling to call upon themselves the full destructive power of the French army, devious plots and conspiracies darkly hatched: it was all very different from 1565. Then the alternatives had been a passage either to Heaven wafted on the trumpets of the Cherubim, or to the homeland crowned with laurels. But in 1798 the trumpets of the Cherubim were drowned by the thunder of Christian guns, and for many of the defenders there were no homelands to return to, no laurels to be plucked. Men must have a cause to fight for; the Hospitallers had watched theirs evaporate as the armies of Europe made peace with the Infidel and the grand cause of Christendom was smothered by the Court of Rome.

Chapter XIX

A RUSSIAN REMEDY

ON 12th June the outer periphery of fortresses was surrendered to the French. Bonaparte decreed the instant
expulsion of O'Hara and St Priest, the only members of the
Russian Priory in the island, within three hours, and of the
Portuguese, as belonging to an enemy power, within two days.
Von Hompesch's intercession secured a delay for St Priest,
but O'Hara began the long trek to St Petersburg to report the
cataclysm to his sovereign. "The Emperor of Russia owes me
thanks," Bonaparte wrote to the Directors on 17th June,
"since the occupation of Malta has spared his Treasury 400,000
roubles. We have served the interests of his nation better than
he." On 13th June *L'Orient* sailed into Grand Harbour and
the French commissaries took over the arsenal, and the
San Zaccaria and *San Giovanni*, rechristened *Dego* and *Berouse*,
joined the French fleet.

Bonaparte lodged for the first night in the Palace of the
Jurats and then moved into the Palazzo Parisio, next door to
the Inn of Castile. There he stayed for six days. He wrote at
once on the 13th to the French minister in Naples offering
to acknowledge Neapolitan suzerainty as soon as Naples
acknowledged that of the Republic of Rome. He then invited
von Hompesch and all his chivalry to wait upon him. The
Grand Master had prepared apartments and supper for him in
the Palace, but instead found himself, the head of the oldest
order of Chivalry in Europe, ordered before an upstart
artillery officer from an island that Pinto had once tried to make
his. No record of the interview survives. The Grand Master
and all those Knights who had not volunteered for service
with the French were given notice to quit and to take nothing

of value with them, apart from 240 francs each, which Bonaparte reluctantly allowed them as travelling expenses. Dolomieu had the wry pleasure of receiving de Loras who "came to beg that I should forget all his past proceedings against me and to demand my friendship."

Von Hompesch ordered the Knights to doff their crosses and allowed those who wanted to take service with the French. Thirty-four "citizens of the Order of Jerusalem," all of them under thirty, some of them veterans of Condé's armies, applied. Jeered at in the streets by the soldiery, and booed by the Maltese, von Hompesch settled to leave on the 17th. He claimed the Grand Magistral jewels, the Palace plate and the Archives. The French refused: the first had a high cash value, the last would be useful for cartridges. Bonaparte offered him 600,000 francs, half of which would be distrained to pay his debts, 100,000 given him in cash, the rest in four drafts of 50,000 drawn on the French Treasury. The pension of 100,000 crowns, in lieu of a Principality, would follow. He was permitted to take with him the holy relics of the Order, of no value to Bonaparte, the splinter of the True Cross, the hand of St John, despoiled of its gold and jewelled reliquary, and the ikon of Our Lady of Philermos removed from its silver frame. The Grand Master and his party left on board a French merchantman for Trieste escorted by a frigate as far as Meloda. With him went St Priest and eleven other Knights and two Servants-at-Arms. "It was not thus," cried Maisonneuve from St Petersburg, "that de l'Isle Adam left Rhodes!"

The Emperor accorded the wretched Grand Master asylum in Trieste while the Empire buzzed with rumours of what had happened in Malta. And in August Litta in St Petersburg received what appeared to be a letter from the Bailiff de Tigné imputing treachery to the Knights of the Council and collusion to von Hompesch. The news was published forthwith in the London Courier, at that moment the most widely read newspaper in the capital.

Litta had been recently joined by Maisonneuve who had at last reached the city to which he should have gone in 1792.

Between them they decided upon the next move. On 26th August 1798, at an extraordinary general meeting of the Russian priory, a manifesto was issued, which listed the counts against the Grand Master and concluded: "Ferdinand von Hompesch and his agents have sold Malta, and they alone have received the price for her." The full council had not been convened or it would never have agreed to this betrayal; it was now scattered. Therefore "We, Knights of the Grand Priory of Russia and others present here, regard von Hompesch as deposed from the rank to which we raised him, and by virtue of our laws we look upon ourselves as absolved from the obedience that we would otherwise owe him as our head. We invite our brothers in the other Grand Priories to join us in our action which honour has rendered indispensable and from which to abstain would be to participate in the opprobrium that Ferdinand von Hompesch, St Tropez and others have so justly deserved. We throw ourselves into the arms of our august and sovereign Protector, Paul I, Emperor of all the Russias." The Convention was sternly repudiated.

On 10th September, Paul received them and declared his Imperial intention to maintain the Order and its institutions, privileges and honours and to employ every means in his power to re-establish it. St Petersburg would temporarily become the chief centre and the other Tongues were invited to accept it in the interests of the whole Order. Condé from his H.Q. at Dubno in Volhynia declared his adhesion on 3rd October, together with 37 novices of his army recently admitted by Litta. On 23rd October, at Heitersheim, led by the Grand Bailiff von Pfurdt, and seconded by Maisonneuve, the Priory of Germany followed suit. The Bavarian, Bohemian and Spanish priories, however, held their hand, while the Grand Prior of Germany, the Prince von Heitersheim, disassociated himself tactfully from the declaration of his Priory.

Von Hompesch, meanwhile, unaware of what was happening, issued his formal Protest from Trieste on October 12th. He ascribed the fall of Malta to French agents in the Order and to those Maltese who had deceived the people and rendered all resistance vain. He protested against the French attack, the Convention, his expulsion and the insinuation that he had resigned the sovereignty of his island, which belonged to the King of Naples, to another power. All acts passed in Malta since the Convention were null and void. It had taken him four months to overcome the opposition of the Emperor and Thugut, who had no desire to ruffle the unpredictable Czar, but it came now too late. Alone the Priory of Castile, meeting in Madrid, affirmed its confidence in and loyalty towards him.

Both Lorenzo and Giulio Litta, the first anxious to preserve the Catholic mission, the second the survival of the Order, informed the Pope of the decisions of the Russian priory. Pius VI was in an embarrassing position: a virtual prisoner in Florence, he had no desire to alienate Paul who had offered him asylum in Russia, nor did he wish to dampen what seemed an almost providential interest in the Catholic cause now reeling from the blows of the French Republican armies. But he could not approve of von Hompesch's deposition while the Grand Master enjoyed the protection of the Empire and of Spain. The Littas were told on 3rd November that Papal approval could only follow the agreement of the other Priories: Lorenzo Litta had done his best on 7th September to convince Cardinal Odescalchi, the Secretary of State, that Paul's concern with Malta was purely disinterested. The possession of the island would be an embarrassment and would compromise his dignity and power. He had already refused offers of Corsica and Minorca from England and an invitation from the Grand Vizier to incorporate Malta into his Empire. He was only concerned to restore the Knights of Malta.

Lorenzo Litta was now Grand Almoner of the Priory, and was lodged in rich apartments in the Palace and did not want to dampen the Czar's enthusiasm. In his effort to present a rosy picture to the Pope he did not bring home to him the extraordinary seriousness with which the Czar took his position as Protector of the Order.

Already the Papal Nuncio was under constant pressure in St Petersburg. The Knights of Condé's regiment were determined to exploit the situation and consented to wait only one month for the adhesion of the Bohemian Priory and the Emperor's approval of von Hompesch's deposition. Paul himself, now daily clad in the full habit of the Order, even when there was no ceremonial function, consumed the days discussing the affairs of the Hospitallers. When no adhesion and no approval came, an extraordinary meeting of the Priory and of as many of its adherents as could be gathered together decided on 7th November to elect the Czar as Grand Master of the Order.

Braving the displeasure of the Pope and of the Emperor, both of whom were scarcely in a position to object too strongly, the Knights of St Petersburg elected a Greek schismatic as head of a Roman Catholic order, an honorary Grand Cross who had never been a Knight, a married man who had taken none of the vows of poverty, chastity and obedience. The tailors of the city working night and day to celebrate the new commercial treaty with Great Britain by putting the Czar's household cavalry into the red trousers and blue reveres of the English Horse Guards, now unpicked their threads and re-dyed their cloth a deep purple, a colour that Paul liked to believe was affected by the highest dignitaries of the Order. On 29th November clad in a silk, tasselled dalmatic of his own design, he was crowned with a great pomp by the Archbishop of Thebes in an elaborate crown, constructed at his own expense.

The Spanish minister, who had absented himself in order not to give the impression that his King had approved of this step, was given only a few days' notice to quit the country. The Bavarian, for daring to mention the Elector's recognition of the Chevalier von Hompesch, was ordered to follow him. The minister explained that he had referred only to the period before the deposition, but two couriers were sent post-haste to Munich to make sure. "Just now," Cobenzl wrote to the Imperial Vice-Chancellor, Colloredo, "the Czar's sole pre-occupation is with Malta. Although this is quite ridiculous, we must toe the line and gain for ourselves the merits of complaisance."

It was inevitable that men should attribute to Paul's mind sinister designs. Was he aiming at a naval base in the Mediterranean? Was he even hoping that, with six Cardinals believed to be making their way to asylum on the Neva, he could hold a snap consistory on the death of Pius, and become Pope Paul VI? The truth was simple: seeing the Knights in the van of the armies against Jacobinism he gave them his support. Dazzled by his mission, he accepted the titles as they came, generously.

His first action on becoming Grand Master was to create eighty-eight commanderies for his Greek Orthodox nobility, as he had offered to do in December 1797. This offer had reached Malta only the day before the French. Two hundred and sixteen thousand roubles were assigned to the Priory for their upkeep. The new Knights were to pay responsions and keep all the rules; the Czar arrogated to himself the quinquennial commandery of grace. Giulio Litta, appointed Lieutenant, was to sift the claims of the candidates.

On 1st January 1799 Paul declared his intentions. In a fulsome manifesto the Czar asserted that as Protector of the Order, he had considered it incumbent on him to save it from ruin and to re-establish it, not only in its old properties and titles but in a new splendour. He appealed to all brave and valiant Christian men, wherever they might be, to become Knights of Malta, if not in their own countries, then in his. "The laws and statutes of the Order inspire love of virtue, form good manners and cement the ties of obedience; they offer a puissant remedy for the evils that have been induced by an insensate mania for novelty and an unrestrained freedom of thought. The Order is for every state a means of increasing its strength, security and glory."

Paul genuinely believed it and the Littas hoped that Pius would believe he believed it. In earnest of his promise to employ his forces in the restoration of the Order, the Czar requisitioned six battleships, two frigates and a host of smaller vessels from both the Baltic and Black Sea fleets to form a special squadron to which he gave the flag of St John. To mollify the Pope, the army of Moldavia was ordered to march to the Dalmatian coast and ship itself to Ancona to bolster the Neapolitans who had just relieved Rome.

Lorenzo Litta tactfully explained to Odescalchi on 2nd January that the new schismatic commanderies were an establishment quite separate from the Russian Priory and would need no authorization from His Holiness. They would be a special foundation like the Lutheran Priory of Brandenburg. Pius VI was bewildered. The sensible world seemed to be collapsing, the French were threatening to remove him further north. The armies of Russia were the most powerful vanguard of the Army of Christ. Neither Austria nor Naples with designs on Italy were to be trusted. He had to be cautious. To Lorenzo Litta he had written on 3rd November 1798 that the deposition of von Hompesch had been too hasty a move. To Giulio two days later he wrote to counsel united action with the other Priories, neither denying the accusation against von Hompesch nor doubting the good intentions of the Czar. Neither had taken any notice.

Von Hompesch, pitifully eking out his days in Trieste, had made his own protest to the Pope and written humbly to Paul denying the accusations of treachery. But the Pope had little sympathy for the craven Grand Master: "Protesting is not proving the falsity of what the Russian Priory advances," he had written tartly on 16th November 1798. "It is up to you to substantiate the truth of what you depose." The election of the Czar, however, had thoroughly upset Pius VI who after all had the sole right of judging a Grand Master. And von Hompesch, with his core of influential Bailiffs, still protested vigorously to the Emperor. The action of the Priory of Russia looked like destroying the Order, not saving it. The Spaniards were believed to be considering sequestration, the new Elector of Bavaria had in February 1799 already carried it out. What would happen if the other Priories demanded the restitution of von Hompesch? The Pope would have liked to approve, wrote Odescalchi on 16th March to Litta, but to do so would be to impair his authority in a matter that affected all Catholic Sovereigns. And what was to be done about Bavaria?

Paul himself dealt summarily with Maximilian-Joseph. The new elector, sadly in need of money, had confiscated the Anglo-Bavarian commanderies shortly after his accession in February. The Czar at once instructed him that unless the Priory were restored 50,000 men under General Korsakov would lay the electorate waste. Though the General was nowhere near Bavaria, the Elector was suspicious of Austria and could not afford to antagonize the Czar; the Priory was re-established in July and a corps of 20,000 men promised in the campaign against France. The Bavarian Priory was also detailed to send a representative to St Petersburg to render homage to the new Grand Master.

All this was satisfactory: the difficulty of reconciling the Pope remained and Lorenzo Litta on 8th March 1799 related to Odescalchi that the atmosphere in the Russian capital was changing. "My situation here is too dependent upon the fate of my brother and as a foreigner he is too exposed to envy and to cabal. Nor is it possible to withstand them, since the Emperor is wayward. He is extreme in both his favour and in his disfavour." But Odescalchi could not make things easier for the two brothers by meeting the Czar all along the line: His Holiness could accept the Czar's protection of the Order but not his Grand Mastership. The Order was in schism, the German priory was now hesitant and likely to join the Spanish and Italian Priories in the process of being "liberated." Paul's greatness of mind and generous spirit should prompt him to accept the situation and not insist on Papal recognition of his title.

But Paul did insist and as the Littas failed to procure it, the Czar's mind changed towards them. The Greek Orthodox, suspicious all along of the Archbishop of Thebes, now found a fellow intriguer against him in the Catholic metropolitan, the Polish Bishop of Siestrzencewicz, who resented the creation of the new Bishoprics and the privilege of the cardinalatial habit accorded the Archbishop of Mohilov. The Littas felt the ground sliding from under their feet.

On 6th July 1799 the Emperor, warned by Cobenzl that a Russian army in Italy was conditional upon Imperial support for Paul's caprices over Malta, at last persuaded von Hompesch to declare his abdication. "May you bring this," he wrote to Francis II, "to the attention of your most intimate ally, the Emperor of all the Russias, under whose powerful auspices the Order will be re-born, whose protection I was the first to invoke and whom I shall be the first to bless for his general efforts for the good of the Religion." With this dignified statement, he despatched the relic of St John the Baptist to St Petersburg, where it arrived on October 12th and the Czar, dressed in his coronation robes, bowed to the ground before it as had, 100 years earlier, the Boyar Boris Czeremetev.

Von Hompesch was out of the way, the relic in the Chapel of the Imperial Palace at Gatchina. Paul was now free to organize his new Order as he liked. Giulio Litta, after some months wringing the dispensation out of a reluctant Pope, had married the niece of Potemkin, the rich widow Skavronski. The Czarevich Alexander was Grand Marshal; the Count de Sievers, Hospitaller; Count Kouchelev, Admiral; General Lamb, Grand Conservator; de Flachslanden and von Pfurdt in their old dignities of Turcopilier and Grand Bailiff. The Chancellor was Count Rostopchin, the Czar's principal secretary. There were 90 commanders, 41 Knights of Justice and 21 family Commanders among the Greek Orthodox members, including a Czeremetev as Grand Chamberlain. The Latin group contained eight Grand Crosses, including the Metropolitan, the Archbishop of Thebes and the Neapolitan Ambassador, nineteen Commanders, mostly Polish, and 80 Knights of Justice, mostly French, and nine Polish family Commanders. The total was 249, exclusive of the Czar's femily and hangers on. In the midst of them all Paul held court in the dual function of Czar of all the Russias and Grand Master of the Knights Hospitaller of St John of Jerusalem.

Chapter XX

MALTA INVICTA

BONAPARTE during his six days set down at once to the administration of liberty to the island of Malta and the appropriation of its wealth. He did not spare himself and in four days had issued the ordinances that consummated the revolution.

On 13th June he set up a commission of government of which de Ransijat was head with Regnaud de St Jean d'Angely the French Commissioner. It consisted of the Bishop's secretary, a French and Maltese merchant, a Gozitan judge, two magistrates and a notary. Doublet was its secretary. Its job was to administer the island, raise taxes, reorganize the tribunals and appropriate the possessions of the Order. On the same day Lannes was instructed to enrol as many Maltese as he could for the expedition to Egypt and all the gold and silver in the various buildings of the Order was to be seized.

Bonaparte also settled other problems that had exercised the Grand Masters: all foreign priests except the Bishop were expelled; no further priests were to be ordained until jobs had been found for all existing ones; the religious houses were reduced to one for each order; clerical immunity was abolished. All the slaves in the island, 1400 Moors and 600 Turks were released, and in Tunis the Bey struck the irons off 66 Maltese in return. The armorial bearings of the nobility were defaced, all titles abolished. The Maltese were to wear the French cockade. Malta was now a democracy.

Bonaparte did not intend to waste the human resources of his new co-citizens. Sixty children of better born parents were to be sent to Paris to complete their education at their parents' expense. Six were for a naval academy, thirty to form an officer cadre for the new regiments. Classes in seamanship were to be set up in each port, and mariners enrolled in a general press. The veterans of the Malta Regiment were ordered to Corfu, the *Cacciatori* reduced to 100; but the bourgeois were enjoined to set up a National Guard and to form four companies of cannoneers.

On 13th June Bonaparte in a day of startling activity laid down in minute detail the terms of reference of the governing commission. He also decreed the substitution of an *Ecole Nationale* for the University with lecturers in mathematics, navigation and the applied sciences and the provision of fifteen primary schools to teach French, calculus, pilotage and the French constitution.

On 19th June, the Army of England sailed for Egypt. About fifty Knights now accompanied it and the better part of the old *corpo di guardia*, the Regiment, the *Cacciatori* and the battalions of the squadron of galleys. Vaubois, with 3,053 men, was left behind to hold Malta.

The Maltese at first took kindly to the unfamiliar efficiency of the government, with their own countrymen in positions of trust. Although all the palaces and streets were re-christened the Government knew that change must not be too rapid. On 14th July—now the National feast instead of SS. Peter and Paul—the celebrations of the union of the Maltese people with the French Republic had a familiar ring about them. The happy peasants were driven into the City to celebrate the honour of being free men and to thank the Hero and his army. Four orphans were married in St John's by the complaisant Bishop and given away by Vaubois himself with a handsome dowry, to become good citizen mothers. A tree of Liberty was planted in the "*Place de la Liberté*" opposite the "*Palais National*" and the crowd addressed by both Vaubois and de Ransijat were promised prosperity and warned about those conspirators against peace and humanity—the English. The marches, games and races were rounded off by the burning of all patents of nobility at the foot of the tree of liberty and a ball, supper and fireworks that continued until 3 a.m. There were few signs of unrest.

But Vaubois was worried. The island's supplies were short and the Sicilians were being very obstructive with Maltese merchants. The sale of the Knights' property was slow and buyers did not come forward. Worst of all, three British frigates were sighted off the island. Then on 1st August, Nelson destroyed Bonaparte's fleet; the Neapolitan court, bolstered by the victory, stopped all commerce with Malta. Alone in the island was there a sufficiency of corn and arms: all else was short. The Commission of Government needed money most urgently of all: in their search for it, the sweetness and concord that de Ransijat and Vaubois had so glowingly described in their despatches to Bonaparte were to be rudely shattered.

A percipient commander would have noticed that the cockades were being cast off in the countryside and that the civil registration of marriages was so unpopular that the Bishop had had to issue a pastoral letter on the subject. Vaubois should have realized that the Maltese would not buy the effects of suppressed convents.

The trouble began on 2nd September. On that day four Maltese commissioners were deputed to Notabile to dispose by auction of the effects of the Carmelite convent and church. It was a Sunday, and the city was full of villagers and the commissioners were met by jeers and catcalls and the ringing of bells which caused a crowd to gather. The French captain, Masson, emerged indignantly from the Jurats' Palace to disperse the mob but was soon forced by stones and rubbish to shelter in a private house. The mob broke in and heedless of Masson's cries to be allowed to surrender, it flung him out of the window and broke his neck. His death was the signal for a general insurrection: within a few hours the countryside was aflame with angry people, hauling down the tricolor. The small garrison of Notabile managed to close the gates, but during the night the walls were scaled by the more resourceful Maltese and Masson's second in command decided to surrender in the morning. Unfortunately a few stray shots fired by one or two of his frightened soldiers after the cease-fire drove the mob berserk; it slaughtered the garrison and burned the bodies on a nearby hill. And from the masts of the walls of Notabile flew the red and white flag that had last been seen in 1775.

The Maltese were not without a leader, a notary called Emmanuel Vitale, who realized at once what was happening. Knowing that reinforcements were bound to be sent up from Valetta, he hurriedly left Notabile and sped to Cospicua. There an insurrection, which must have been planned, followed at once. In Notabile, the mob now leaderless did to death a number of collaborators and an elderly Knight who was identified with the shameful capitulation of 11th June.

The insurrection in Cospicua was scotched when Vaubois moved the *San Zaccaria*, now *Dego*, into the old galley creek, and the Maltese were disarmed in the Four Cities, on whose gates a strong guard was set. The rising, which Vaubois had feared from the start, had given the garrison an unpleasant shock by its suddenness and violence. The Maltese, checked in the Four Cities, at once set up a junta, and Vitale consented to share command with Caruana, the Bishop's secretary and a member of the Commission of Government. As an army of irregulars could not hope to contain a garrison of 3,000, they decided upon instant submission to the King of Naples whom they begged earnestly to send them arms and men. The cannon was wheeled from the coastal forts all the way to the Porte des Bombes and under spasmodic fire from the beleaguered French, trenches and earthworks were thrown up against Fort Ricasoli and Corradino.

Vaubois, unable to understand the reasons for the insurrection, ascribed it to a Neapolitan plot. Had he been more perspicacious he would have seen it as entirely spontaneous. The grievances of the Maltese were many: troops had been billeted on the wealthier families and payment deferred; all the debts of the old régime had been cancelled; interest rates at the *Monte di Pietà* had been raised to 6 per cent; the distribution of alms and bread to the poor had been stopped; the Hospital had been cleared for French sailors; the families of those impressed for Egypt were repeatedly denied their share of the men's pay. But it was the cynical spoliation of the churches that supplied a naked flame to the touchpaper passions of a devout and Catholic people. "The priests have fanaticized the people," Vaubois told the Directors on 13th September, "and they call down upon us the angel of extermination." The French had only themselves to blame; their pressing need of money had ignored the susceptibilities of the people. The priests were not ordinary "citizens", they were fathers in Christ; a marriage celebrated before the altar needed no registration in a civil court; above all the peasant, who had contributed his mite towards the purchase of jewels for his Madonna, saw with angry eye the French hand that rose to seize them. The Order of St John's had been a long dying cause, but the cause of the Order of God and all His Saints brooked neither delay nor caution. The very arms that the French had distributed to the *Cacciatori* and the National Guard were now turned against their own breasts. By 4th September Vaubois had decided to call all the French into Valetta and to settle down behind the impregnable walls. He had not the resources to do more.

On 19th September the Portuguese Marques de Niza and four seventy-fours, sent by Nelson anchored off shore, where they were joined on the 23rd by Captain Saumarez in H.M.S. *Orion*. The Maltese at once asked him for arms and ammunition. He let them have what he could, sent a demand for surrender to Vaubois which was curtly refused and returned to Naples with a request from the rebel leaders that the island be subjected to a total blockade.

From that moment all connections with the outside world were severed and Vaubois was short of meat, rice, wine, vinegar, and fresh vegetables. Though the Wignacourt aqueduct had been cut, water if strictly rationed was sufficient. He was not ill provided with corn or powder, but short of ball. A welcome relief had come in the arrival of the *Guillaume Tell*, and the two frigates *Diane* and *La Justice* which had limped home from Aboukir Bay and which brought invaluable cannon and cannoneers to the garrison. The insurgents were short of corn, and had no bombs and mortars and only small cannons.

Neither side could do much damage to the other while the superb walls intervened. It would be a matter of how long each could last.

The Neapolitan court was slow to respond to the submission of the Maltese and the chief Minister, Gallo, who had met and been flattered by Bonaparte at Campo Formio, struggled for power and friendship with France against the generalissimo from Shropshire, John Acton. While Gallo's policy prevailed, the Sicilian ports were closed to the vessels of the Maltese. Acton, with Nelson at his elbow all the time, whetted the King's appetite for Malta. Nelson, with Minorca safely captured, had no ambitions for the island, and Acton played on the King's fear that, if he did not move, the Russians would become its masters. But the King did not make up his mind until December. In the meantime Nelson kept the insurgents going with powder and shot and detached Captain Alexander Ball of H.M.S. *Alexander* to command the blockading fleet on 25th October. Vaubois and the ill-fated Villeneuve refused a generous offer of repatriation and Ball had to content himself by accepting the surrender of Gozo. On 6th November Gallo, steadily being edged into war with France, was persuaded to send some mortars and small cannon to Malta. With these Ball tried to keep the Maltese morale high, and the two generals, Vitale and Caruana, from quarrelling. He became in fact the chairman of the junta and spent as much time on land as at sea trying to prevent the nimble Sardinian brigs and Maltese *speronari* from slipping the blockade. Nelson had lain off Malta until December 30th, and despatched Niza to Naples whither he himself followed, leaving H.M. ships *Alexander*, *Audacious* and *Goliath* with two frigates to watch the island.

In Naples Nelson heard that Admiral Ouchakov had sailed through the Dardanelles in command of Paul's "Maltese fleet" and that a Russian army was marching to the Adriatic. Ouchakov's orders were anything but clear but Nelson was convinced that his object was the reduction of Malta. Ball was put on his guard and told to warn the Russians that if they landed all Neapolitan ports would be closed to them. Without consulting London, Nelson had made himself the champion of the Neapolitan crown and was preparing to use his fleet against an ally in the Second Coalition. The captured French standards from Gozo had already been presented to Ferdinand who was told that he had 16,000 new subjects.

But by December the Neapolitans who had triumphantly entered Rome were in full flight and the King was preparing to leave for Sicily. The Maltese, who had accepted Caruana's reasons for submitting to Ferdinand, now had second opinions. If the French surrendered, they asked Ball, would His Britannic Majesty consider a condominium of England and Naples in Malta! But with quarrels and sickness in the ranks of the insurgents, a French surrender was not imminent.

Indeed on 11th January French patrols had thwarted a brave and ambitious plan on the part of a largish body of Maltese irregulars hiding in the fosses of the Lazaretto to rush one of the main gates by night. Their leader, an ex-privateer called Guglielmo Lorenzi, had a Russian flag upon him to raise on the walls. Ball informed Nelson at Palermo, adding "the Maltese have a great dislike to the Russians and are so prepossessed in favour of the English that they are continually inviting me to hoist the British colours all over the island".

Nelson once more instructed Ball to see that no Russian flag was hoisted; this would be a "very unhandsome manner of treating the legitimate Sovereign of Malta . . . and also me, who command the forces of a power in such close alliance with the Russian Emperor."

Paul, however, reported Whitworth, the British Ambassador in St Petersburg, was just as suspicious of Great Britain. Grenville, then Foreign Secretary, had instructed Whitworth to see that Malta did not prejudice Russia's entry into the Coalition, and by December Paul was ready: he told Whitworth that he had no objection to a purely temporary Neapolitan garrison in the island should it surrender, but it would only stay until the Hospitallers were restored. Ideally, a triple garrison of Russian, British and Neapolitan troops should hold it, and Whitworth agreed on 29th December. The Czar now busied himself with the war and with organizing a dramatic sweep across Europe, but in January 1799, he casually gazetted the appointment of Prince Dmitri Volkonski to command in Malta. On Whitworth's protest the Czar amended this to read Commander of the Russian troops in Malta, of which there were to be 3,000 as soon as they had been despatched through the Dardanelles, opened by the Turks to allow the restoration of Malta to an Order they had sworn for 250 years to destroy.

The Russian and Turkish fleets captured Corfu in February but made no moves to sail on to Malta. There the besiegers and besieged were engaged on a struggle of attrition, neither side able to attack, and both sides suffering the most appalling privations. Naples sent scarcely any assistance and the Maltese had recently received all the useless mouths expelled by Vaubois from the Four Cities. They were so short of food, that the irregulars were now walking skeletons, and scurvy, syphilis and dysentery carried off twenty people a day. An occasional ship managed to slip into Valetta and enabled the indomitable general to prolong the struggle. The price of bread was raised to squeeze money from the rich whom he had not expelled. No one could kill a mule or horse, reserved for the use of the Hospital. "We have not six sincere friends in the city", Vaubois wrote on 28th June to the Minister of War.

The enthusiasm of the patriots was now waning. Caruana was repeatedly sick and his men starving and in rags. Nelson, do what he could, was unable to obtain reinforcement from Sicily or Minorca where the Commander-in-Chief, General Fox, was frightened to move without orders. Ball was worn to a shadow by pity for the misery of the Maltese and by trying to eke out his inadequate resources. He had five hundred marines from H.M. ships *Lion* and *Success*, a few Portuguese and fifteen hundred Maltese, of whom six hundred alone might be fit to fight at any one time. The Maltese kept up the struggle because they were sure Ball would not desert them. Emma Hamilton, at his insistence, was able to get £3,500 out of the Neapolitan royal family, but what the Maltese wanted was an assurance that the British flag would fly in Malta when the

French surrendered. Nelson was able to give this in February, but had to revoke it in April because Ferdinand objected.

On 10th April Ball informed Sir William Hamilton in Palermo that Paul I was preparing to ship a million ducats to Malta and that it was imperative Great Britain should assume the sovereignty of the island. The next day the Congress of Maltese Deputies wrote to Nelson with a prayer that whatever happened, Alexander Ball should be left in charge of the island. Him they knew and trusted; they knew nothing of the Russians. Ball, however, had no option but to co-operate with them if they came, and indeed received orders to do so.

In May Ball was obliged to lift the blockade for two months when news came that Admiral Bruix had broken out of Brest, and was sailing for the Mediterranean. The French took advantage of his absence to raid the Maltese fishing fleet and to bring in a boat bearing beef. Their morale rose while that of the Maltese dropped to a new low. On 29th June, a *speronaro* put ashore three Knights who had formed part of Von Hompesch's party in Trieste. They were the Maltese-speaking Bailiff de Neveu, a respected and benign ex-commander of the *Cacciatori*, the Commander Schauemburg and the Servant-at-Arms Prepaud. Their arrival caused a mild sensation; they brought money, they said, and a promise of supplies. They were promptly arrested by Ball's lieutenant, an artillery commander called Vivion. Finding that they had brought little else than hundreds of copies of Mayer's account of the Fall of Malta, flattering to von Hompesch, he sent them back to Messina under protest. It was the last despairing throw of the discredited Grand Master: had the party been successful and raised a strong Maltese faction in his favour, the Bailiff Caracciolo, minister in Naples, was to make von Hompesch's submission to Ferdinand in the hope that the promise of a vassal more subservient than George III or Paul I would induce him to send men and supplies. Von Hompesch, anxious about Austria's reactions, had stipulated that his return could only be made under the same conditions as those of the Donation of Charles V. De Neveu had full powers (Caracciolo did not know this) to negotiate a truce with Vaubois. It was a forlorn hope and von Hompesch, still beguiled by the spell he had once worked on the Maltese people, alone could have thought it had any chance of success. Its failure marked the destruction of this last hope that had until now prevented him from abdicating.

Vivion was able to restore Maltese morale by skilful feint attacks on the ramparts, giving them action to distract them from the pamphlets that Vaubois was sending out, containing the "true" account of British intentions in Malta. In return he began to fire newspapers into the city containing the news of French reverses in Egypt and Italy.

On 5th July Ball returned to everyone's immense relief; he was now officially Ferdinand's Viceroy and Commander, but this apart the King sent scarcely anything that Ball wanted. Besides, restored to Naples after the nightmare of the Parthenopean Republic, he was inclined to agree with Acton that the English intended to supplant him in Malta. British ships were blockading Valetta, true, and British powder keeping the Maltese guns firing, but the Court of Naples was always being badgered for corn and money all of which was needed at home. As if that were not enough, the Court of St James had made a compact with the Court of St Petersburg to land a Russian force in the island, and the Court of Naples had been invited to submit. Why continue to pay good money— he had spent £40,000 already—for the prestige of being feudal sovereign of Malta if somebody else was going to be in possession?

In September Ouchakov's fleet sailed into Palermo, and Nelson was convinced he had come at last to reduce Malta. Acton was convinced on the other hand that Ouchakov and Nelson were confederates. Nelson was in despair. If the Russians turned up, the Maltese, he was sure, would give up the struggle. He was prepared to mortgage the Duchy of Brontë and to sell the Czar's diamond-studded snuff-box, presented to him after Aboukir Bay, to get corn from Agrigento. But as General Fox in Minorca prevaricated over sending Sir Charles Stuart's Messina garrison to Malta, he had to accept the prospect of Russian aid and even began to encourage Ouchakov to sail. But the Admiral's orders had been confused in the first place and further confused by the Russian minister at every port he had visited. Now he refused to budge, saying his ships were unseaworthy and, though Nelson offered to transport his marines and sailors to Malta and to order Ball to see that the flag of St John alone flew from Valetta when it fell, Acton outsmarted him and was able both to keep Ouchakov at Palermo and to persuade Hamilton and the Russian minister, Italinski, to agree to share the expenses of keeping the "loyal Maltese from starving."

In November fifteen hundred Russian troops arrived in Naples destined for Malta, but Ferdinand who thought that they had come for the defence of his capital persuaded Ouchakov not to transport them. In December the cautious C.-in-C. in Minorca had reluctantly consented to part with Brigadier Thomas Graham and two regiments of foot, three hundred troops in all, who arrived in Malta with orders not to engage in any adventure likely to cost men or money. They were not an attacking force and became a serious burden on the already strained resources of the island. Troubridge, now in charge of the blockading ships, was so shocked at the condition of the Maltese that he wrote to Nelson on his birthday: "Many happy returns of the day to you. I never spent a more miserable one. I am not very tender hearted, but, really, the distress here would, if he could see it, move even a Neapolitan."

Troubridge had no respect for the "deceitful traitors" of Sicilians, Neapolitans and Russians and on 6th January, hearing that the granaries at Agrigento were full, he sent H.M.S. *Stromboli* to get supplies and not to take no for an answer. The enterprising captain commandeered two ships laden with corn, and Nelson was left to explain the theft away. The immediate crisis was over but Ball now feared a bread war among the Maltese insurgents themselves.

Ouchakov, worn down by the ceaseless badgering of his

allies, at last consented to ship some of the Russians to Messina but no further, and it was believed he had been got at by the Austrians. The tergiversations of the court of Vienna were not over: relations between the Russian and Austrian armies were at their worst and Paul was becoming restless at spending so many men and so much money in furthering Hapsburg dynastic aims in Italy. On 11th January 1800, without warning, Ouchakov was ordered to Corfu. No one knew it, but the Czar was preparing to withdraw from the Second Coalition.

Ferdinand, emboldened by the departure of the Russian fleet, at last consented to send twelve hundred troops, all of them bad, to Malta. On the 16th, Nelson broke up a relieving French squadron from Toulon and had the satisfaction of capturing *Le Genereux*, one of the two battleships that had escaped him at Aboukir Bay. Admiral Perré, who, mortally wounded, surrendered his sword to his victor, saw the convoy with supplies and the two thousand troops he had hoped to throw into Valetta dispersed before the winds.

The failure of the expedition and the absence of any attack convinced Vaubois that he was going to be starved into surrender. In a desperate attempt to save the *Guillaume Tell* for the Republic, he loaded her with sick soldiers and sailors and ordered her to make for Toulon and lead another relief expedition. He had corn enough to last till August. On the night of 24th March, the *Guillaume Tell* was intercepted by H.M.S. *Foudroyant*, chased for 30 miles, and, crippled and outmanœuvred, struck after a gallant fight.

The gloom in Valetta was partially relieved by the arrival of a provisions ship in June that slipped past H.M.S. *Penelope*. Vaubois, ready to defend the city to the last, though his garrison was depleted by dysentery, worms and scrofular— the cannonades of the insurgents caused him no anxiety— took pity on the wretched civilian population, and began the expulsion of those Maltese who had elected or been forced to remain in the Four Cities. Graham made a painful decision. They should not come out. Vaubois had offered them asylum and there they should stay, to help eat up the supplies of the garrison.

In July the cautious Fox in Minorca was replaced by Sir Ralph Abercrombie and the Commander-in-Chief, though asked for men by Lord Keith to help reduce Genoa, decided to send fifteen hundred men to Malta under Major-General Pigot. They arrived on 18th July. Pigot was a professional soldier who had a poor opinion of sailors. He at once conceived a curious dislike for Ball whom he found on shore where no sailor should be and decided to ignore him, even though he was the Neapolitan viceroy. He had orders to see that the Russians did not take possession of any of the forts in the archipelago: in everything he did he acted as if he were the sole authority.

He had good reason to be suspicious of Russia. On 6th January—five days before Ouchakov's departure—Italinski had arrived in Malta with instructions which he showed to Ball, and which allotted Valetta, Floriana and St Elmo to the Russians, Cotoner to the Neapolitans and Forts Ricasoli and Tigné to the British. Ball had protested that as there was as yet no Russian garrison in the island, the terms were preposterous. Italinski, who was a good fellow, was visibly embarrassed but Graham wrote to Dundas to put him on his guard. Whitworth still affirmed the purity of the Czar's intentions, but Dundas in April insisted to Grenville that Malta should only be restored to the Order at a general peace and that while England was at war with France it would be folly to deny herself the use of Malta as a harbour. But the Russians never came and increasingly it began to look as if any force that did come would come as the allies not the enemies of the French.

Paul's lukewarmness for the Austrian alliance was patent by the end of 1799, but Whitworth and Serracapriola, the Neapolitan ambassador, who did homage for the Priories of Capua, Barletta and Messina, "the Sicilian Priories", had managed to get him to revoke Suvarov's recall in November. But the Austrians still continued so to annoy him, interfering in Italy and grudging supplies, that Bonaparte assumed the aura of a romantic and generous foe. The French émigrés were keenest on the Austrian alliance, but Condé and his brother d'Enghien, for trying to escape "the obscure life of a colonel of Russian dragoons in a cantonment in Volhynia" by transferring to English pay, were summarily dismissed by Paul in March, 1800. Suvarov was recalled in January: Whitworth, created a Knight of Malta but forbidden to wear the Cross by Lord Grenville in case it argued Britain's formal recognition of the Imperial Grand Master, found the Czar increasingly cool with him. His despatches were opened and read; he knew that negotiations were in train with France and then, in June, he was recalled at the Czar's request. "The fact is," he wrote in cypher, "the Czar is not in his senses. This truth has been for many years known to those nearest to him, and I have myself had frequent opportunities of observing it. But since he came to the throne, his disorder has gradually increased." Frequent rages, psychopathic sensitiveness to the merest report or rumour, blind fanaticism over the shape of a hat, the cut of a uniform, wilful prejudices, a brain turning under the solvent of undiluted power: his advisers trembled and the world admired. A coalition could be sacrificed, a campaign thrown away, a former enemy and anti-Christ turned into a latter-day Alexander the Great. The lunacy, it was thought, had begun with his coronation as Grand Master. Hard politics suggested that he was disappointed in his allies. The Holland expedition with England had been a costly failure and he was increasingly jealous of England's successes at sea. Economics, too, as expounded by the new Chancellor, Count Rostopchin, demanded peace not war.

Then, on 5th September, Valetta fell.

Chapter XXI

MALTA BRITANNICA

At midnight on 24th August Vaubois made a last desperate attempt to save something for the Republic. The frigates *Diane* and *La Justice* made a dash for it. On the 27th the general watched *Diane* towed back by her captor, quite dismasted. He was now able to hold out for another fortnight and the British from documents taken on board the frigate knew it. It was no surprise to them, therefore, to receive a deputation, and on 5th September, two years and three days after the insurrection had begun, Valetta surrendered.

At once Pigot and Ball found themselves at loggerheads. Pigot had orders to raise the British flag, Ball the Hospitallers'. Pigot refused to recognize Ball as a signatory to the surrender; Ball as viceroy of the King of Naples and commander of the Maltese believed he should sign it on their behalf. But Pigot rudely snubbed him and in doing so snubbed the Maltese too. It was an ungenerous decision and in no way mitigated by Vaubois's refusal to recognize Ball as a signatory. Vaubois was, after all the vanquished, not the vanquisher, and it was the Maltese not Pigot who had sustained the siege. And Vaubois secured very good terms: his men were not to be prisoners of war, but to be transported at British expense to Marseilles and exchanged for an equal number of British. He was not permitted to take any of the ships with him, but he took nearly everything else. The Maltese, on the other hand, were ignored.

Pigot hoisted the British flag and brusquely refused to allow General Fardella, the Neapolitan commander, to sign the capitulation. But the siege over, other problems loomed. Was a Russian Deputy Grand Master to be allowed to land? Was von Hompesch to return where his creditors waited for him? Whose was the island? Ball regretfully wound up the provisional government and dissolved the Maltese Congress. But Ball was the ruler the Maltese wanted. Did he not understand them, had he not listened to them like a father and spent himself on their behalf? What should they do without him? Abercrombie sensibly retained him for a while as Civil Governor, but transferred all effective power to Pigot and in February 1801 Ball was recalled to the fleet. Everyone, but Pigot, was sorry to see him go, and Ball himself was disappointed. He had while serving ashore foregone any share of prize money he might have had at sea and he was seriously out of pocket from spending his own pay on the Maltese. But this was a pale grievance beside his bitterness at seeing the Maltese battalions denied their share of the prize money for the capture of Valetta. This was a fine way, he wrote scornfully to Dundas on 6th March 1801, to treat men who had replaced British deserters and sustained the siege in posts that the British and Neapolitans had refused!

In July Charles Cameron arrived as properly constituted Civil Governor with orders to administer the island as it had been administered under the Knights. Ball's last advice to him was to ensure that none of them returned or there would be trouble. Cameron, acting on it promptly, ordered a party of Spanish Knights coming from Barcelona to be diverted to Messina. He soon realized how wise Ball had been, when the Bailiffs and Commanders who had been shut up in Valetta emerged from the siege truculently demanding their old privileges and immunities.

The British government was beginning now to have second thoughts about Malta. In March Naples had been forced to sign a humiliating treaty with France in which she was forced to close all her ports to the English. News from Russia was confused and fearful. Possession of Malta was not, therefore, to be lightly lost. There could be no question of an early return of the Hospital.

Paul's first reaction to the news of Valetta's fall was to

demand the admission of a Russian garrison as had been agreed on in 1799. When he received no reply from London he impounded the goods of English merchants in St Petersburg and threatened an Armed Neutrality. Until England ceased to usurp the rights of the Order in Malta, she could expect to feel nothing but the Czar's displeasure. Paul had already been attracted by the prospect of a French alliance; for nine months, since January 1800, the Prussian minister, Haugwitz, had been acting as a go-between for Talleyrand, who had in March signified his readiness to recognize the Czar as Grand Master, "a title he could enjoy quite as well at St Petersburg or Rhodes as at Malta." After Marengo, Bonaparte had stepped up the diplomatic offensive using released prisoners of war, but it was not until the fall of Valetta that the Czar threw his own influence against the pro-Austrian Chancellor Panine in favour of his favourite Rostopchin. He informed Talleyrand of his terms. They included a settlement in Germany and Italy, the restoration of the King of Sardinia, the inviolability of the Kingdom of Naples, the integrity of Bavaria and Wurtemburg, where rich commanderies acknowledged the Imperial Grand Master, and last but not least the restoration of Malta to the Knights of St John.

The British capture of Valetta meant, however, that this was just what France could not ensure, but Bonaparte played on Paul's obsession. In return for Malta he wanted a Russian army in Hanover "to close the Weser", a Russian fleet in the Mediterranean to discipline Ferdinand of Naples, a Russian demonstration off Ireland and finally a Russian invasion of India. But by the time these preposterous terms reached St Petersburg, Paul I was dead.

He was murdered on the night of 23rd March 1801. The plot was well-laid and included his own family and creatures. He was strangled brutally in his bedroom, dying not bravely but pitifully. He had been condemned by his courtiers because they were afraid his dementia would destroy them; he was murdered by his own ministers who believed that he was reversing the traditional policy of the Empire for a chimera. In the middle of his grandiose plans for a settlement of the world he was murdered in a plot that included four of his own Knights of Justice.

He died as Nelson was sailing to the Baltic for a show of force against the possible adherents of an Armed Neutrality. At the last moment Bonaparte was denied a Tilsit, to be obtained without a Friedland. On the 27th Alexander I declared that he took the Order of St John under his Imperial protection and promised to employ his utmost means to reinstate it in all its rights, honours, immunities and privileges. But he had no intention of being Grand Master and he appointed as Lieutenant the Bailiff Field Marshall Count Nicholas Soltikov until a Great Council, as he called it, could be convoked and, if the great powers agreed, a new Grand Master elected by a Chapter General. The Order had once more become a European responsibility.

Overtures for a general peace were now in the air. In order not to prejudice the chances, Great Britain was prepared to evacuate Malta if she could have a reasonable guarantee that it would remain independent, particularly of France. Who could provide it? Grenville was prepared to accept a Russian guarantee, but Talleyrand was not. By October 1801, they had only managed to agree on the return of the Order under the protection of a third power. This news was received badly in Malta, where the inhabitants had no desire to return to the status of second class citizens; if they were to pass under foreign rule, let that rule be British. Though Pigot had behaved shabbily, Ball stood forth as a shining example of the true character of Britain, which was not dimmed by the actions of the British troops that treated the island as a conquered province. By an ingenious thesis that, as Alfonso V of Aragon in 1397 had bartered Maltese submission for money and declared that any alienation of the island from the Crown of Sicily could be legitimately resisted by the islanders, then the Maltese were masters of their island, submitting voluntarily to the cession of Malta to the Knights of St John on the understanding that, if the Order left, the island could revert to the Sicilian crown, not by right, however, of that crown, but by election of the Maltese people. They did not now so elect. Their leaders, therefore, addressed a humble petition to His Britannic Majesty and offered him the sovereignty of their isle. The Maltese had won it from the French who had won it from the Order; they now made a free offer of it to King George III. If Russia and France wanted to restore the Order, why should they not choose another island?

To reinforce their case, six of them went to London. They met the King, who was gracious; they met Lord Hobart, who was no less gracious but who was more practical. In the interests of a general peace, he told them, everyone should be prepared to make sacrifices. Britain and France had made theirs, and that of Malta should be to receive back the Order—not, however, as subjects but as equals, for there was to be a Maltese Tongue, and the high offices of state would be open to its members. Since the contracting powers had apparently made up their minds, the Deputies returned empty-handed. The Bailiff Carracciolo in Naples hastened to assert that the Deputies had represented, not the people who wanted the return of the Order that had done so much for them, but their own class, the nobility and clergy who had been traditionally opposed to the rule of the Hospitallers.

The Maltese people were, for the greater part, willing to be led either way. They had shouted huzzahs for Von Hompesch; they had enjoyed themselves at the *Fête Nationale*; they had suffered the utmost misery for Caruana and they venerated, along with the Holy Family, cheap lithographs of Captain Ball to be found in the lowliest hovel. The mercantile community on the other hand betrayed a surprising knowledge of Locke, and believed in the advantages of British rule.

But their fate was not in their hands. On 27th March 1802 the Treaty of Amiens was signed. In Article X, it was decreed that the Order should be restored after a Chapter General had met in the island and elected a Grand Master. The future constitution of the Order should contain neither a French nor an English Tongue, but a Maltese. The British garrison should

261

evacuate the island after three months, releasing it to the Neapolitans, who should hold it until a force was raised, half to be recruited from among the Maltese, and half from the countries with Tongues in the Order. The port should be open to ships of all nations who would pay dues for the upkeep of the Maltese Tongue. Malta's independence should be guaranteed by Great Britain, France, Russia, Austria, Spain and Prussia.

Bonaparte was not alone in thinking these arrangements "a romance that could not be executed." Lord Grenville, now out of office, thundered in the Lords that the Order impoverished in finance and degraded in reputation must soon sink into a gang of low, needy and unprincipled adventurers. Of the six guarantors, four had no navies, Prussia was a thrall of France, Naples was virtually a French vassal and the Italian Priories at the disposal of the First Consul, while the King of Spain, at the first promptings of Bonaparte had appropriated the lands of the Spanish Tongues. The German Priories threatened to secede if Maltese were admitted to the Order. What was the Order to live on? Who would support the new Grand Master if there were one? How could two thousand Neapolitans prevent the naval might of France, her ally Spain and her satellite Holland from seizing the island if Bonaparte had a mind to it?

In Malta, few came forward to take the Cross in the new Tongue, and in an effort to create confidence the British government deputed Alexander Ball as Plenipotentiary to the Order. He arrived on 10th July and was followed a month later by the French plenipotentiary, General Vial. But there was still no Grand Master to whom they were to be accredited.

The arrangements for the election were in the hands of Maisonneuve, now Vice-Chancellor, and he was to instruct the Priories to send a list to Rome from which the Pope would select a name. Von Hompesch, now destitute at Porto di Fermo, whither he had moved from Trieste, once again tried to resurrect his claim before the Emperor, but when that failed, the Bailiff de Suffren de Saint Tropez made the long journey to Paris to beg Bonaparte either to pay the pension promised in 1798 or to support his restitution. He had sold all he had to finance de Neveu's futile expedition, and he had but one treasure left—the sacred portrait of Our Lady of Philermos, and with that he would not part.

Pope Pius VII waited six months before choosing, to allow the ferment to settle in Russia. There, for two years, Paul's aberration had mesmerized Europe, but it had kept the Order alive. Though the Czar had intended it as "a novitiate from which the nobility of all the countries of Europe might learn the lessons of loyalty and honour," it had witnessed a sad degradation at the Court of St Petersburg. Paul's mistress, Madame Lapoukine, had obtained a Grand Cross first for her husband and then for herself. Her supplanter, the French siren Madame Chevalier, nightly awaited her lover to call upon her in the habit of the Grand Master. Lorenzo Litta had succumbed to the machinations of his enemies and been expelled; Giulio, a victim of the Czar's anger at Pope Pius VI's refusal to recognize him, had been exiled to his wife's estates. The Czar lavished the Cross on all and sundry. The worthiest recipient was Ball himself, the most unexpected Lady Hamilton—for services rendered to the Czar's Maltese subjects. With Paul's death, the Order's Roman Catholicity could reassert itself.

Pius VII, at last in September 1802 chose as Grand Master the forty-seven-year-old Bailiff di Ruspoli, Captain-General in 1784. Ruspoli was in London at the time and could not be reconciled to his appointment. First Article X of the Treaty of Amiens had stipulated that he should be the choice of a Chapter General; instead he had been chosen from a list submitted to the Pope by the Russian Priory which the Court of St James did not wish to recognize. Secondly he received shortly after a summons from Talleyrand to proceed straight to France without meeting the English ministers. Alexander in the meantime was being awkward. He resented the imputation of the Treaty that he was to be a Guarantor and not a Protecting Power, and refused to consider the admission of Maltese Knights without proofs. The appeal to a Chapter

General without his prior consent he took as a personal slight and refused to contribute any money to the defence of Malta until the Order was restored, or to be a Guarantor. Ruspoli in the end turned down the dignity. He valued his freedom and could foresee only trouble.

In the absence of the Czar's guarantee the British government refused to evacuate the island. Spain had sequestered the Spanish commanderies, Portugal was thinking of doing the same and the Prussians had sequestered the Priory of Silesia. Article X had no chance of being implemented. Bonaparte, whose activities in Holland and Switzerland were also in defiance of the Treaty and whose designs on India and Egypt were increasingly patent, decided to camouflage them by making an issue of Malta. In the meantime the Pope, having appointed the Bailiff Caracciolo Lieutenant on Soltikov's resignation, proceeded to the election of the Bailiff Tommasi on 9th February 1803. Tommasi, though one of the Bailiffs who had received Junot on the fateful 11th of June, enjoyed the approbation of both Alexander and Ferdinand. He had been one of Pinto's pages and was now seventy-one. His title was largely hollow; he had been chosen because he had held high office when the Order ruled in Malta, but had not formed one of von Hompesch's circle. He held a General Assembly of all available Knights in the prioral church at Messina where he received their homage, but he had no prospect of an early return to Malta. He set up his court in an Augustinian convent in Catania and despatched the Chevalier Busi to negotiate with Ball the Grand Master's return. Ball prevaricated by saying that there was no building in a fit state to receive him and that he would do far better to stay where he was until he had received orders from London instructing him to receive His Eminence.

General Vial, on the other hand, warmly encouraged Tommasi to come. Great Britain's continued occupation of the island in defiance of the Treaty of Amiens was provocative and malicious. Twelve days after Tommasi's election Bonaparte had informed Whitworth, now Ambassador in Paris, that he would rather see the English in the Faubourg St Antoine than in Malta. The British government was unmoved. Tommasi's promise, made to the Maltese through Busi, to lower the price of bread fell on deaf ears—the price of bread was already lower than in any other place in Europe. The Maltese greeted the prospect with no enthusiasm.

Until the Czar made up his mind to adhere to the articles of the Treaty of Amiens, the British government felt justified in hanging on to Malta. And by March 1803 the talk was once more of war. One last compromise was suggested whereby Great Britain should retain Malta for ever and indemnify the Order; in return she would recognize the new Italian Republics. But Bonaparte must evacuate Holland and Switzerland as he had promised in the Treaty of Lunéville. Talleyrand had now put on the shining armour of Protector of the Hospital. "The French government," he wrote to Lord Hawkesbury on 3rd April, "will never consent to anything that may prejudice the independence of the Maltese Order in its island." In pursuit of this policy, General Vial invited Tommasi officially to Malta and persuaded Acton to provide transport. Tommasi, despite Bonaparte's assurance that he would suffer himself to be "cut in pieces before consenting to Britain's possession of the island," decided not to risk the inevitable rebuff that would follow when he arrived.

There were several other arrangements that the British proposed, but they all sought to ensure that Great Britain remained in Malta. She should hold the island for ten years and allow the Knights to be installed in Lampedusa until the period was up and the fortifications of Malta had been levelled; she should permit the Knights to administer the island in civil matters while retaining the harbour and forts. In return Bonaparte should evacuate Holland.

Talleyrand refused and in doing so showed the cloven hoof. "The re-establishment of the Order was not so much the point to be discussed," Whitworth told Hawkesbury on 23rd April, "as that of allowing Great Britain to acquire a possession in the Mediterranean." The Addington ministry could under no circumstances leave Malta and so virtually evacuate the Mediterranean, and all these proposals were mere verbal finery. Despite the representations of a peace party led by Joseph Bonaparte, the First Consul was adamant. A Russian, Prussian or Austrian garrison must be admitted forthwith. The British government knew that Prussia and Austria could not and that Russia would not provide one. The real possibility of war was finally brought home to Bonaparte and he·made a last desperate concession: Britain could retain Malta if the French were given Taranto and Otranto in Puglia. It was still-born. An ultimatum to evacuate Holland was presented and on 18th May 1803 Great Britain and France went once more to war.

Bonaparte had hoped for a diplomatic intervention from the Czar and held out too long. The Order throughout was a mere cypher, kept in existence only by the protection of the Czar. Bavaria, despite pressure from France to sequester the Priory, dared not upset Alexander. Ferdinand IV would have sequestered the Sicilian Priories but for a similar awe of the imponderable. Though he was least consulted, there was one man who could keep the Knights together—the Pope. Alexander had accepted his nominee and ordered the Russian Priory to do homage to Tommasi. On the rock of St Peter the Order was to cling and to be saved.

Tommasi died in 1805 and the Pope did not elect another Grand Master. He was not anxious to provoke anybody and a General Assembly meeting in the Prioral Church at Messina had declared that the election did not lie with the Pope anyhow. They selected and Pius VII approved a Lieutenant, the Bailiff Guevara, a sixty-one-year-old Neapolitan. It was his job to try to reign among the débris. He succeeded in persuading Ferdinand once more to defer the sequestration of the Sicilian Priories, now urged on him by Lord William Bentinck, but he could do little more. He died on the eve of the Congress of Vienna. His successor, the Bailiff di Giovanni, deputed two Knights to Vienna, de Rohan's old Italian secretary, Miari, and the Commander Berlinghieri. They were to request another Mediterranean island from which the Knights could continue the *Corso* and on which they could maintain a Hospital. They were politely ignored. By the Treaty of Paris, 30th May 1814, Malta passed to the empire of His Britannic Majesty and on 12th May, the Neapolitan plenipotentiary signed away the rights of the Kingdom of Naples.

Di Giovanni reigned until 1821, to be succeeded by the Bailiff of Armenia, Antonio Busca. It seemed a propitious moment. The Greeks on a special mission to the Pope to ask for assistance in their struggle against the Turks offered to re-establish the Order on one of the islands of the Aegean. The Knights endeavoured to raise a loan in Paris of ten million francs in expectation of such an event, but at the Congress of Verona, though the powers recognized the surviving commanderies in Europe, they refused to take a decision on this matter. In 1825, the Sicilian commanderies were finally expropriated and the Lieutenant removed his sorry court to Ferrara in 1827. Hope had died among the Knights. Three years later Cardinal Lambruschini in Paris tried to persuade Charles X to instal the Knights in Algiers but their hopes, such as they were, were snuffed out by the July Revolution.

In 1834 the temporary sojourn in Ferrara came to an end and the Order moved to Rome to take over a palace on the Aventine Hill. Their glory had now departed and in their distress they returned to their first avocation as Hospitallers. In 1879, as a reward to the Order whose head was also titled the Servant of the Poor for many years of rescue and relief work in the former Papal states, the Pope once more appointed a Grand Master. For seventy-two years three Grand Masters ruled over an Order of two Tongues, the German and Italian, until the death of Prince Chigi della Rovere Albani in 1951. Thereafter Pope Pius XII refused to appoint a successor and, ever since, the future of the Order, still aristocratic, still subject to its ancient statutes has been under review. In the 20th century it must be hoped that a new Order will emerge to meet the new times, and despite the arguments of the entrenched stalwarts of the establishment, the wheels of change are turning and the last stronghold of the titled aristocrats is crumbling. There is a Peasant Pope. Why not a Peasant Grand Master?

In 1810 the King of Prussia, trying to carry out the reforms forced on him after Jena, suppressed the Lutheran Priory of Brandenburg. In 1853, at the request of the Prussian nobility starved of ceremonial at the austere Hohenzollern court, it was revived, but when the Lieutenant Grand Master refused to revive the old fraternal links forged by Pinto and Prince Ferdinand, it became an independent Protestant organization, numbering in two years 500 Knights. (The Order then numbered 100 Knights of Justice and 800 Knights and Ladies of Devotion.) By the last quarter of the century it supported 19 hospitals, a house at Beirut and a hospice in Jerusalem.

During the Greek War of Independence, when for a short time a return to Rhodes seemed possible, a group of French Knights, knowing the consent of England would be essential, crossed to England to see if they could revive the English Tongue. A number of Roman Catholic gentry established an English Priory under Sir Robert Peat who became Prior in 1831, but when it was not accepted in Rome financial stringency forced it to recruit Protestants. The Priory announced its complete independence in 1858 and under its Prior the Duke of Manchester (1861–88) it acquired for itself a constitution that received a royal charter. In 1874 it established the Life-Saving Medal; in 1882 it founded the ophthalmic hospital at Jerusalem. In 1888 it set up the St John's Ambulance Service. It bought the ancient property of the Priory of St John of London, at St John's Gate, Clerkenwell, and became the Venerable Order of St John of Jerusalem of the British Realm. The white cross of St John is now seen at fêtes and bazaars, usually, though not exclusively, worn by an elderly lady, a matron substitute for the veteran warrior who once escorted the pilgrims to Jerusalem. The warriors of this latter day, Lord Alexander of Tunis, Lord Portal of Hungerford are its Knights Commander, but their laurels, like those of the Bailiff de Suffren, were won on other fields and in other armies.

The Sovereign Order is as staunchly Roman Catholic as ever, and renowned in Catholic lands for its works of mercy. In 1956, when the Suez attack had caused the ejection of all British subjects from Egypt, it was the Plenipotentiary of the Order in Lebanon that negotiated a safe exodus for the Maltese.

What of our main protagonists? Von Hompesch lingered on until 1805. One year before he died the Imperial treasury was ordered to start paying him the annual pension of 300,000 francs he had been promised in 1798. His faithful apologist Mayer continued to defend his memory and assiduously collected documents for his rehabilitation, but he vanishes from the scene unheeded and discredited by the violence of his partisanship. De Loras, after dictating his own version of the surrender of Malta, died suddenly in Catania in 1799. De Ransijat returned to France with Vaubois and died, aged 69, in 1812. He wrote his own apology. De Fay and Toussard went with him to die ingloriously in the service of the Empire. Dolomieu is left, and the Maltese who went with him to Egypt. The last, with boots split and discarded, fought France's battles bare-footed in the sand. Some deserted and melted away into the mass where their Maltese vernacular would allow them to pass through the Egyptian crowd. Those who remained neither broke nor ran and earned the grudging respect of their commander.

Dolomieu was shipped home for health reasons in 1799. Forced by bad weather into Messina he was arrested as a traitor for his part in the events of June 1798. He was thrown into a dungeon where he lay for twenty-one months, deprived of books, deprived of light, but writing in the margin of his Bible with the smoke of his lamp for ink and a splinter of wood for pen, a dissertation on *La Philosophie Minéralogique et sur l'Espèce Minérale*. He was released after the Franco-Neapolitan treaty of March 1802, but his unsteady health had been fatally undermined. He died on 26th November, fifty-one years old. He was indomitable to the last. Not, in fact, the least among the Hospitallers.

Bombs have destroyed the Inns of France and Auvergne in Malta and have gutted the Hospital. A Maltese Parliament sits in Perellos's tapestry chamber and a Maltese Prime Minister lives in the Inn of Aragon. A Maltese Bishop sings Mass in the Conventual Church; a NATO C.-in-C. presides in the house of the Grand Admiral; destroyers with Turkish flags float in the creek of the galleys and a Turkish flag flies over Floriana. On high days and holidays, in the many casales of the island, flies too a standard of a white cross on a red ground, a living reminder that Malta will remain indissolubly united to the memory of the Order of the Knights Hospitaller of St John.

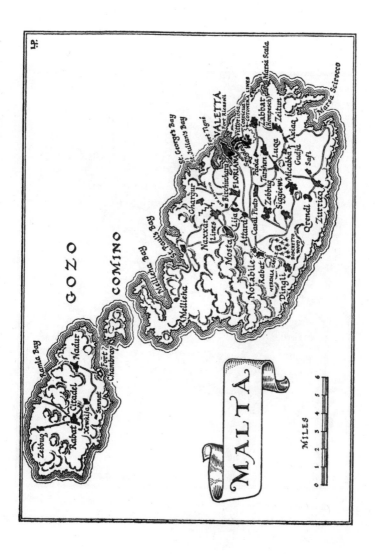

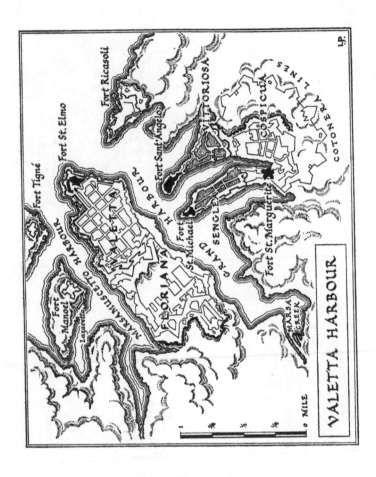

VALETTA HARBOUR

AUTHORITIES

KEY

AOM=Archives of the Order in Malta.
VLM=Valetta Library Manuscript.
   (The manuscripts are numbered according to the standard index used in
   the Royal Library of Malta in 1958.)
L.=London; P.=Paris; M.=Malta; R.=Rome.

   Page references in Archive and MS. sources have not been given as these are
likely to be renumbered in the future when the new catalogue is produced.
Dates have been given.
   The notes have been given under the separate chapters. They are each given
a page reference and the subject matter in brief to which the note refers. The
first section of notes is given over to amplifications of the text, the second to
sources.

The following are printed, contemporary authorities mentioned specifically in the
text, and reference to them will not be made in the source notes:

BOISGELIN, THE CHEV. LOUIS DE, *Ancient and Modern Malta*, 4 vols., L., 1804.
BORCH, COMTE DE, *Lettres sur la Sicile et sur l'Ile de Malte*, 1777, 2 vols., Turin, 1782.
BRES, HONORATO, *Recherches Historiques et Politiques sur l'Isle de Malte*, P., An IX
   (1799).
BRYDONE, PATRICK, *A Tour through Sicily and Malta*, 2 vols., L., 1774.
DENON, V., *Voyage en Sicile et à Malte*, P., 1788.
FRENCH VISITOR IN 1678, A, *Nouvelle Relation d'un Voyage et Description Exacte de
   l'Ile de Malte*, P., 1679.
PLATIÈRE, ROLAND DE LA, *Lettres Ecrites de Suisse... et de Malte*, Vol. 3, Amsterdam,
   1783.
SPRETI, CHEV. CAMILLO, *A Treatise on Knightly Behaviour and Description of the
   Island of Malta*, trans. A. Mackenzie-Grieve, L., 1949 (original *VLM* 1200-2).
YOUNG, SIR WILLIAM, *Journal of a Summer Excursion to Malta*, 1772, L., 1774.

Page
18   *For light offences:* For dodging divine services, absenting oneself from the
     Assembly of the Tongue, for interrupting a speaker in Council, for eating in
     the Inn without wearing the habit, for calumniating a fellow Knight—the
     Settena: seven days' close confinement on bread and water, a daily beating
     before the altar of the Tongue in the conventual church administered by the
     Grand Prior or his deputy. For failure to do military exercises, for dicing,
     gambling, eating in taverns—the Quarantena: forty days' solitary, with daily
     beating and an obligation to take the penitential bread and water on the ground.
     Both penalties were abolished in 1776 as they had not been enforced for years.
34   *The election of a Grand Master:* In the early days of the Order the newly-
     elected Grand Master's house was thrown open to pillage by the Knights, but
     later these perks were substituted by a bonus payment of three scudi to each
     elector in Convent.
36   *Ambassadors:* France first received a Maltese emissary with that title, and he
     always received most cordial and friendly treatment. Over the unimportant
     matter of the Grand Priory of France which Louis XV wished to confer on the
     Prince de Conti, the Ambassador had six audiences of the King—as many as,
     if not more than would have been accorded the Ambassador of a major power.
     AOM 1239, Froullay to Pinto: 13 Jan. 1749. In 1744 Maria Theresa accorded
     the Maltese minister the same reception as the Venetian Ambassador and the

Page

Pope in 1747 admitted the minister in Rome to *accesso pubblico, sala regia e la comitiva alla regia capella* as the Benjamin of the Diplomatic corps. In the same year Ferdinand VI of Spain followed suit. A request from the King of Portugal to have an embassy was turned down on grounds of expense, since it was feared that all the Italian states would imitate him. *AOM* 269, Liber Conciliorum Status: 22 May 1744; *AOM* 270, LCS: 12 May 1747; 9 Oct. 1747

37   *Consul:* The consul in Malta was always the nominee of the Grand Master and so subject to him. "The Grand Master should be considered as the Consul, that is, as the Consul General for all nations and the common father of all nationals." Public Records Office, L. SP 86/2, Pinto to Lord Egremont: undated, 1763. Both Versailles and London asked at regular intervals to be allowed to appoint a patented official, but the Grand Master refused to permit anyone in his realm to have virtual diplomatic and personal immunity; he had enough trouble as it was with the patentees of the Bishop and Inquisitor. The British consul at Messina was authorized to appoint his deputy in Malta but in effect he accepted the Grand Master's nominee. This position was never properly understood in London. *AOM* 1216–17 and 1561–2, Correspondence between Grand Master and Ambassador in Paris: 8 Sept 1711; 21 Oct., 26 Nov. 1712; 18 Feb. 1713. The consul had no salary, but a consulage duty of 50 shillings sterling from every ship of his nation that entered the port. The English consul was often consul for Holland, Sweden, the Netherlands and Prussia as well.

38   *Quarantine:* Most rigorously kept. Any ship suspected of having been in contact with the plague was subjected to a full 40 days, and its crew and passengers were lodged in the Lazaretto. In 1781 a ship carrying some plague victims was wrecked off Taormina; at once it was decreed that any vessel proceeding from any point within 90 miles of Taormina should be subjected to full quarantine. Anyone attempting to break out of the Lazaretto could be shot on sight, and no right of sanctuary was enjoyed in churches. Marseilles, which suffered a serious outbreak of plague in 1723, sent observers to Malta to see the Quarantine regulations at work. *AOM* 273, LCS: 5 June 1781.

38   *Monte di Redenzione:* Set up in 1607 at the instance of a Capuchin, and administered by a French, Spanish, Italian and German Knight. It assisted with ransoms, preference being given to those who had been enslaved in the Order's service. A maximum tariff had been fixed at 700 scudi (roughly £70). The Monte was not permitted to ransom Knights or Servants-at-Arms; the sums were only intended to assist the slaves whose families could not afford the ransoms. *VLM* 404, *passim.*

38   *Monte di Pietà:* Government pawn shop, founded by a Portuguese Knight in 1598 to prevent the poor from falling into the hands of moneylenders. It grew into a bank, obliged to give money on pledge. So popular did its short- and long-term loans become that it needed constant injections of money. Zondadari reduced the interest rate from 4 to 3½ per cent and allowed clothing to be deposited as a pledge. When short of funds, the Monte borrowed from the Università. Pinto in 1763 gave it 12,000 scudi and lent it 38,000 at 3 per cent to allow it to pay its debts. De Rohan in 1787 incorporated the Monte di Pietà with the Redenzione as the latter had more money than it needed. In 1798 its funds were nearly 50,000 sc. in hand and 274,000 in pledges. The French in that year by an unscrupulous use of the Monte were reputed to have raised 420,000 sc. or 42 sc. per head of the population. Fairly and easily come by money was a contributing factor in the prosperity of the Maltese in the 18th century. *VLM* 379, *passim.*

39   *Consuls:* These were legal functionaries; in the Consolato they could give summary judgments in cases concerning less than 10 sc.; otherwise they were judges in the first instance. Each nation had an interpreter with no judicial influence, usually the Consul of that nation, who might also be the Judge Consul in litigation not concerning his own nationals. The Consuls of those nations with Knights in the Order could set up their own courts in their office to adjudicate in cases concerning their own nationals only, with the right to imprison refractory sailors. The British consul had no such right, and had to

bring every dispute before the Consolato. *VLM* 392, Consolato del Mare; PRO SP 86/2, Dodsworth to Sec. of State: 16 Mar. 1754.

43 *Quittance from Capitation Tax:* Amounted to a contribution of 39,600 livres, from the Vingtième to 120,000 livres p.a. while the Tongues of France, Provence and Auvergne contributed 28,000 livres direct to the King. The total was 186,000 livres. By 1790, when the total revenue from the Order's lands in France was 4,284,651 livres, these contributions had been brought up to one-tenth—428,465 livres. Camus (Développement de la Motion rel. à l'Ordre de M.) assessed the total capital of the Order in France at 112,006,250 livres.

49 *The purchase of weapons:* In 1714 rumours of a threatened attack from Turkey panicked the Order in the purchase from the arsenals of Marseilles and Toulon of armaments worth 50,000 livres. Orleans cancelled the debt in return for the admission of one of his bastards as a Knight. In 1734 the Order purchased 24 cannon from Toulon at a time when France was at war and French ships denied access to Grand Harbour.

49 *Law:* When Law's credit scheme collapsed, an attempt was made to bolster the shocked and failing currency by seizing all available bullion in exchange for *billets de liquidation* or I.O.U.s. The Receivers of the Order were obliged to hand over their specie for *billets* that were unredeemable for four years and lost value every month. At their pre-cash value, the sum owed to the Order was over a million livres. In 1720, Demesmes, the Ambassador in Paris, made secret approaches to Orleans to prevent the redeemable value of these *billets* being fixed at 50 per cent and was told that if the Order were content to wait, a 100 per cent redemption might be made. In 1723, however, new threats of a Turkish armada made purchases of arms and powder necessary and because the Order had no cash in France, Demesmes once more approached the Regent who promised to exempt the Religion from any final ruling that would settle for less than 100 per cent redemption. Emboldened by this promise, Demesmes purchased on credit 400,000 livres worth of stuff, which the Grand Master hastily reduced to 210,000. Orleans, on consulting Paris Duverny, the financial minister, then found that he could not keep his promise, while Dudon, the Comptroller General, averred that the Order's claims were old debts and bills raked up from a period long before Law's crash. Orleans' death put off any settlement until June 1724, when, partly to get ready payment for the Order's purchases and partly to oblige it, a settlement was made whereby the purchases would be paid for by the government's accepting *billets de liquidation* at their face value. The remaining 900,000-odd livres should be met by a contract on the *taille* for the next 50 years from which the customary 39,600 livres capitation tax should be extracted. As the Order in the meantime had run up debts to meet its obligations, there being no acceptable money coming from France, it was decided in 1725 to sell these contracts outright and to liquidate the debts that were standing at 3 per cent interest, while the contracts brought in only 2 per cent. Once again, in preference to other institutions the Order was favoured. Dudon's suspicions were false, but it had driven a hard bargain. It could not afford to do anything else. *AOM* 266, LCS: 4 June 1724; 12 Jan. 1725. *AOM* 1481, Perellos to Receiver in Genoa: 28 July 1720; *AOM* 1219, Amb. in Paris to Vilhena: 16 Jan., 20 Feb. 1723; 8 July 1724.

227 *O'Hara:* Anthony Mary Marcellus O'Hara, son of Charles O'Hara, colonel in the Russian army, and his Russian wife. His uncle was M.P. for Sligo and had obtained from the Ulster King-at-Arms formal acknowledgment of his nephew's nobility, so that he could become a professed Knight of Devotion, sponsored by Cardinal Henry of York and Catherine II. Pius VI issued his bull conferring the cross in June 1790. In March 1797 Paul made him, now a colonel in his army, Psaro's successor in Malta, where he arrived in July. He was believed to be in hopes of the Grand Priory of Ireland and to this end he made solemn profession of the triple vow in April 1798 to become a Knight of Justice with a commandery in the Russian Priory and a commandery of grace. With his salary from Paul, he was worth thus 15,000 sc. a year. He also wanted to combine William England's post with his own and prevailed on Lord Whitworth,

Page

British Ambassador in St Petersburg, to recommend him to the Court of St James. Napoleon intervened to prevent it. O'Hara, V.A., "A Knight of Malta: the Chevalier O'H.", *English Review*, May 1932.

260 *Four of his own Knights of Justice:* Paul Stroganov, Commander *de famille*; Commander Pahlen; Commander Adam Czartoryski; Commander Ouvarov, Paul's A.D.C. and Governor of St Petersburg.

Chapter I

For the history of the Order before the 18th century:

BOISGELIN, L. DE, *Ancient and Modern Malta*, L., 1804.

BOSIO, G., *Dell'Istoria della Sacra et Illustrissima Religione di San Giovanni Gerosolomitano*, R., 1594–1602.

ENGEL, C. E., *L'Ordre de Malte en la Méditerranée*, 1530–1798, Monaco, 1957.

LUKE, H., *Malta*, L., 1949.

MIÈGE, *Histoire de Malte*, 4 vols., Brussels, 1841.

PORTER, W., *A History of the Knights of Malta*, L., 1858.

SCHERMERHORN, E., *Malta of the Knights*, L., 1929.

VERTOT, ABBÉ R. A., *Histoire des Chevaliers Hospitaliers de Saint Jean de Jerusalem*, P., 1726.

VILLENEUVE-BOUGEMENT, L. F. DE, *Monumens des Grand-Maîtres de St J. de J.*, P., 1829.

Chapter II

Passim: VERTOT, op. cit.

Codice Gerosolomitano, 1776–82, e Compendio, 1783. M. *Istruzzioni sopra gli obblighi piu principali de Cavalieri di San Giovanni Geros⁰*, Alessandria, 1758.

ARGENS, CHEV. D', *Reflexions Politiques sur l'Etat et les Devoirs de l'Ordre de Malte*, The Hague, 1734.

12 *Nobility: Proteste à S.A.R. le Duc d'Orleans du part des Chevaliers de la Langue de France*, P., 1715.

14 *Hooliganism among novices: AOM* 1526, Pinto to Amb. in Rome: 31 Jan. 1770.

20 *French romans:* Engel, C. E., "Le Chevalier de Malte, type littéraire au 18ème siècle", *Revue des Sciences Humaines*, July–Sept. 1953.

21 *Coleridge on Malta:* See Letters, L.1932; Table Talk, L.1917; "The Friend", a series of essays, L.1890.

Bosredon de Ransijat: Journal du Siège et Blocus de Malte, P., An IX (1801).

23 *Tencin's will: VLM* 265.

Abela: VLM 12, Giornale di I. S. Mifsud, 2 Dec. 1756.

24 *Ciantar:* Author of *Malta Illustrata* (a new edition of the work first produced in 1647 by G. F. Abela), M., 1772.

Vassali, M. A.: Mylsen Phoenico-Punicum sive Grammatica Melitensis, R., 1791.

25 *Dolomieu: La Vie et Correspondance*, ed. P. Lacroix, 2 vols., P., 1921.

26 *Sumptuary Laws: AOM* 264, Liber Conciliorum Status (hereafter LCS): 15 Feb. 1697.

AOM 1568, Pinto to Grand Priors of France; 4 Feb. 1741.

27 *Sardinia and the Priories of Italy: AOM* 273, LCS: 23 June 1781; 8, 9 May, 17 June 1782.

AOM 274, LCS: 20, 29 Apr., 9, 14 May 1784.

AOM 2153–4, Procedimenti della Lingua d'Italia, 1782–5, *passim*.

Frederick II and Silesia: AOM 1503, Pinto to Minister in Vienna; 29 Feb. 1744.

28 *Complaint from Ambassador in Paris: AOM* 1219, Demesmes to Vilhena: 26 Nov. 1722.

Chapter III

Page
Passim: VERTOT, op. cit.; *Istruzzioni,* op. cit.
37 *Grand Master's Court:* HÉRITTE, L., "Essai sur l'Ordre des Hospitaliers ... et de son Gouvernement Civil et Militaire à Malte au commencement du 18ème siècle", P., 1912.
39 *Consolato del Mare: VLM* 392, Establishment of C. del M.
41 *Entry into Notabile: AOM* 269, LCS: 29 Oct. 1741. Pinto's entry.
42 *Death of Grand Master:* Le Nouveau Mercure, P., 1 Mar. 1720.
44 *The Order of St Anthony: VLM* 268, Correspondence upon the Incorporation of the O. of St A. into the O. of St J. of J., 1774-6.
45 *Houel, J.: Voyage Pittoresque aux Iles de Sicile et de Malte,* 4th vol., P., 1787.
47 *Louis XIV:* Quoted by BRES, *Rech. Hist.,* etc.
48 *1728 War with Tripoli: AOM* 1220, Amb. in P. to Vilhena; 7 Jan. 1729.
1741 War with Tunis: AOM 269, LCS: 16 June, 14, 16 Sept., 24 Nov. 1741.
49 *Honours of the Louvre:* Ibid. Amb. in France to Pinto: 30 May 1742.
50 *Charles VII and Concordat: AOM* 1500, Pinto to Amb. in R.: 24 July, 7 Aug., 30 Sept., 30 Oct. 1741.
    AOM 1501, Pinto to Pro-Amb. R.; 26 Mar., 23 Apr. 1742.
    AOM 1502, Pinto to Amb. in R.: 2 Oct. 1743.
    AOM 1550, Amb. in R. to Pinto: 29 Oct., 9 Nov. 1743.
51 "*Like the United Nations*": See O'FARRAN, C. D', "The Sovereign Order in International Law", *The Internat. Law and Compar. Law Quarterly,* April 1954.

Chapter IV

Passim: HUGHES, Q., *The Building of Malta,* L., 1956.
52 *Louis XIV:* Quoted by BRES.
54 *Teonge: Diary of Henry Teonge,* 1675-9, L., 1825.
58 *Conventual Church:* SCICLUNA, H., *The Church of St John in Valetta,* R., 1955.
62 *Sacred Infirmary: VLM* 377, Regulations of S.I.
    HOWARD, J., *An Account of the Principal Lazarettos of Europe,* L., 1791.
64 *Ximenes's visit: VLM* 1146, Giornale di Notizie: 6 Mar. 1773.
    Number of patients: AOM 273, LCS: 13 Apr. 1781.
67 *Gobelin tapestries: AOM* 1216, Amb. in P. to Perellos: 20 Dec. 1708.
68 *Theatre: VLM* 1398, BORG, *Cronistoria della Opera Lirica a Malta.*
    VLM 1146, Giornale di Not.: 23 Apr. 1772, commissioning of professional company of twenty.
69 *Birth of Dauphin:* "Compendio del Giornale di Fra Gaetano Reboul" (Archivium Melitense), 14 Nov. 1729.
    Marriage of Louis XIV: VLM 1146, Giornale di Not.: 11 July 1770.
70 *Messina earthquake:* BOISGELIN, op. cit.
72 *Freemasonry:* DOUBLET, P. J. L. O., *Mémoires Historiques sur l'Invasion et l'Occupation de Malte,* ed. Panisse-Passis, P., 1883, pp. 81–108.
    BROADLEY, W., *F. in Malta,* L., 1880, Chap. 1.

Chapter V

76 *Carnival,* 1765: *VLM* 14, Giornale di I. S. Mifsud: 3 Feb. 1765.
78 *Slavery in Malta: AOM* 270, LCS: 23 June 1749, regulations.
    Reciprocity: AOM 1484, Vilhena to Apost. Prefect, Tunis: 1 July 1924; to Bey, Apost. Prefect, Consul of Tuscany: 28 Aug. 1724—over closure of churches and ill-treatment of priests in Tunis.
79 *Ransoms:* Archives of French Consulate, Valetta, contain the documents of innumerable transactions.
80 *Turks seek slavery in Malta: AOM* 266, LCS: 18 Nov. 1714.

Page

81 *Bey of Benghazi: AOM* 1511, Pinto to Bey: 8 June 1754.
Recognition of Tripoli pass: AOM 1487, Vilhena to Basha of T.: 22 Oct. 1726.
Maltese passes to Tripoli traders: AOM 1532, de Rohan to Bey of Benghazi: 14 Feb. 1780.

81 et seq. *Corso:* Cavaliero, R. E., "The Decline of the Malt. C. in the 18th century", *Melita Historica*, 1959.

85 *Cotton: VLM* 628, 4 vols. Records of the Douane for 1776, 1791, 1792, 1797–8.
VLM 429, Bandi e Prammatiche: 7 May 1757; 20 Apr. 1769; 23 May 1770; 3 Oct. 1777.
VLM 388, Letter from Lord Hobart to Chas. Cameron, Civil Governor in Malta: 14 May 1807.

86 *French trade in Malta:* Godechot, "La France et M. au 18ème siècle", *Revue Historique*, July 1951.
Reduction of tax: AOM 1568, Vilhena to Amb. in P.: 12 Mar. 1733.
Trade dues: VLM 429, Bandi, etc., Règlements de la Douane Magistrale, 5 Nov. 1723.

87 *Free port:* Ibid.: 22 Jan. 1754; 23 Feb. 1761; 25, 28 Sept. 1765; 3 Oct. 1773; 9 Dec. 1779; 2 Aug. 1784.
Corn concession: Ibid.: 12 Aug. 1723–31 Mar. 1724.
Warehouses: Ibid.: 22 Jan. 1754.
Marsilian complaints: AOM 1573, Pinto to Amb. in P.: 3 Nov. 1751.
Maria Theresa dollar: VLM 429, Bandi, etc.: 3 Jan. 1777.

88 *Director of Farms: AOM* 1576, Pinto to Espanet, Marit. Agent in Marseilles: 4 Dec. 1753.
Turgot: AOM 1240, Turgot to de Rohan: 6 Feb. 1777.

89 *Harbour dues: VLM* 1057, Statement of Customs Duties paid by merchants importing goods to M.
Quarantine: Godechot, op. cit.

90 *Riedesel, J. H.: Voyage en Sicile et dans la Grande Grèce*, Lausanne, 1773.
Carnival—masks: VLM 429, Bandi, etc., 26 Feb. 1722.
Carnival—d. of Pope: VLM 137, Journal de l'Abbé Boyer, 10 Feb. 1775

93 *Patentees—leaseholders: AOM* 1464, Perellos to Amb. in R.: 20 Jan., 5 Mar. 1703.
Patentees—militia: VLM 5, protest of clerics of M. against serving in the Militia, 1761.
Patentees—Consolato: AOM 1528, Pinto to Amb. in R.: 6 July 1772.
Patentees—1706: AOM 1467, Perellos to Amb. in R.: 1 June 1706.
Patentees—1750: AOM 270, LCS: 6 June 1750, Papal Brief.

94 *Sanctuary: AOM* 273, LCS: 3 Dec. 1777, Papal Brief.

95 *Venerable Cong. of Poor: VLM* 429, Bandi, etc.: 20 Feb., 3 Mar. 1730.
Guilds: Mifsud, A., *I nostri Consoli e le Arti ed i Mestieri*, M., 1917.

96 *Public morals: VLM* 429, Bandi, etc.: 1 Jan. 1790; 19 Nov. 1794; 20 Feb. 1777.
Adulterers: Ibid.: 23 Jan. 1786.
Sieur du Mont: Nouveau Voyage au Levant, à Malte et en Turquie, The Hague, 1699.
Walsh, T.: Journal of the Late Campaign in Egypt. L., 1803.

97 *Baptized slave: VLM* 12, Giornale di Mifsud: 19 Dec. 1757.

98 *Justice:* Royal Commission on Malta, 1812: "The Laws". *VLM* 429, Bandi, etc.: 2 June, 1 Dec. 1786.

99 *Università:* Mifsud, A., *Provigionamento e l'Università di Malta*, M. 1917.
Royal Commission on Malta: "The Università." *VLM* 1146, Giornale di N.: 21 Apr. 1773, credits.

100 *Bread: VLM* 429, Bandi, etc.: 22 Feb. 1741; 25 Feb., 17 Mar. 1737.
Lacroix, *Vie et Corres. de D. de Dolomieu*, D. to Chev. Gioeni: 10 Sept. 1785.

Chapter VI

Page

102 *Visit of Czeremetev: Journal du Voyage*, 1697–9, trans. Prince Galitzin, P., 1859. *AOM* 264, LCS: 8, 9, 12, 13, 14, 18, 19 May, 28 July, 1, 27 Aug. 1798.

105 *Expeditions of 1635–94:* See ROSSI, E., *Storia della Marina dell'ordine di San Giov. di Ger. di Rodi e di Malta*, Rome-Milan, 1926.

Expedition of 1696–7: AOM 264, LCS: 2 Oct. 1697, relation of Capt.-General.

106 *Loss of Capitana and San Paolo:* Ibid.: 12 Mar. 1700. *AOM* 265, LCS: 13 June 1700.

Inauguration of Line Squadron: AOM 264, LCS: 31 Mar. 1700.

AOM 265, LCS: 16 Jan. 1701.

VLM 1146, Giornale di N.: 1 Apr. 1705.

Toulon vessels: AOM 1215, Amb. in P. to Perellos: 23 May 1704.

107 *1716 Expedition: AOM* 266, LCS: 25 June 1716; 14 Sept. 1718.

Recognition of Philip V: AOM 265, LCS: 17, 25 Apr. 1701.

108 *The War of Spanish Succession: AOM* 1215–17, Amb. in P. to Perellos: 1701–

et 1713, *passim*.

seq. *AOM* 1561, Perellos to Amb. in P. *et al*.: 1705–13, *passim*.

AOM 1466, Perellos to Dutch Consul, Leghorn; 20 Mar. 1705. *AOM* 1469, Perellos to Bailiff Riggio: 17 Feb. 1707. *AOM* 1470, Perellos to Dutch Consul, Leg.: 13 Mar. 1709. *AOM* 1474, Perellos to A. Giovanni: 13 July 1713.

109 *Chauvelin: AOM* 1221, Amb. in P. to Vilhena: 16 Dec. 1733.

Alberoni and Conquest of Sicily: AOM 1479, Perellos to Amb. in R.: 13, 27 July 1718; to Receiver in Turin: 27 July 1718; to Receiver in Messina: 1 Aug., 2, 15 Sept., 11, 26 Oct. 1718; to Receiver in Palermo: 3 Nov., 11, 19 Dec. 1718; to Receiver in Genoa: 16 Aug., 21 Dec. 1718.

AOM 1480, Perellos to Receiver in Naples: 21 June 1719; to Admiral Byng: 26 June 1719; to Receiver in Venice: 19 July 1719; to Amb. in R.: 2 Aug., 21 Sept., 8 Nov. 1719. Zondadari to George I, 16 Dec. 1719.

AOM 267, LCS: 26 June 1719; 27 Apr. 1720; 29 Oct. 1722; 7 Aug. 1723. La Val's report.

AOM 1779, Diverse Scritture sulla neutralita del Porto: Decree of 23 Nov. 1719; Mémoire of Chev. Castellane, 27 Nov. 1719.

PATTEE BYNG, *Journals*, Navy Records, L., 1950.

111 *Oran: AOM* 265, LCS: 31 Dec. 1706, relation of de Langon, dated 12, 26

et Dec. 1707, relation of Saint Pierre, dated 5 July, 17 Oct. 1707.

seq. *VLM* 262, "Voyages à Barbarie—by a Redemptionist Father"; *Journal de Chambray*, 1707, pp. 27–42, L., 1736.

AOM 1561, Perellos to des Pennes: 21 July 1712; *AOM* 266, LCS: 6 Feb., 20 Mar. 1715;

AOM 1562, Perellos to Pontchartrain: 30 Mar. 1715; to Regent Orleans: 18 July 1717.

AOM 1216, Amb. in P. to Perellos: 20 June 1716.

112 *Difficulties of Treasury: AOM* 266, LCS: 16 Oct. 1710.

1714 War Scare: Ibid.: 18 Nov., 11 Dec. 1714; 5, 26 Jan., 12 Apr., 10, 19 June 1715.

Chapter VII

General: RAFAL, MARQUES DE, *Grandes Maestres de la Orden de M. partenecientes a las Lenguas de Castilla y Aragon en los siglos XVII y XVIII*, Madrid, 1932.

113 *Contemporary diarist: VLM* 1146, Giornale di N.: 14 Jan. 1720.

Dispute with Inquisitor: AOM 1482, Zondadari to Sant 'Agnese: 29 Oct. 1721; to Amb. in R.: 11, 24 Nov. 1721.

114 *The Aga Abdi: AOM* 267, LCS: 7 May, 2 Aug. 1722.

AOM 1484, Vilhena to Amb. in R.: 2 June, 29 July, 15 Aug. 1722.

115 *Sant' Agnese: AOM* 267, LCS: Reports from Amb. in R.: 26 Sept. (entered 13 Oct.); 3 Oct. (1 Nov.); 9 Nov. (29 Nov.) 1722.

AOM 1484, Vilhena to Amb. in R.: 20 July, 15 Sept. 1722.

AUTHORITIES

Page
115 *Spain's offer and Von Schade in Germany: AOM* 267, LCS: Letter from Amb. in R.: 7 Sept. (7 Oct.) 1722.
    AOM 1333, Amb. in R. to Vilhena: 29 Dec. 1722; 16 Jan., 7 Feb., 6, 8 Mar., 30 Apr., 1, 8 May 1723; 14 Jan. 1724.
116 *Projected truce with Turkey: AOM* 267, LCS: 19 Apr. 1723.
117 *Chambray: VLM* 262, *Journal*, pp. 1–250.
118 *Stock and Pilier: AOM* 267, LCS: 19 Apr.–6 May 1724. "Relation de la Fonction Solennelle de l'Estoc et du Chapeau donnés par le Pape à D. Antoine M. de Vilhena", P., 1725.
119 *Bey of Tunis: AOM* 269, LCS: 10 May, 7 June, 29 Dec. 1737.
    AOM 1496, Despuig to B. of T.: 19 June 1738.
    Giornale di G. Reboul: 7 Oct. 1740.

Chapter VIII

121 *Obituary Notice: VLM* 12, Giornale di Mifsud: 21, 25 Dec. 1758.
122 *Judge Cumbo:* LEOPARDI, E. R., "Judge Cumbo and the Baker", *Sunday Times of Malta*, 2 Dec. 1956.
123 *Pinto on Palm Sunday: VLM* 14, Giornale di Mifsud: 15 Apr. 1764.
    Cagliostro: Mémoire pour le Comte de Cagliostro (from the proceedings of the trial of the Cardinal de Rohan), P., 1786.
124 *Ethiopia: AOM* 269, LCS: 6 Apr. 1735; 22 Mar. 1740.
    PASTOR, *History of Popes*, vol. xxxv, p. 396.
126 *Corsica: VLM* 421, Remise à S. E. le Duc de Choiseul: 4 Nov. 1763.
    AOM 272, LCS: 30 Aug. 1769.
127 *Crusade Bull: VLM* 1170, Bolla Crociata.
128 *Ecclesiastical Visitor: AOM* 1510, Pinto to Amb. in R.: 10, 20 July, 21 Aug., 4, 18 Sept., 17 Oct., 14 Dec. 1752.
    AOM 1576, Pinto to Amb. in P.: 12 Aug.; to Chev. de Grieu: 16, 22 Sept., 29, 31, Oct., 13 Dec. 1753.
    AOM 270, LCS: 19 May, 4 June, 18 July, 6 Aug., 16 Sept., 1753; 8, 21 Jan., 14 Mar., 10 Apr., 8 May 1754; 7 Jan. 1755.
    AOM 1374, Benedict XIV to Card. Tencin: 11 Sept., 2 Oct., 14 Nov. 1753; 16 Jan., 19 Apr. 1754; Card. Tencin to Benedict XIV: 25 Oct. 1753; Amb. in R. to Pinto: 15 Oct., 16 Nov., 28 Dec. 1754; 6 Jan. 1755; Card. Valenti to Card. Tencin: 13, 20 Feb., 3 Apr. 1754; Receiver in Turin to Amb. in R.: 13 Mar., 1 May 1754.
    AOM 1511, Pinto to Amb. in R.: 11, 21 Mar., 21 May, 8 June, 2 July 1754.
    AOM 1226, Amb. in P. to Pinto: 8, 9 Jan., 7, 11, 14 Feb., 22 May, 18 Apr., 19 June, 21 Oct. 1754.
    AOM 271, LCS: 24 July, 6 Nov. 1755; 17 Jan. 1756.
129 *Patentees—1755: AOM* 1577, Pinto to Amb. in P.: 10 Aug. 1755.
    Patentees—Homicide, 1766: AOM 1522, Pinto to Amb. in R.: 31 Oct. 1766; *AOM* 1524, ditto: 11 Jan. 1768.
    Sanctuary—Limitation: AOM 271, LCS: 30 May 1761, representations in ibid.: 10 May 1759.
    Sanctuary—Gang of footpads: AOM 1515, Pinto to Amb. in R.: 10 Feb., 5 May, 2 June, 23 Aug. 1759.
    Sanctuary—Prostitute: AOM 1474, Perellos to Amb. in R.: 29 Mar. 1713.
130 *Expulsion of Jesuits:* MIFSUD, A., *L'Espulsione dei Gesuiti da Malta*, M., 1914.
    University—warehouses: AOM 273, LCS: 16, 22 Sept. 1773.
131 *University—responsibility of Treasury:* Ibid.: 22 Apr. 1779.
    Priests of the diocese: AOM 1525, Pinto to Minister in Naples: 22 Oct. 1769.

Chapter IX

132 *Dodsworth:* CAVALIERO, R. E., "John Dodsworth, a Consul in Malta" *Mariners' Mirror*, Nov. 1957.
    ERSKINE, *Augustus Hervey's Journal, 1746–59*, L., 1953, pp. 187, 285.

380

AUTHORITIES

Page
138 *New British Consul: VLM* 1255, de Rohan to Lord Caernarvon: 20 May 1789; England's Commission sgd. 6 June 1794.

339 *The Conspiracy of the Slaves:* Giornale di Reboul: 7 June 1749.
et *VLM* 1146, Giornale di N.: 6 June–12 Nov. 1749, Relazione del Congiuro
seq. dei Schiavi, M., 1749.

  AOM 1225, Amb. in P. to Pinto: 27 Jan., 7 Apr., 3, 10, 23 Sept., 12, 26, 29 Oct., 16, 25 Nov., 10 Dec. 1749.

  AOM 270, LCS: 1 Feb. 1748; 5 May, 14, 23 June, 24, 28 July, 14 Aug. 1749.

  AOM 1573, Pinto to Amb. in P.: 23 July, 6, 31 Oct. 1748.
142 *"The Ottoman Crown": AOM* 271 6, 18 Oct., 14 Nov. 1760; 18 Feb., 2 Mar., 6 July, 27 Aug., 12 Sept. 1761.
143 *Maltese privileges in France: AOM* 272, LCS: 7 Mar. 1766—Registered by Parlement: 12 July 1765.

Chapter X

  General: CAVALIERO, R. E., "The Affair of Ostrog", *Journal of the Faculty of Arts,* Royal Univ. of M., 1958.
147 *Sagramoso:* BERTOLI, A., *La Vita del Marchese S.,* Pavia, 1793.
148 *Cavalcabo:* BOSWELL, *On the Grand Tour, Germany and Switzerland,* L., 1953, pp. 58–9, 64, 67–8, 113.

  AOM 272, LCS: 11 Jan., 13 Nov. 1770; 18 Apr. 1771.

  AOM 1579, Pinto to Catherine II, to Amb. in P.: 6 Apr. 1770.

  VLM 1146, Giornale di N.: 18 Feb., 11 Mar., 1 May, 21 June, 16, 31 July 1770; 17, 18 Jan., 3, 5 Feb. 1771.

  AOM 1526, Pinto to Receiver in Naples and Messina: 7 Jan. 1771.
149 *de Pins: AOM* 1526, Pinto to Amb. in R.: 20 Feb. to 10 July 1770.

  AOM 1579, Pinto to Amb. in P.: 23 Feb. 1771.
151 *d. of Pinto and career of de Rohan:* Villeneuve-Bougement: Monuments des Grand-Maîtres Pinto et de Rohan.
152 *de Rohan persona non grata: AOM* 1578, Pinto to Louis XV: 30 Aug. 1766; Choiseul to Pinto: 17 Oct. 1766.

Chapter XI

153 *The Priests' Revolt: AOM* 6499, Relazione della Ribellione dei Preti.
et LAFERLA, *Una Giustizia Storica,* R., 1926.
seq. *AOM* 1529, G.M.'s Auditor to Bishop: 17 June 1774.

  Ximenes to Amb. in R.: 13, 22 Aug., 2 Sept. 1774.
157 *Chev. di Masino:* GREPPI, G., *Un Gentiluomo Milanese, Guerriero Diplomatico,* Milan, 1896.

  Russia—Knight for galley fleet: AOM 1520, Pinto to Amb. in Vienna: 1 May 1764.

  Russia—R. officers in M.: AOM 1578, Pinto to Receiver in Marseilles: 1 May 1766.

  AOM 1521, Pinto to Amb. in Vienna: 2 Dec. 1765.
158 *Cavalcabo's recall:* DOUBLET, op. cit., pp. 4–5.

Chapter XII

  For Poland, see CAVALIERO, op. cit.
161 *Spanish resentment: VLM* 137, Journal de l'Abbé Boyer: 4 Aug., 7, 8 Dec. 1775; 5 Jan. 1776.
162 *Chapter-General:* Ibid.: Mar.–Apr. 1776, *passim.*

  VLM 1259, Mémoire apologetique sur la conduite qu'à tenir à Malte dans le dernier C.G. M. le Chev. Bosredon.

  AOM 309, Capitulum Generale, 1776.

Page
166 *Germany and Bohemia: AOM* 1580, de Rohan to Chapter of G.: 25 Jan. 1778; to Bailiff d'Argenteuil: 10 Feb.; to the Grand Prior of Bohemia: 13 Feb.; to the Grand Priors of St Gilles and Toulouse: 18 Feb.; to Amb. in P.: 21 May 1778.
    AOM 1366, Spedalieri, Proto-Amb. in R. to de Rohan: 11 Mar., 1, 3, 8 Apr., 26 May, 17 June 1778.
    AOM 273, LCS: 26 Aug. 1778.
    AOM 1531, de Rohan to Bailiff Mandelli: 6 Mar. 1779.
167 *Psaro: AOM* 1535, de Rohan to Min. at Naples: 26 Apr. 1783.
    AOM 1582, de Rohan to Min. at Naples: 28 July, 6 Dec.; to Amb. in P.: 16 Aug., 25 Oct.; to Bailiff Sagramoso: 16 Aug.; to B. de Loras: 11 Oct. 1783.
    AOM 1583, de Rohan to Amb. in P.: 28 Feb. 1784.
    AOM 6406, Journal de l'Arrivée à M. et de la Reception de M. le Chev Psaro: 13 May 1784.
168 *Rumour in Naples: AOM* 1583, de Rohan to Amb. in P.: 1 May 1784.

Chapter XIII

169 *Dolomieu: Lacroix, Vie et Lettres.*
    AOM 1525, Pinto to Card. Torriggiani: 30 Jan. 1769.
    Regiment: DOUBLET, op. cit., pp. 17–18.
    Dol. as Marshal: LACROIX: D. to Picot de Lapeyrousse: 10 Apr., 30 Sept. 1783.
170 *Dol.—banned from Naples: AOM* 1584, de Rohan to Amb. in P.: 15 Apr. 1786.
171 *Bavaria: AOM* 273, LCS: 25 Mar., 9, 22 Apr. 1782.
    AOM 274, LCS: 30 Aug. 1787; 26 Oct. 1790.
    Squabble over Turcopilier: Ibid.: 13 Aug. 1783; 12 July 1784.
    AOM 1583, de Rohan to Amb. in P.: 30 Aug., 28 Nov.; to Min. in Naples: 6 Sept. 1784.
172 *Squabble over pensions: AOM* 1584, de Rohan to Amb. in P.: 24 Apr. 1786; de Loras to Grand Prior of R.: 29 Apr. 1786.
    Briefs for Grand Cross: AOM 1585, de Rohan to Sagramoso: 15, 29 Sept. 1787.
    de Suffren: AOM 1584, de Rohan to de Suffren: 13 May 1786.
173 *des Pennes:* Ibid., ditto: 16, 22 Sept.; 1 Nov. 1786.
174 *Kaunitz:* Quoted DOUBLET, op. cit., p. 11.
    de Loras's diplomatic history: AOM 1241, de Loras to Treasury: 25 Nov. 1784.
175 *de Loras's reply: AOM* 1585, de L. to Sagramoso: 24 Nov. 1787.
177 *Dolomieu on de Loras:* LACROIX: D. to de Fay: 10 Aug. 1786.
    D. and the Complete Council: AOM 1584, de Loras's address to the Council of the Tongue of Auvergne (enclosed in a letter to de Suffren): 18 Dec. 1786.
    AOM 1585, de Loras to de Suffren: 6 Jan. 1787.
    LACROIX: D. to de Fay: 17, 28 Mar. 1786.
    des Adrets: AOM 1622, de Rohan to de Suffren: 23 Mar., 16 Aug. 1788.
    AOM 1538, de Rohan to de Brillane: 2 Aug., 27 Sept., 22 Nov. 1786.
    AOM 274, LCS: 1, 10 Oct. 1788; 3 July 1789.
178 *"Capuchins":* LACROIX: D. to de Fay: 29 Apr. 1788.
    "tertian ague": Ibid., ditto: 12 July 1788.
    "dissensions": AOM 1622, de Rohan to de Suffren: undated, June 1788.
178 *Cagliostro: AOM* 1241, de Loras to de Rohan: 10 June 1789.
et   ANON, *Vie de Joseph Balsamo,* R., 1791.
seq.   HARRISON, M., *Count C.,* L., 1942.
    TROWBRIDGE, C., *The Splendour and Misery of a Master of Magic,* L., 1910.

Chapter XIV

181 *"common cause with them": AOM* 1585, de Rohan to de Suffren: 17 Aug. 1786.
182 *de Brillane in Paris: AOM* 1241, Cibon to de Rohan: 26 Mar. 1789.
    Knights in Estates General: DOUBLET, op. cit., p. 119.

Page
182 *de Virieu's letter: AOM* 1241, to de Loras (?): 11 May 1789.
     de Brillane's letter: DOUBLET, p. 120.
183 *Camus's reply: Le Moniteur,* P., 30 Nov. 1789.
     Adverse leaflet: "A Quoi Bon l'Ordre de Malte?" P., 1790.
184 *The reply:* "Réponse à un libelle anti-patriotique", undated and anon., P., 1790.
     The Order's position: AOM 6406, Examen de la Motion relativement à l'Ordre de Malte et Réponse Sommaire par un Citoyen de l'Ancien Ordre du Tiers Etat (believed to be Flachslanden): Feb. 1790.
185 *The Chambers of Commerce: Observations de la Chambre de Commerce de Marseilles . . .*, P., 1789.
     Camus: Développement de la Motion de M. Camus relativement à l'Ordre de Malte, P., 1790, p. 7.
186 *The caisses of the Priories: AOM* 1623, Questions à soumettre aux Assemblées des 6 Grands Prieures du Royaume. D'Estourmel to Treasury: 12 June 1790.
     Don Patriotique: Ibid., in same letter.
       CAMUS, *Développement, etc.,* p. 9.
     Camus's compromise: Ibid., pp 26–35.
187 *"Our cause is . . .": AOM* 6406, de Rohan to Ministers in Vienna, Venice, Naples, Rome, etc.: (?) Mar. 1790.
188 *Balance of Accounts: AOM* 888, Bilancio Decennale, 1778–88.
     De Ransijat's proposal: AOM 6406, de Ransijat to de Rohan: undated, 1790.
     his mémoire: DE RANSIJAT, *Siège et Blocus,* p. 296.
189 *Cagliostro: AOM* 1241, de Loras to Card. Zelada: 9 Jan. 1790.
     SILVAGNI, *La Corte e la Società Romana nei secoli XVIII e XIX,* vol. i. Florence, 1881 (for séance at Villa Malta).
     LACROIX: Dolomieu to Chev Gioeni: 30 Dec. 1789; 19 Jan., 8 Feb., 16 Mar., 2 Apr., 5 June 1790; to de Fay: 15 Dec. 1790; 4 June 1791.
     D'Estourmel's proposal: AOM 1623, D'Estourmel to Treasury: 12 June 1790.
190 *de Virieu's motion and Camus's reply:* Ibid., ditto: 16 Aug. 1790.
     Deputies Extraordinary: Rapport des Dép.s Ext.s à l'Assemblée Nationale sur la Preservation de M., P., 1790.
     Inventory: AOM 1623, d'Estourmel to Treasury: 22 June 1790.
     de Foresta: AOM 1625, de Foresta to Treasury: 29 June 1790.
191 *Avignon:* Ibid., ditto: 27 Jan. 1790.

Chapter XV

192 *The murder of Segond: AOM* 6410, L'Affaire Segond.
     AOM 1540, de Rohan to Min. at Naples: 6, 25, 30 Mar., 1, 8 May, 26 June 1790.
     AOM 274, LCS: 21 Apr., 11 June 1790.
     DOUBLET, pp. 109–11.
     AOM 1625, de Foresta to de Rohan: 21 July 1790.
193 *Bureau de Conciliation:* Ibid., de Foresta to Treasury: 21 July 1790.
     ". . . silver crowns": Ibid., ditto: 30 July 1790.
     The assignat: AOM 1623, D'Estourmel to Treasury: 23 Oct. 1790.
194 *Lawful currency: AOM* 1625, de Foresta to Treasury: 3 Dec. 1790.
     Malta and Marseilles: Ibid., ditto: 2 Dec. 1790; 11, 19, Apr. 1791.
     Municipality of Aix: Ibid., ditto: 19 May 1791.
     St John Lateran: AOM 1623, D'Estourmel to Treasury: 9 Apr. 1791.
     Toulouse: AOM 1628, Montauzet to Treasury: (?) Feb., 29 Mar. 1791.
195 *D'Estourmel and Varennes: VLM* 1130, *Relation du Bailli de la Tour du Pin,* pp. 10–11.
     Frigate from Marseilles: AOM 1625, de Foresta to Treasury: 14 Aug. 1791.
     d'Estourmel's optimism: AOM 1623, to de Rohan: 31 July 1791.
     de Virieu's motion: AOM 1625, de Virieu to de Foresta: 27 Sept. 1791.
     Charbot's motion: AOM 1623, D'Estourmel to Treasury: 14 Nov. 1791.
     Financial position of Treasury: AOM 274, LCS: 21 Sept.; 3 Oct. 1791.

Page
211 *Russian Priory: AOM* 275, LCS: 7 Aug. 1797.
  MAISONNEUVE, *Annales, etc.,* pp. 78–83.
212 *Racʒynski in Ancona:* Archives of the Vatican (Arch. Vat.) 344 I Min. Nunziatura
  di Polonia: Annexe to letter, Lorenzo Litta to Cardinal Doria: (?) June 1797.

Chapter XVII

General: HARDMAN, W., *A History of Malta,* 1798–1815, L., 1909, which col-
lates original documents.
Except where stated otherwise, the materials for this chapter are to be found
here.
213 *De Rohan's death: AOM* 923, Libro dei Debitori verso il fu de Rohan.
  AOM 926, Gli Spropriamenti di G.M. de R.
  AOM 1099, Conte per morte di de R.
214 *Godoy: Correspondence de Napoleon I,* vol. iii, p. 65.
  Election of von Hompesch: VLM 1130, *Journal du Bailli de la Tour du Pin,*
  pp. 23, 191–3.
  VLM 429, Bandi e Prammatiche: 17 July 1797.
  PRO FO 49/2, England to Grenville: 20 July 1797. Mémoire of Alex Ball:
  24 Oct. 1800.
  BOISGELIN, vol. iii, p. 43.
  MAISONNEUVE, pp. 88–9.
216 *Vassalli's conspiracy: VLM* 1020, Procès de Vassalli.
  VLM 1130, *De la Tour du Pin,* p. 18.
  VLM 418, Anon. to Mayer: 30 Aug. 1797.
218 *"the Crosses of de L'Isle Adam": AOM* 275, LCS: 7 Aug. 1797.
  Litta presents the Crosses: AOM 2196, Il Priorato di Russia: Discours de
  Conte Litta: 29 Nov. 1797.
  Condé, Grand Prior: Arch. Vat. 344, L. Litta to Card. Doria: 31 July, 20 Nov.
  1797.
219 *The Russian Priory: AOM* 2196, 1 June 1797, Report of Commissioners.
  ". . . productive of the greatest actions": Arch. Vat. 344: 24 Nov. 1797.

Chapter XVIII

General: For the capture of Malta, see HARDMAN, BOISGELIN, DOUBLET,
MAISONNEUVE and MAYER, *Revolution de Malte en* 1798, Trieste, 1799.
221 *Giulio Carpegna:* Archives of the French Consulate, Valetta, Carton 1796–8,
  Dossier 394.
228 *Dolomieu and Rochefoucauld:* LACROIX: D. to de Fay: 4 Oct. 1792.
  ". . . I protested loudly": Ibid., D. to Governor of Messina: 5 June 1799.

Chapters XIX–XXI

General: HARDMAN, BOISGELIN, DOUBLET.
SCICLUNA, H., *The French in Malta,* 1798–1800, M., 1923.
VASSALLO, G. A., *La Storia di Malta,* M., 1854.
WALISZEWSKI, K., *Paul I of Russia,* L., 1913.
Arch. Vat. 343, Nunziatura di Polonia: Cardinal Odescalchi to Lorenzo Litta.
Arch. Vat. 344, N. di P.: L. Litta to Card. Odescalchi.
Cambridge History of the British Empire, vol. ii, chap. ii, Cambridge 1940.
238 *The Bavarian minister:* Arch. Vat. 344, Litta to Odescalchi: 20 Dec. 1798.
  Cobenʒl's letter: dated 10 Dec. 1798, quoted in Appendix, GREPPI, op. cit.
240 *Pius VI's letter to G. Litta:* VILLENEUVE-BOUGEMENT, *Monuments des G.M.s*
  vol. ii, p. 415. Letter dated 5 Nov. 1798.

AUTHORITIES

Page
242   *von Hompesch to Francis II:* Ibid., p. 418.
      Hand of St John: DENARO, V., *The Hand of St J. the B. Revue de l'Ordre Souverain Militaire de M.,* R., Jan.–Mar. 1958.

For the history of the Order outside Malta to the present day, see VILLENEUVE-BOUGEMENT, op. cit., vol. ii; LAVIGERIE, BARON O., *L'Ordre de Malte depuis la Révolution Française,* P., 1889.

INDEX

Abdi, Aga, 114
Abela, French consul, 23
Abercrombie, General Sir Ralph, 255, 258
Aboukir Bay, battle of, 247, 252, 254
Academy of Inscriptions, Parisian, 24
Acre, St Jean d', 2
Acton, General John, 193, 248, 252–3, 265
Adam, Villiers de l'Isle, 3, 218, 235
Adrets, des, novice, 177–8, 180
Adriatic, 46
Agrigento, 252, 253
Aigle, l', French privateer, 108–9
Aix en Provence, 194
Albermarle, William Keppel, 3rd Earl of 128
Alberoni, Cardinal, 109–10
Alexander I, Czar, 219, 242, 260, 263, 264, 266
Alexander VII, Pope, 93, 113
Alexander, H.M.S., 248
Alfonso V, King of Aragon, 260
Algiers, 5, 6, 46, 48, 78, 106, 111, 114, 117, 149, 155, 196, 267; Bey of, 111
Alsace, 193
Amalfi, 1
Amati, Chevalier de, 229, 231
Ambassadors of the Order, 10, 36, 43–4, 204; in Paris, 28, 48, 109, 115, 126, 133, 152 (*see also* Suffren); in Rome, 14 (*also* Brillane, Camille de Rohan). *See* note to pp. 36, 49; in Spain and Empire, *see* note to p. 36
America, United States of, 25, 87, 194, 215
Amiens, Treaty of, 261, 263–4
Ancona, 212, 240
Anglo-Bavaro-Polish Tongue, 171, 182, 212
Antinori, Bailiff, 189
Aragon, Tongue of, 10, 11, 27, 102, 107; Spanish Priories, 236; Spanish Tongues, 262; Pilier of, 35
Arles, 199
Artemis, L', 216
Artois, Duke d', *see* Charles X
Assistance, H.M.S., 54
Audacious, H.M.S., 248
Audience, Court of the, 39
Augusta, 49, 135
Augustine, St, 1

Augustus II, King of Poland, 145
Aurora, H.M.S., 208
Auvergne, Tongue of, 10, 164, 168, 172, 175, 178, 225 (*see also* note to p. 43); Pilier of, 34, 169, 175
Auvergnat Club, 164, 170–2, 175, 188
Austria, *see* Empire, Holy Roman
Avignon, 191
Azov, 102

Bailiff (also Grand Cross), definition, 34; Rome holds up briefs for, 172–3; of Acre, 34, 114; of Armenia, 267; of Brandenburg, 214; of the Holy Sepulchre and of Morea, 34; of Negroponte, 34, 79
Bajazet, Emperor, 1
Bakaffa, Emperor of Ethiopia, 124–5
Ball, Captain (later Sir) Alexander, 247–249, 251–3, 255, 257–8, 260–4
Baraguey-Hilliers, Brigade commander, 224–5
Barbara, Vincenzo, 216–17, 220, 225
Barbary (also Regencies), 6, 7, 28, 41, 45, 46, 48, 70, 78, 80, 82, 85, 87, 110, 115, 116–17, 126, 127, 128, 132, 140, 190. *See also* Tunis, Tripoli, Algiers
Barcelona, 3, 39, 45, 86, 258
Bardonenche, Chevalier, 217, 230–1
Barletta, Priory of, 255; as Sicilian Priory, 266–7
Barres, Bailiff des, 164–5
Basle, Congress of, 208
Bavaria, 259; Elector of, 115, 170–1, 238, 240–1, 266; Priory of, 27, 170–1, 215, 236, 240–1, 266; Inn of (La Bavière), 215
Belli, Agostino, 189
Belmont, Bailiff de, 151, 198, 213, 224
Benedict XIII, Pope, 118
Benedict XIV, Pope, 92, 127, 131
Benghazi, Bey of, 81
Bentinck, Lord William, 266
Berlinghieri, Commander, 267
Bernis, Cardinal de, 173, 177, 189
Berry, Duke de, 182
Berthier, General Louis-Alexandre, 224, 229
Bishop of Malta, the, 23, 41, 55, 90, 92–94, 129, 153–4, 232, 243, 244, 245, 270 and note to p. 37
Bocage, Bailiff de, 140–1

INDEX

Colloredo, Count, Imperial Vice-Chancellor, 238
Cologne, Elector of, 115
Commandery, definition, 9; smutition, 10; of grace, 36; responsions, 43
Composition des Rhodiens, the, 43, 50, 186
Concordat, the (1741), 50, 127
Condé, Louis Joseph de Bourbon, Prince de, 203, 218–19, 235, 236, 237, 256
Condorcet, Marquis de, 169, 196
Congregation of Armaments, 38; of Galleys, 38; of Ships, 38; of State, 32, 163, 173; of War, 38, 170, 231
Consolato del Mare, 39, 56, 83, 93, 133, and note to p. 39
Constantinople, 78, 111, 114, 116, 140, 142, 147
Consul, in Malta, 37, 39, and note to p. 37; for slaves, 80; British, 100, 132, 138, and notes to pp. 37, 39, (*see also* Dodsworth, John, and England, William); French, 100, and note to p. 37
Conti, Prince de, 146, 163, and note to p. 36
Convent, definition of term, 9
Conventual Chaplains, 13, 22, 23, 153, 164, 171, 212
Conventual Church of St John the Baptist, 33, 38, 42, 58–62, 103, 112, 118, 188, 213, 218, 244, 270, and note to p. 18
Corfu, 106, 216, 219, 244, 250, 254
Corinth, 105
Corradino, 246
Corsica, 126–7, 190, 237
Corso, the, 6, 81–5, 89, 113, 116, 267
Cospicua, 40, 232, 246; *see also* Four Cities, Three Cities
Cotoner, Grand Masters Niccolò and Raffaello, 16, 59, 115, 123; Casa, 103, the C. lines, 52, 224, 227, 231, 255
Cotton in Malta, 85–6
Council, Complete (Consiglio Compito), 31, 150, 176, 178, 192; Popular (C. Popolare), 40, 155; Sacred, 31, 34, 173, 182, 209; Venerable, 12, 31, 133, 134, 135, 136, 156, 157, 199, 202, 226, 227–8; of Notables, 177, 181
Craggs, James, Secretary of State for Southern Affairs, 110
Crato, Grand Priory of, 27
Crete, 6, 85, 114
Crimea, 148, 205
Crusade Bull, 127
Crussol, Bailiff de, 182
Cumbo, Judge, 122
Cyprus, 2
Czartoryski, Prince Augustus, 145–7, 161; Prince Adam, 219, and note to p. 260

Czeremetev, Boyar Boris Petrovich, 102–4, 216, 242; family of, 242

Dal Pozzo, 6
Damas, a hatter, 227
Damietta, 3, 117
Danube, 46, 103
Dardanelles, 5, 105, 248, 250
Denmark, King of, 68, 147
Denon, Dominique Vivant, Baron de, 74, 75, 77
Desaix, Joseph-Marie, 225
Despuig, Ramon, elected Grand Master, 119; helps Bey of Tunis, 119; death, 120; and Ethiopia, 125
Diane, La, 247, 257
Dimech, Joseph, 156
Dodsworth, John, 132–8, 157, 207
Dolomieu, Déodat de, 25, 71, 100, 168, 169, 170, 172, 175, 176–7, 178, 179, 180, 188, 189, 190, 196–7, 198, 228, 230, 235, 269; Casimir de, 197; Guy-Joseph de, 197
Don Patriotique, 186, 188, 189
Donat, definition of term, 13, 23
Doria, Cardinal, 219
Doublet, Ovide, 72, 122, 123, 175–6, 195, 198, 201, 208, 209, 217, 222, 223, 224, 225, 229, 230, 232
Dubois, Cardinal, 115
Dudon, French Comptroller General, see note to p. 49.
Dundas, Henry (1st Viscount Melville), 255, 258

Egypt, 96, 124, 170, 215, 220, 243, 244, 246, 252, 269
Elizabeth I, Czarina, 148
Empire, Holy Roman, as protecting power, 12, 37; offers to help Malta (1722), 115–16; and Ethiopian project, 125; and the Chapter-General (1776), 167; France declares war on, 197; France suspects designs on Malta, 215–16; and Malta at Rastadt, 221; news of fall of Malta reaches, 235; protects Hompesch, 237, 251; suborns Admiral Ouchakov, 254; and Treaty of Amiens, 262; and Malta (1803), 266
Emperor, the (Leopold II) 199; (Francis II) 215, 216, 235, 237, 238, 242, 262. *See also* Joseph II, Maria Theresa
Enghien, Louis de Bourbon, Duke d', 256
England, Tongue of, 10, 27, 35, 164, 171, 261, 268; Pilier of, 35, 171
England, William, 207–8, 215, and note to p. 227.
Esclan, Chevalier d', 182

* Additions to Index